12-15 feet   25 feet or more

Fruits for the Home Garden

Fruits
for the
Home Garden

by KEN and PAT KRAFT

DRAWINGS by KATHLEEN BOURKE

WILLIAM MORROW & COMPANY, INC.
425 Park Avenue South • New York, N.Y. 10016

To the memory of the home gardeners' friend,
LUTHER BURBANK

Acknowledgments

We have drawn particularly on the expertise of pomologists and nurserymen in order to round out our practical experience and to produce a really helpful book for home fruit gardeners. The goal we set was the kind of book we'd have liked to have found years ago for our own use—a book that kept its eye fastened on the home gardener and his desires and limitations. These are often quite apart from those of the commercial orchardist, who has his own sources of know-how.

The Stark Bro's Nurseries, now with 152 years of experience in working with home fruit gardeners and trying to answer their questions, has been most cooperative. Our sincere thanks are due them and their home community, Louisiana, Missouri. Pomologist Paul Stark, Jr., checked the manuscript for horticultural accuracy and put us in touch with horticultural progress in Europe and the Southern Hemisphere. Short of mentioning everyone in the Stark organization who helped us, since everyone did, we should like *particularly to mention John Stark Logan, Lloyd C. Stark, Paul Stark, Sr., and Lloyd S. Stark, Jr.; Harry Guengerich, Paul Reller, Jim Law, and Don Stinson; Miss Nellie Lee Hagen, Mrs. Ada Dorward, Miss Ada Virginia Muirr, Mrs. Leona Elliott, and Mrs. Melvia Woodward.*

In addition to specialists too numerous to name in the United States Department of Agriculture and in state organizations, we are especially grateful for help received from the following: Professor Emeritus H. B. Tukey, Professor Stanley Johnston, Dr. Jerome Hull, Jr., and Glenn P. Lumis, of Michigan State University; Dr. George L. Slate, and Professor Nelson Shaulis, of the New York State Agricultural Experiment Station at Geneva; Dr. J. P. Overcash of Mississippi State University; Dr. Richard A. Hayden of Purdue University.

Our editor, Helen Van Pelt Wilson, has been a world of help and encouragement, and the accuracy and artistry of

Kathleen Bourke's drawings have enhanced this book. Other individuals to whom we are also most grateful for freely giving us their time and expert advice include Grant Merrill, Robert A. Nitschke, John Bregger, Dr. David Armstrong and John Armstrong, Henry Weinland, Gordon Baker Lloyd, Floris Hartog, H. Jack W. Rayner, and Bill Erickson.

The Nutrition Foundation, Inc., was helpful in our research, and our thanks are due also to Chevron Chemical Company.

Finally, we are grateful indeed for the help given us by the Harrison Memorial Library of Carmel, California, in locating and getting many of the uncommon references we needed, especially the efforts of Mrs. Ruth G. Thornburg and Mrs. Edith J. Chester.

Carmel, California   KEN and PAT KRAFT
January, 1968

Contents

Illustrations

The Joy
of a
Fruit Garden 1

Several years ago we decided to change climates and to leave the Missouri farm we had bought six years earlier. The farm was about forty miles southwest of St. Louis, just edging into the foothill country of the beautiful old Ozark Mountains, and we loved the place.

About half the rolling land was wooded, largely with oak and hickory and red-cedar. Late in December we'd cut a plump red-cedar—this was *Juniperus virginiana*—frosted with tiny blue berries for our Christmas tree, and then saw two to three feet off the bottom because our eyes were always bigger than our living room. There were glades of dogwood that welcomed each springtime with constellations of blossoms, and in the front meadow were more wild blackberries than the birds and we could eat. On a slope just above a little spring where we'd planted water cress there was a persimmon grove that our cattle thought they owned.

We hated to leave all this, and we missed the good feel of watching our small herd flourish on the lespedeza and redtop we'd sown, and we missed the lake we'd built. It covered an acre, was twelve feet deep at the toe of the dam, and alive with fish. In the winter it was a skating rink and in summer an immense swimming pool. It was from this lake that we'd dipped hundreds of bucketfuls for the thirsty little fruit trees we'd planted to flank in double rows the bluegrass lawn. This sloped down from the house to the water. We still feel guilty about going off and leaving those little trees in the hands of strangers.

We knew our trees expected better of us for a fruit tree has a personality—and it's a different personality from every other fruit tree. Luther Burbank once said that "Plants have minds—subconscious minds, but at any rate, minds."

We think so, too. And we think fruit trees also have feelings, and tempers, and they do better for people who appreciate them. This is an attitude botanists deplore, with reason; it confuses research, adulterating chemistry with behaviorism. Gardening is not botany, though. And the only plants that prosper on hate are the weeds.

Our old apple tree

Just beyond the front-yard gate of our farmhouse there was an old apple tree. It would make good firewood, people kept telling us when we bought the farm. We would as soon have sawed up the walnut secretary we'd bought when we were married and had used that first year for a china-cabinet-desk-sideboard-everything.

The old apple had a strong cant to the north. Its trunk was battered and knobby and had a mean rotting patch halfway up. Its top was a thicket of crisscrossing branches and of water sprouts.

We had no idea how old it was but we knew apple trees lived about as long as a man does. We also suspected it was a seedling, for an early mistress of the place had Johnny-Appleseeded the grounds, we'd heard, and there were plums and more recently planted seedling peaches and nectarines in the kitchen garden. Planting a peach seed often produces a nectarine tree, the two being closely related varieties of the same species. In the yard there were two pie cherries.

We took care of all these trees and they produced fruit for us during our years on the farm. It was not the choicest fruit, but it was welcome as we waited for our new orchard to reach bearing age. We treated the old apple, described in Chapter four, scraping the trunk, cleaning out the rotted wood, the dead and diseased limbs, spraying it, spading up the earth in a twenty-foot circle around it. We ended up by spreading a nourishing mulch of old manure. On the barn's earth floor it was more than a foot deep and we thought it would last forever.

And the tree gave us bushels and bushels of apples. Looking

after it was the kind of work that leaves you glowing with satisfaction. An enthusiastic French gardener put it this way:

> A fruit tree any tree, is a great, great person. . . . Do you realize that a single apple tree can very well yield hundreds of pounds of apples! . . . Because of all this, a tree has a right to the most special care.

The gardener here is Fernand Lequenne, and the quotation from *My Friend the Garden.* He added this caution:

> Nevertheless it is often neglected, this good, silent provider. People are apt to say, as is said of so many other plants, that a tree "grows by itself."
>
> One thing is certain: the best tree, even from the best nursery, doesn't take long to become disgusted. From the start, it is watching you; it knows right away, like any well-bred thing, if it is in the hands of a clumsy or insensitive master. . . . You will soon see.
>
> Be careful not to make of it a rebel or a worthless beauty.

Lequenne's rapport with his plants (for a tree is a plant even though the word seems too little for it) is an enthusiasm every gardener knows. But just to show how differently two gardeners can look at the same thing, listen a moment to an equally enthusiastic plantsman, a Canadian, Isaac Lucas: "I sometimes found a gardener busily engaged doing all the wrong things to his trees, but doing them thoroughly and with enthusiasm. For him I predict success and ultimate joy in his trees."

Our own experience tells us there is something in both points of view. You can *over*-tend a tree, too. We knew a man, a restless retired executive, who cultivated his young orchard so often he didn't live to see the trees bear. They were paper-shell pecan trees, which have shallow feeder roots; his cultivating kept chopping them up. The trouble was he had bought a little tractor and just loved to run it.

The rule of five

Now let's talk about you, about you and your fruit garden. If you haven't one already, the chances are you want one, since you're reading this, so you'll be glad to hear that:

> Home fruit gardening has been simplified.
> Fruit trees have been more miniaturized.

FOUR POSSIBILITIES for growing fruit on your home grounds if space is limited: the smallest dwarf trees; an espaliered dwarf, taking no more room than a vine; a dwarf tree in a planter; a row of dwarfs serving as a divider or screen.

Chemistry has simplified things in the past few years through easier controls of tree health and behavior, and science has made many small fruit trees even smaller. In fact, the newest dwarf peach in its early bearing years could fit comfortably under a card table. Yet these tiny dwarf trees load themselves with fruit, and the fruit is even larger than on standard (regular-sized) trees, and also of better color.

We know that some gardeners have the space to plant standard fruit trees, and that some prefer standards, perhaps because of their greater production or for their special landscape value. And, too, every fruit is not yet available in dwarf size. But where you have the choice of a dwarf, we suggest you think twice before passing it up. We go into this more in the next chapter. Meanwhile we'd like to pass along a quick and simple way to help you determine what to put into your fruit garden. We call it the Rule of Five. It covers taste, space, climate, time, and price.

TASTE.   This refers to your own preference. What fruits do your family like? What fruits do you buy? Make a list now. If there's a reason you can't, or shouldn't, grow some of them, the points that follow will bring this out. But first consider your own likes and dislikes.

SPACE.   This is the problem that plagues more hopeful fruit gardeners than any other. What with shrub plantings, flower beds, shade trees, lawn, all competing for room, where can you possibly put fruit trees that require an open space with several hours of sun? And if they have to compete for food and water with nearby shade trees, they won't do as well as if they had adequate room.

Furthermore, many fruit trees require another of the same species nearby for cross-pollination or they won't set fruit. This isn't as big a problem as it sounds, because bees, which do most of the pollinating, search out all the fruit trees in the neighborhood, and chances are fair that if you have but one solitary fruit tree, it will get pollinated. But planting a second suitable variety is good insurance. You'll find more on this in the chapters on each fruit.

If there seems to be just no space for fruit on your place, then here are five suggestions: (1) First and most obvious, consider the very smallest dwarf trees. They take up no more room than a lilac.

(2) Try an espalier on a wall or fence; these flat trees grow in an area only a vine could use. (3) Consider tub planting; you can grow a dwarf tree in an eighteen-inch-diameter container set on a concrete walk or in a patio. (4) Plant fruit trees as architectural units to screen off service areas or for divider strips. (5) Finally, consider the small fruits. If you have room for nothing else, remember "runnerless" strawberries. You can edge a walk with them or border a flower bed. Strawberries are one of the best-liked fruits in the world, and they grow all over the world, even within the Artic Circle.

5

A border planting of strawberries another way to grow fruit on your home grounds.

CLIMATE.   When you plant a fruit tree you want it to bear. Of course, if you're awfully cautious, you'll lose a lot of the adventure, but there are limits. For instance, a Napoleon cherry in Minnesota won't get you any cherries. The tree will die the first winter or go moping along for a few barren years. Temperature isn't the only factor here. A tree has to have time enough to set fruit; that is, a long enough growing season. (We know that somebody in Minnesota is going to read this and say that he has a Napoleon cherry and it bears every year. And we'll believe him. But we are not talking about the one-in-a-million exception.)

Another limiting factor is what pomologists call the chilling requirement. Most apples and pears require a cold winter. Too mild or too short a winter fails to break their dormancy, and they limp along with poor growth and no fruit. In this regard, science has recently made notable progress and gardeners in Zones 8 and 9 will find new varieties of apples, pears, Japanese plums, nectarines, and peaches that get along with less cold and will accept some foggy weather in place of chilly weather. Check your local nurseries for variety names. In this matter of climate, you will need advice and the best advice comes from close by. (We discuss this in the last part of Chapter four.)

What we are going to say now may sound contradictory. When in doubt as to whether your climate is *exactly* right for a plant, go ahead and try it. The odd fact is, the climate between your yard and even your next-door neighbor's may differ enough so that you can grow something he can't. Even the practical-minded United States Department of Agriculture, describing the high mountain areas of the West as having "climatic conditions in general too severe for the growing of fruit," adds that "in especially favorable locations" of these cold mountains certain hardy varieties may be tried.

TIME. It is plain common sense not to plant what you don't have time to care for. But this is something every gardener decides for himself, most of us by planting exactly what we please and then finding out how much attention it takes. The tendency is to overdo. We know, because we do.

The trees that take the least care are the nuts, especially black walnuts, pecans, chestnuts, and hazelnuts. Quinces come next. Grapes appreciate care but don't demand it the way some other fruits do. This is also true of strawberries, blackberries, and raspberries. Plums, cherries, and apricots take more attention, but less than apples, peaches, nectarines, and pears.

But perhaps it is more to the point to say that the time your fruit trees will require is mainly a few hours scattered through spring and summer. Compared to vegetables and flowers, the demands of fruit trees are indeed few—and fairly far between.

PRICE. A good fruit tree from a reliable nursery costs about the same as a good dinner in a downtown restaurant, somewhere between three and six dollars. Fruit varieties that are quite new often cost a little more, as may trees on which much grafting or other skilled handwork is done. Dwarf trees are usually more expensive, mainly because of more handling.

Transportation is usually not figured into catalogue prices of trees. A fairly common practice is to have the customer add ten percent to the price of his order to cover shipping. Some nurseries ship collect, and two of the biggest, Inter-State and Stark Bro's, add to your order free stock of a value equal to shipping costs.

Most nurseries offer groups of fruit trees—package deals—at savings that usually amount to your getting one tree free. These assortments have two other advantages: Shipping several trees by express may cost no more than shipping a single tree; and the assortment is made up of varieties that help each other to fruit by cross-pollination.

Stark Bro's and Burbank

In writing this book, we have had the help of pomologists and nurserymen who supplemented our own practical experience. We have made particular use of Stark Bro's Nurseries and Orchards Company because of their uncommonly long experience in helping home fruit gardeners. Furthermore, we already had a working relationship with them that came about in 1965 when we were doing research for a biography on Luther Burbank.

Stark's had been one of Burbank's early customers and had introduced many of his new fruits over the thirty-five years preceding the plant wizard's death in 1926. The next year Stark's took over all his unfinished experiments, and still carry such important Burbank developments as his 'July Elberta' peach, 'Van Deman' quince, and several plums. The Plant Patent Act of 1930 enabled Stark's to do what Burbank died too soon to do—patent a new plant and prevent competitors from pirating it. This single law, which Paul Stark, Sr. helped into existence, has been an enormous factor in speeding up plant improvement during the past four decades.

In 1966, when Stark's celebrated their one hundred fiftieth anniversary, we were invited to their headquarters in Louisiana, Missouri, to speak on Luther Burbank. There we took a close look at the inner workings of a horticultural search and experiment station operating on an international scale. It is an organization considerably older than the United States Department of Agriculture, which was not established until 1862.

Since almost everybody who plants home fruits deals with a nurseryman, we thought it sensible to consult with nursery pomologists and technicians on a book for home fruit gardeners. We knew that nobody more earnestly wants them to succeed than does the good nurseryman. This man is a combination of daring and caution, always swooping on something new and exciting for you to grow, and then tossing ninety-nine out of one hundred experimental trees on the scrap heap when tests reveal faults you'd bless him out for if he sold you his new near-wonder.

We also want you to succeed, and to enjoy growing fruit at home. It is one of the world's healthiest and most interesting pastimes, and one of the most rewarding.

These Amazing Dwarfs *2*

We were visiting a man who owns a spectacularly sited front yard—a shelf cut into a mountain that slopes steeply down to the Pacific Ocean about thirteen hundred feet below. Out there, three warships that looked like toy boats were firing at a floating target, and far out near the horizon we watched a freighter heading north for San Francisco. As we looked almost vertically down from the edge of the lawn, a whale swam through the dark green waters, a great gray whale on its annual journey to warmer deeps. The breakers were foaming on the headlands nearer shore, the kelp was russet lace among the tide pools, and—

"Come along now," our host said. "See a marvelous sight." We followed him to a small garden area, and there this owner of a matchless ocean view halted before a little apple tree heavy with fruit. "I planted it only three years ago," said he, "and would you look at that crop!"

The apples were a bit bigger and better colored than those from standard trees, which is typical of dwarfs. The owner's enthusiasm was typical also. Typical, that is, of the home fruit gardener, and more and more that means the dwarf-tree gardener. If fruit is the royalty of the garden, the dainty dwarf trees are the princesses.

But aside from the charm of the miniature and the plain-as-your-nose fact that a bit of a tree that makes a perfect bouquet of itself every spring and a juicy horn of plenty at harvest time can't help being loved and admired, just what are the good points about the dwarfs? And are there any bad ones?

"An apple tree!" a wife exclaimed as her bedazzled husband

read a nursery catalogue. "Why, just one solitary apple tree would fill our whole yard." Quite right. A standard apple tree grows 25 feet high or more and needs a 40-by 40-foot plot of ground to itself, a fair-sized back yard.

Ah, but these dwarf trees. . . . If by some miracle, you do have an available 40-by 40-foot piece of ground, then instead of one standard apple tree you can plant *sixteen* dwarfs. Each tree needs only a 10-by 10-foot plot, so even a carport-sized piece of ground will take two. The dwarf is so accommodating a little thing that in a pinch it is perfectly willing to borrow space in a flower bed or to beautify a house or garage wall as an espalier while bearing a good crop of high quality fruit.

Then there's the matter of earlier bearing age. "How soon will I get some fruit?" home gardeners always want to know. Standard trees take from three to fifteen years to produce first fruits. Dwarfs are so eager to start, you may have to save them from themselves by nipping off fruit buds the first season. Actually you can let half a dozen fruits develop in the center, but try to let the little trees devote most of their energy to developing strong frameworks. It isn't unusual for a dwarf to pay for itself with its very first real crop.

When they reach full production, dwarf apples and pears often yield three to four bushels a season, and may bear up to six bushels. And a bushel of apples weighs fifty pounds. What do apples cost at your supermarket? At ours, from three to five pounds for a dollar, depending on the season.

Perhaps you have heard that dwarf trees are short-lived and that this marvelous production soon stops. Forget it. Many reports you hear about dwarf trees no longer apply. The day when a dwarf fruit tree was a charming lawn ornament and of little earthly use otherwise has passed. Give your dwarf tree ordinary good garden care and it will produce high-quality fruit for as long as a standard tree. And for an apple or pear that means a working life as long as a man's or longer—upward of forty years.

If you have ever pruned and sprayed a tall standard fruit tree, an apple or pear, the convenience of taking care of a dwarf may be its greatest appeal. And the care costs less. A big apple tree may require ten or more gallons of spray for a single treatment and fifty dollars' worth of equipment to put it on. A dwarf apple tree will need a quart or less and you can apply it with your rose-bush sprayer.

To prune a big tree also takes other equipment, including a ladder—which you'll need again for thinning and for harvesting. You stand on the ground to tend a dwarf tree. And if the ripe fruit drops, the shorter fall from a dwarf is less bruising.

We said earlier that the 40-by 40-foot space a standard apple requires will accommodate sixteen dwarfs, which take 10-by 10-foot squares, so another advantage of dwarfs appears—the greater variety of fruits you can enjoy. And this also means you can space your harvest through the season. For instance, if you had one standard apple tree taking up all your space and it happened to be an early variety that didn't keep well—early ones often don't—you'd be glutted with apples for a few weeks and then have nothing for a year. Another point, dwarfs spread the risk. If you have one big tree and disease kills it or lightning hits it, you're finished.

So . . . plainly we are prejudiced in favor of dwarfs for the home

COMPARISON OF SPACE REQUIREMENTS. *On the same amount of ground needed for a single standard apple tree—40 by 40 feet—you can actually grow sixteen dwarf trees.*

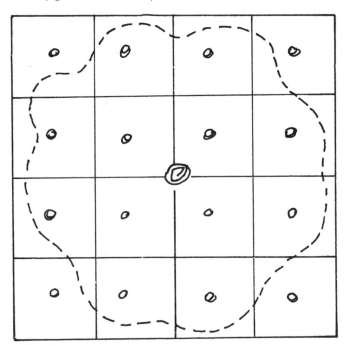

gardener. But not so prejudiced that we won't admit dwarfs do take a little more looking after than standards. They also cost more, usually a dollar or two more per tree.

What makes a dwarf?

Do dwarf trees naturally grow that way or are they made to do so? There are and always have been natural dwarfs but they almost always occur as ornamentals. Today's dwarf is a worker, and the dwarf you get from a nursery will be an assembly job—a root from one type of tree, a top from another, and perhaps part of the trunk from a third. This horticultural carpentry is one of the mysteries of the nursery business. Nevertheless it has been going on for at least three hundred years.

Dwarf trees have been in and out of favor several times during those three centuries and much of the credit for their present return to favor must go to English pomologists at the East Malling Research Station in Kent. They collected from many countries all the natural dwarf apples they could find, then tested them until they weeded out the undependables. They ended up with sixteen varieties known as Malling (or EM) I, II, III, etc., each exerting a different effect on a standard apple grafted to it. Four Mallings are now the most popular rootstocks for dwarfing. Malling IX is used to grow the smallest trees, 6 to 9 feet high, Mallings II, IV, and VII to grow larger dwarfs. Another name you may run across is Malling-Merton. This refers to a rootstock that has been produced by breeding one of the Mallings to another variety of apple in order to get a valuable combination of characters, such as resistance to a troublesome disease and better root anchorage.

Perhaps this is the place to mention that if you buy a dwarf apple tree from Stark Bro's it won't have a Malling root. Stark's believe that dwarf apples on Malling roots do not develop strong enough root systems to take the severe weather of many parts of North America—drouth, heat, and wind. In 1943, Stark's planted a test orchard of trees grafted on the entire Malling series, and by the fall of 1961 only one tree was left standing, a Malling IV.

Stark's develop their dwarf apples by inserting a piece of dwarfing wood into the trunk. This frees them to select something huskier than a Malling for the roots. They use a French crabapple for them, and then grow an extra set of roots by grafting a hardy apple so low on the crabapple rootstock that the grafted piece is partly underground and so sprouts roots the way a cutting does. While this little two-piece tree is still growing in the nursery, Stark workers put the top part together on a work bench as if they were building furniture. They splice a stem of the variety that will become the top of the tree and bear the fruit onto a dwarfing stem-piece of the apple selected for this purpose, as in the case of a double-dwarf 'Golden Delicious'.

This two-piece splice is then grafted onto the sturdy little two-piece whip tree in the nursery that is growing on French crabapple roots. The dwarfing section is in the middle—a part of the trunk, not of the roots. After another year of growing, with some manipulation by experienced nurserymen in the field, these roots and stems of four separate trees will have grown together into one tree. This is now well branched and ready to be dug for a customer.

The dwarfing trunk section is called a Clark stem-piece. It was named for an amateur fruit gardener who found the original Clark dwarf apple tree growing in the yard of an old lady in Muscatine, Iowa, and realized the possibilities of a dwarf apple that could take Iowa's cold winters. Still hardier stem-pieces are now being developed through research as more is learned of their behavior and advantages.

The remarkable spur-types

Because the apple is such a popular and widely grown fruit, progress in dwarfing apple trees has been immensely more important than it has been with, say, sweet cherries. So by great good luck the newest thing in dwarfs today is a type of apple tree. It is called a spur-type or fruit-spur type.

A spur-type apple tree is a natural, or genetic, dwarf. It is shorter than a standard—about 15 feet high, making it a semidwarf. This is good, but even better, the tree bears big crops because it has fruit-bearing wood, called spurs, not only far out on the branches in the usual way but bristling all over them and even on the trunk.

Stark's first successful spur-type was a 'Starking Red Delicious', discovered in 1956 in a commercial orchard in Hood River, Oregon. Stark's paid $25,000 for it, then a record high. Later they changed the name to 'Starkrimson Delicious'. They now have seven more spur-type varieties, including a 'Golden Delicious' which cost them $51,000. They are hopefully on the prowl for spur-type trees in other apples and other fruits.

It is Stark's belief that spur-type fruit trees have probably always occurred but were dismissed as freaks, for some bore fruit of poor color or shape. Or they were ignored or weeded out, "rogued," as horticulturists say, when they remove an unwanted plant. This indifference sounds extraordinary in view of the current enthusiasm for spur-types among pomologists, but it is common experience in every area for good things to be neglected because they are ahead of their time.

Discovery of the spur-type apple tree is important to home gardeners who want a tree that will give ten to fifteen bushels of fruit and yet grow appreciably smaller than a standard, needing only a quarter of the ground area or less—about 12 by 20 feet. Perhaps more important, a spur-type top on a stem-piece dwarf tree makes a still smaller dwarf, 6 to 8 feet high. Stark's call them double-dwarfs. They are well-mannered little trees, strong and upright, probably the nearest thing to perfection in a fruiting ornamental deciduous plant. And if you dislike pruning, these are the trees for you. Once they grow up and start bearing, they require practically no pruning at all.

The dwarf orchard

It used to be that you could buy a dwarf apple tree and a dwarf pear, but not much else. Times have changed and are changing more. Customer enthusiasm for new dwarf fruit trees has professional researchers and nurserymen striving, watching for mutations and for better combinations of scions and rootstocks (as the tops and bottoms of grafted trees are called), and performing some odd-sounding manipulations with irradiation and even with viruses. Here is how the dwarfs that we have right now, in addition to the apple, are made:

PEAR. To dwarf a pear, nurserymen graft it on quince roots. Peculiar, but it works. They once used only the 'Angers' quince but the 'French Provence' is now favored, having a stronger root system and being more productive. As with the 'Angers', some pears won't live when grafted on the Provence, so a compatible variety is grafted to the Provence and the incompatible one is grafted on top. The compatible variety acts as a bridge between the other two, and the method works nicely.

PEACH.   Rootstocks of the Western sand cherry, *Prunus besseyi*, have been used to dwarf peaches, as has the Nanking cherry, *P. tomentosa* and the 'St. Julien A' plum, related to the Damsons. More recent breeding has been done with a dwarf peach from China called 'Swatow'. The Armstrong Nursery in Ontario, California, developed and introduced a very dwarf peach with Swatow blood, the 'Bonanza', and Stark's have a variety called 'Stark Starlet'.

These little trees, still quite new on the market, bear good crops when only about 3 feet tall, and are one of the best fruits to grow in planters. They are also early bearers, fruiting the year after planting. At maturity they are 5 to 6 feet high. They are as compact as shrubs, their blossoms worthy of an ornamental grown for flowers alone, and the foliage is dense and attractive.

APRICOT, NECTARINE, PLUM.   These fruits are all dwarfed by being grown, like peaches, on rootstocks of the Western sand cherry and the Nanking cherry.

CHERRY.   A variety of sour cherry that was originated by the Minnesota Fruit Breeding Farm is called 'North Star'. It is a natural dwarf, growing 6 to 9 feet tall. It has been used as a rootstock for dwarfing some sweet cherries.

The ground cherry, *Prunus fruticosa*, has also been used as a rootstock for both sweet and sour cherries, making trees the size of double-dwarf apples. There are several good semidwarf cherries, 10 to 12 feet tall. Both sweet and sour cherries can be dwarfed by using 'North Star' as a stem-piece, and splendid hundred-pound crops have been borne by nine-year-old 'Van' and 'Gold' trees so dwarfed.

QUINCE.   By nature this is a compact tree with a picturesque and twiggy branch growth. Quinces are planted about 10 to 15 feet apart, an indication of how restricted their growth is.

Planting of dwarfs

When planting a dwarf tree, take care not to bury the lower graft union. It looks like a kink in the trunk at the point where the dwarfing rootstock joins the top. The reason for this is that the top part may form its own roots if it finds its lower end in the earth. Such so-called scion-rooting will then cancel out the dwarf root system and your "dwarf" will grow into a big tree. To avoid this, plant the tree at the same level it grew in the nursery, as shown by the lighter color of the part of the trunk that grew above ground.

Stark's dwarf apples are an exception. Since the stem-piece and not the root is the dwarfing agent, the Stark dwarfs can be safely planted 3 to 4 inches lower than they stood in the nursery.

As you fill in the hole, firm the earth at several levels by packing it down with your feet and a hoe handle. Support the dwarf tree by tying it to a stake if it is on Malling roots or in a very windy location. Rope is good for tying the tree to the stake. Wire is the worst choice. In fact, the name tag should be removed from the tree at planting time so that the little wire holding it won't be forgotten and later kill the limb by girdling; the effect is the same as if a tourniquet were wrapped around your arm and never loosened.

Pruning at planting time, fertilizing, mulching, and the general care of dwarf trees are the same as for standards. Culture is discussed in the next two chapters. As a rule, you can plant dwarf trees 10 feet apart. Twelve feet apart is a spacing frequently used, and dwarfs are sometimes planted as close as 8 feet. The best policy is to give them liberal spacing for the sake of good air circulation.

You may wonder if you can move a dwarf tree later on, as English tenants are said to do when changing houses. Though a dwarf tree is more apt to survive a move than a standard, providing you prune the top severely, to move any fruit tree of bearing age is to risk killing it. In this case, the gardener who grows his dwarfs in planters has an advantage.

Dwarf trees in planters

Little fruit trees that you shift about like outdoor furniture can be the starlets of your garden. With such portable landscaping, you may place your trees wherever fancy suggests or weather

PLANTER FOR A DWARF TREE. You can build one of redwood or cypress, 18 to 24 inches square, a few inches less deep; finished with a collar of 1- by 4-inch strips. For a dolly, fasten heavy casters or mower wheels to a 2-inch-thick plank platform, slightly bigger around than the planter.

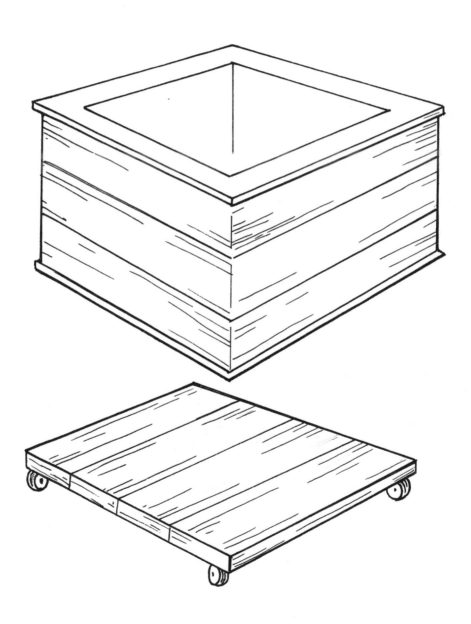

coarse gravel in the bottom. Make a potting mixture of two parts of good garden soil and one part of stable manure, compost, or moist peatmoss. The potting mixture should be medium-coarse. Have it just moist enough for a handful to hold shape when squeezed. Don't add fertilizer now but apply soluble fertilizer at half the recommended strength once a month during the growing season.

Set the tree in the upper two-thirds of the planter, tamping the earth firmly with a piece of broomstick or lath. Finish with a thorough watering and a mulch of damp peatmoss, wood chips, or small white stones.

Trees in planters need a thorough soaking from the hose every week or ten days in dry weather, and an occasional light top-watering with the hose nozzle set for a fine spray.

When planting, prune as directed in Chapter 3 for each species. For later pruning, follow the same practice as for trees in open ground, detailed in the chapters on each fruit, but prune more severely so as to keep the height and spread of a tree in a planter at 4 feet or less. The best way to do such pruning is with your fingers while the tree is in active growth. Pinch off the ends of shoots when they are 5 to 6 inches long, to slow them down. Get rid of misplaced growth entirely by rubbing it off with your fingertips as soon as it appears.

Some of this pruning will take care of some fruit thinning by removing fruit buds, but you'll need to do more thinning with a planter-grown tree than with others. Allow apple, pear, and peach trees to ripen no more than ten fruits the first bearing year. Each season thereafter you can let them increase the number by about five. For apricots and plums you can double these amounts.

Transferring to a larger planter is best done in spring before new growth starts. Water the tree well the day before. Loosen the top few inches of earth and slip a blade, such as a saw, down the sides of the planter to loosen the ball of earth. Lay the planter on its side and slide the tree out onto a cloth with a steady pull on the base of the trunk. Scrape away a third of the ball of earth and prune the larger roots back by one-third. Replant with a fresh soil mixture at the same depth as before.

A less troublesome substitute for repotting every two or three years after a tree is in its permanent container is to replace the top four inches of soil with a fresh mixture. When doing so, prune off the roots exposed. Repotting is better for the tree, of course. but sometimes impractical for the owner.

Another substitute for repotting is to make a complete change of scene. Transfer your little planter tree to a permanent spot in the open ground and replace it in the planter with a different fruit. Make such a change in spring before new growth starts, and take the opportunity to scrub out the planter well with soapy water and dry it in the sunshine.

One warning: If you live in a cold-winter climate, it may be advisable to protect a container-grown tree during extremes of temperature, as a planter gives less protection to roots than does planting in the ground. Merely wheeling the planter into an unheated garage at these times will give considerable protection. In less severe weather, a planter can be protected by placing it close to a house wall where it will be shielded from strong wind.

Getting
Started

3

If you have a choice, select for your fruit garden a spot that gets all-day sun, slopes gently down toward the north, is protected from wind but has good air circulation, has good humus-filled garden soil that is slightly acid, and is well drained.

Most of us must compromise. This is possible. The sunshine can be six hours a day; the slope can be ignored; if needed, wind protection can be provided by hedges and fences. This leaves soil and drainage, and you can't do as much compromising here but you can put things to rights if they are wrong.

Soil

To add humus to soil, dig in stable manure or compost at the rate of a cubic yard to five hundred square feet of surface. This is good advice but if you can't get stable manure and don't have a compost pile, it won't do you much good. In that case, peat moss is an excellent substitute. Sometimes called the city gardener's best friend, it also makes chemical fertilizers more effective.

There are always local substitutes, too. We can buy spent mushroom soil at three dollars a cubic yard if we furnish the truck. Other substitutes are shredded corncobs, spoiled hay, and sawdust. To each of these, and to peat moss, add half a pound of ammonium nitrate for each bushel, or ten pounds to the cubic yard, to maintain the nitrogen balance in the soil.

Another way to add humus is to plant a legume such as clover or alfalfa. Sow it in June. Turn the crop under with a spade or rotary tiller (you can rent one) in early fall, and plant your fruit trees the following spring.

Drainage

Laying a tile line two to three feet underground, leading to a lower outlet, as a ditch or storm sewer, is the classic way to drain soggy soil. It is a hard way for the home gardener. It really takes a professional to do a job you can depend on, though when well done it is a permanent cure.

You may be able to bypass this method by elevating the proposed fruit-garden area with some loads of topsoil well mixed with humus, such as peat moss. This is not a cheap way to cure sogginess but it is less expensive than tile drainage, much less devastating to the yard, and it presents you with the kind of soil that gardeners dream of and fruit trees love. Raise your site by about two feet if you can. You may have to build a retaining wall, but sloping the sides will usually hold such a pile of earth in place.

If the land isn't too awfully soggy, a layer of rocks at the bottom of each planting hole may take care of drainage. Dig a hole deep enough to accommodate the extra bulk of the rocks.

Nursery stock

Your fruit trees will arrive by express, by parcel post, or in some cases by a parcel-delivery service. It depends on the nursery you are dealing with, the size of the order, and so on. The practice is to ship stock bare-rooted but well protected from drying out by a wrapping. Most nurseries give shipping details in their catalogues, and since practices vary among nurseries, it is important to read the catalogue on this point.

If your trees arrive in a moisture-controlled cardboard packing case, so labeled, put this in a cool, dark place (not below freezing) until the day before you plant. Then unpack and stand the trees with their roots in a tub of water until just before planting. With any other packing, open it at the bottom, moisten the roots with a gallon or two of water if they feel dry, and cover them with damp burlap. Then unpack and stand in water before planting.

Some gardeners prefer to "heel in" trees pending planting. To do this, unwrap and untie them first. Then dig a trench deep enough to hold the roots, place trees half upright in the trench, and cover the roots with damp earth.

WHEN NURSERY STOCK ARRIVES. *If in moisture-controlled packing, store unopened in cool place. With other packings, moisten dry roots, cover with damp burlap, store in cool place. Or unwrap and "heel in". Before planting any stock, unwrap, and stand roots in water 24 hours.*

Planting

Most fruit trees are planted in spring. Fall planting is tricky, except in Zones 8 and 9. The ideal day is mild and overcast, the earth just moist enough to work easily—but better too dry than too wet. Dig a hole large enough to hold roots without crowding. Keep the topsoil separate from the subsoil, because when you refill the hole you are going to put the topsoil at the bottom.

Prune off any broken roots, set the tree in the hole, and lay a board across the hole to check where the soil level will come on the trunk. It should be at or a little higher than where it was when the tree was growing in the nursery. You can tell by the darker color of the part that was underground. If you need to raise the level of the earth in the hole, add topsoil and tramp it firmly before resetting the tree. By placing it at the depth it grew in the nursery, you'll be sure to have the graft union above ground.

A slightly shallower planting is all right, but planting too deep can cause the grafted top (the scion) to send out roots on its own, changing the character of your tree. Deep planting can even kill a tree, especially in heavy soil. The bark is more sensitive than you might think, and burying it can bring on disease.

Don't put fertilizer in the hole *at this time* unless you use one of the new slow-release nitrogen types, which have shown very good results. Hold the tree upright in the hole and throw in a few spadefuls of topsoil. Jiggle the tree a bit to sift the soil about the roots. Then fill the hole two-thirds full, tramping the earth *hard* several times as you go and poking it in well with your hoe handle.

Now pour a bucket of water into the hole. Add soluble fertilizer at half strength unless you have used the dry slow-release nitrogen type. The water here is vital, but not everyone agrees that fertilizing is also necessary. However, Stark's have found it grows better trees for them. The soluble fertilizer they use is Tre-Pep: 22.75 percent nitrogen, 24 percent phosphorus, and 12 percent potash. The first year they give additional feedings at full strength (2 tablespoons to 1 gallon of water) at three-week intervals until midsummer. Over the first season, test-blocks of newly planted trees in their nursery have made 25 percent more growth when so fed than have untreated ones.

Finish filling the hole when the soluble fertilizer has soaked in. Complete your planting with the last soil that came out of the

PLANTING. A. Dig the hole large enough to take the roots without crowding. Set the tree with the graft union (ringed) above ground level; sift in a little soil around the roots while jiggling the tree slightly. B. Fill hole two-thirds, firm soil with your feet and by poking it with a hoe handle. C. Pour in a bucket of half-strength fertilizer solution. D. Let soak in, fill up with topsoil, prune, and if needed, drive in a stake now for support against wind.

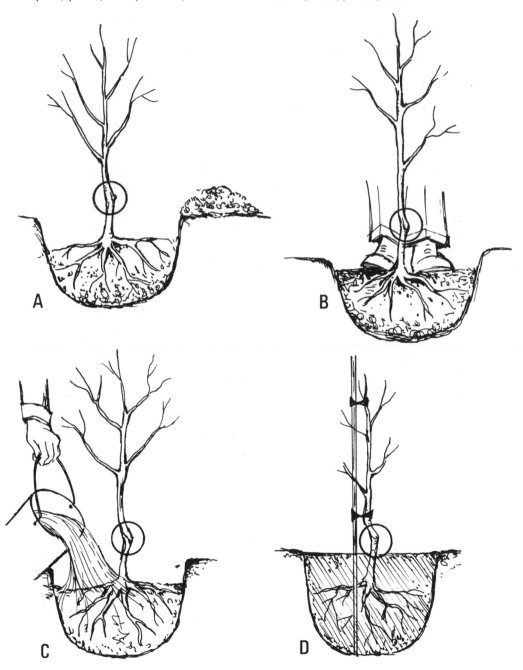

hole as you were digging it. When all is done, the tree should be set as solidly as a post. This is the time to drive a stake if you want it for support against wind.

Pruning

You prune a newly planted tree to make it grow better. Taking off some of the top gives more nourishment to what is left and also forces branching, making a better shaped plant.

Prune your newly planted trees, both dwarfs and standards, like this:

APPLE, PEAR, CHERRY, PLUM. Select three to five branches at different spots up and down and around the trunk, and prune them back to about 10 inches. What you want is a well-balanced tree, not a flat or lopsided one. Now prune the top of the main leader, or trunk, back to about 12 inches above the highest branch that you are retaining. (For plums, cut off the top about 24 inches from ground level.) Finally prune off all other branches where they join the trunk, leaving no stubs. The cut ends do not need painting.

PEACH, NECTARINE, APRICOT. Select three branches spaced around the trunk at about the same height, and prune these to 2 to 4 inches, letting each have one or two buds. Prune the top of the trunk to 1 to 2 inches above the highest branch you are keeping. Remove all other branches.

QUINCE AND NUTS. Simply cut off one-third of the top.

GRAPES AND SMALL FRUITS. See the chapters on each.

SPUR-TYPE TREES. Prune as for non-spur trees.

Opposite Top: PRUNING AT PLANTING TIME. Left: Establish vase shape for peaches, nectarines, apricots by selecting about three branches spaced around the trunk at approximately the same height, and removing others. Center: Remove top third of nuts and quinces. Right: Prune apples, pears, cherries, plums to pyramid form by selecting three to five well-spaced branches, cutting each to 10 inches, the leader to 12 inches above the highest branch; remove other branches. For plums, cut off the leader at about 24 inches above ground. Bottom: TRUNK PROTECTION. To keep rodents from gnawing bark, enclose trunks of newly planted fruit trees with a cylinder of hardware cloth—5 inches wide, about 15 inches long—sunk a few inches into ground.

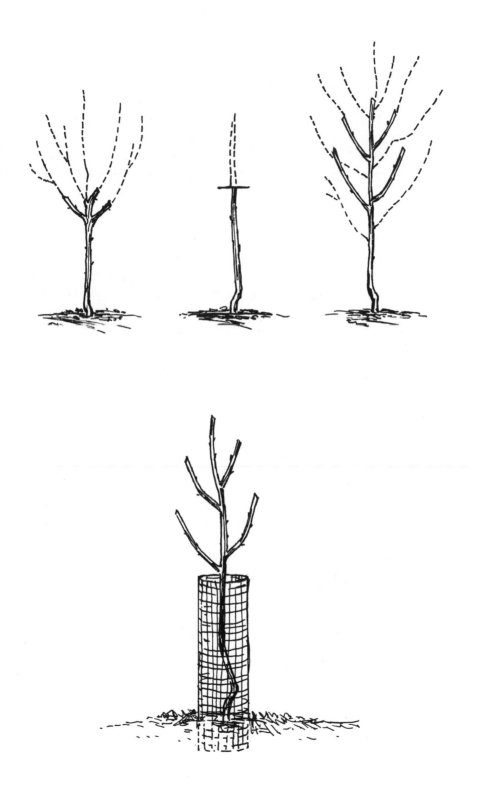

Trunk protection

The bark of newly planted fruit trees is a delicacy to field mice and rabbits. They often eat out a ring clear around the trunk and so kill the tree. This is called girdling. To prevent it, as soon as you finish planting, place a cylinder of wire screen or hardware cloth 5 inches in diameter and 15 inches high around the base of the tree. Push the lower part 2 to 3 inches into the ground.

Moisture control

The day after planting, if the earth is dry enough to work, cultivate the area extending 3 to 4 feet out from the trunk. Keep this circle cultivated until the weather turns warm. Then spread a mulch on it, 2 to 6 inches deep. The idea is to hold moisture in the soil. Soil behaves like a wick, and the water in it will rise to the top and evaporate into the air unless checked. Mulch also keeps the root system cooler in summer. Any mulch will reduce the amount of water that all young fruit trees need during their first season if rain is scanty.

Some gardeners swear by one mulching material, some by another. There is probably less difference than they think. This was indicated in tests at the Brooklyn Botanic Garden where seven different mulches varied by no more than 4 percent in ability to keep moisture in the soil. The same tests showed that a mere 2-inch mulch could carry a garden through a month-long drouth with soil moisture holding nearly steady. So choose your mulch according to what you can get, what looks good, and the nature of your fruit-garden site.

If you can get stable manure, use it. Compost is also good, but both materials are in such demand for other garden needs that your mulch will more likely be grass clippings, sawdust or wood chips, pine straw, or something of the sort. We used to mulch with pond weeds, thus helping the fishing while we helped the trees.

Except with manure and compost, add some balanced fertilizer to offset nitrogen loss from decomposition of the mulch. Two or three handfuls sprinkled on top of the mulch for each tree will do it.

One way to obtain mulching material is by use of a garden-sized motor-driven shredder that chops up leaves, small branches, bark, vines, stalks, and roots. If you can justify the investment, this is a

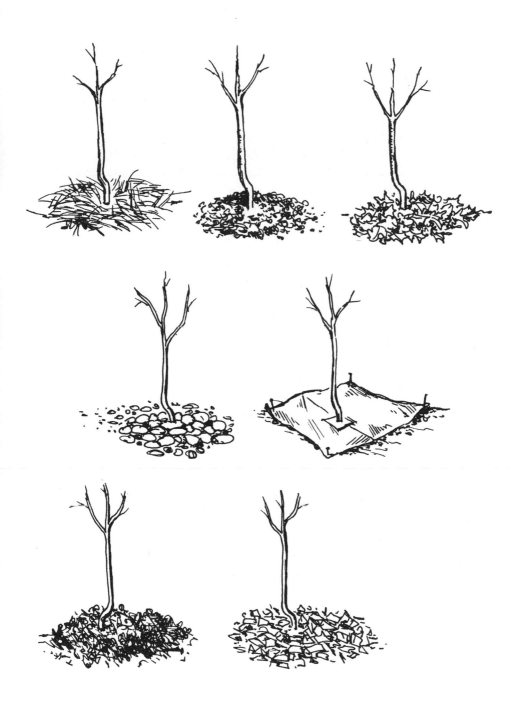

MULCHES. To *help hold moisture in soil and keep down weeds, mulch your fruit trees. Various materials are used for this purpose—straw, peatmoss, leaves, pebbles, (stable manure, or wood chips) one of the sheet plastics sold for mulching,*

labor-saver and a garden-groomer. But utility companies that use such machines to get rid of tree trimmings will often sell the chips to gardeners.

Your fruit-garden site will affect your choice of mulch and the amount. You want the mulch to stay in place so a sloping site or a windy one needs heavier mulching than a flat area. Some gardeners on slopes resort to a mulch of pebbles. If you use them, check the earth beneath every now and then; slugs, sowbugs, and various other insects collect under stones. Synthetic mulches of sheet plastic and other materials are so far mainly of interest to flower and vegetable gardeners, but fruit plantings are logical areas for such products when they have been developed with the requirements of fruit in mind.

Item: Don't spread mulch right up to the trunk of a fruit tree. It makes the bark tender and invites rodent damage. Leave a clear space of about 6 inches around each trunk.

But after all this you may be thinking, what if I don't want *any* mulch; what if I want a lawn under my fruit trees? Go ahead and have a lawn. Grass and fruit aren't an ideal combination but they get along. Just increase the amount of plant food and water given the grass under your trees.

Spray the new tree?

Must you spray fruit trees before they are old enough to bear fruit? Yes, for you want to prevent insects and disease from slowing growth. This is the period to build a strong framework that will bear future fruit.

Control this first year is simple. Use a combination spray that will take care of several things at once. There are a number of these "all-purpose" sprays on the market, also dusts. Spray or dust young trees three or four times at two-week intervals, starting when new growth is about an inch long. When trees set blossoms, an indication that they are ready to begin bearing, switch to the simple spray schedule given in the chapter on each fruit.

Keeping track of your trees

This is something we learned from a hobby fruit gardener years ago. We had asked him how early his everbearing strawberries were ripe, and he produced a small file card and read off the exact dates for each spring crop of the ten years just past. We recommend such a records system. We keep ours on 3- by 5-inch file cards, one card for each tree in a small planting, and one for each planting of small fruits, such as raspberries. A page for each in a loose-leaf notebook would be as good or better. Here are the facts most interesting to record:

> Date tree was planted.
> Date first blossoms opened each year.
> Dates and kinds of sprays used, and weather conditions.
> Dates and kinds of fertilizing and mulching.
> Date fruit was thinned.
> Date first fruit was picked.
> Date last fruit was picked.
> Total amount of fruit.

Such records take a good deal of guesswork out of your fruit gardening. In some cases, they give you the answer to puzzlers you might never get otherwise. For example, the date of first blossoming is a clue to pollination, since a scanty crop can be the result of bloom too early to receive pollen from a later blooming specimen. If so, the remedy is to plant another early bloomer of a compatible variety, or to bud such a variety onto the first tree. The budding way is more chancy but, if it works, you'll have the pleasure of growing two kinds of fruit on the same tree. (You can even buy such a tree—with up to five varieties on one.) The date of any budding should also be made on the index card along with subsequent details.

Another good use of your records is to observe, in the quiet of some winter evening, just how well your various trees are repaying your care. As there are lazy hens in a laying flock, there may be lazy trees in any sized orchard. Or, to be more charitable, trees that can't get along well in your climate or on your soil. Checking on comparative harvests will show them up, clearly and unmistakably.

About
Culture 4

The water rat in *The Wind in the Willows* said there's no pleasure "like messing around with boats." Change boats to fruit trees and do we hear an aye? We do. Tens of thousands, from gardeners who are always hearing that mild slur: "You certainly are lucky with . . ." and you fill it in—"apples, pears, peaches. . . ." Luck? Well, we all need a little luck. Luck enough to get a few good soaking rains in season, to have neighbors who don't let noxious weeds go to seed windward of our garden, or plant rhizome bamboo where it will burrow under the fence line and pop up among our fruits.

But what makes a gardener good isn't luck. Nor is there any mystery about it. His secret is simple—personal interest. He takes a personal interest in his garden. "The foot of the owner manureth the land." And the owner of the foot is curious, and often surprised, and intrigued even by failures.

The gardener who walks his garden may see, sprouting from the middle graft on the trunk of a double-worked tree, unwelcome shoots while they are still mere buds. Whereupon he beheads them with fingertip instead of saw. He scrapes a little earth away from a trunk and, if he sees the start of any scion-rooting, he clips the roots before they change his dwarf into a giant. He sees and removes, while they are young, any suckers, as the shoots arising from roots and underground stems are called. And he does a little garden housekeeping as he goes, clearing away fallen leaves, limbs, or fruit, watching that branches aren't rubbing against each other, or growing in the wrong direction. He's a man looking for trouble, but if you listen, you'll probably hear him whistling while he works. Because there's nothing quite like messing around with fruit trees.

Equipment

If a fruit gardener loves gadgets he's going to buy gadgets, but the basic tools of home fruit gardening are the basic tools of any gardening. You probably already own them: a spade, a fork, a rake, a hoe; a heavy hammer, pruners, buckets, a sprayer, a hose, a wheelbarrow. With these and an occasional item from the toolbox, you can do practically everything. Gardening is a healthy pastime and exercise is one of the dividends. Having said that we'll have to add that good new tools for gardening come on the market from time to time. Some of them save work and time and are interesting to use.

If you grow non-dwarf or standard trees, you may need a tall ladder, also a pole pruner. If you do some grafting, a grafting knife is a convenience. And, being a gardener who intends to succeed, you supply yourself with baskets and boxes for gathering and storing the harvest.

Windbreaks

A fruit tree needs good air circulation but it doesn't care for hard and persistent winds, and they can delay bearing. Summer winds are especially damaging, snatching at leaves and banging fruit about, bruising it, or knocking it off entirely. Wind also causes excessive water loss through the leaves. If your garden is exposed to strong wind, screen it with a fence or a planting. Such a windbreak need not be taller than six feet to do a good job, even with standard trees.

A hedge of privet makes a good screen, and evergreens chosen according to locality are popular and effective. The time to plant such a screen is a year or so before the fruit trees go in. One of the best is arborvitae.

A building—your house, garage, garden house—can serve as windbreak if you can plant on the leeward side. A board fence is the most space-saving windbreak and goes up fast. Make it of foot-wide boards set at an angle to form louvers. This is attractive and lets a little air through so the fence doesn't restrict circulation too much.

Frost

The hedge or fence that protects your fruit garden from wind will
also give some protection from frost, and so will the wall of your
house if the fruit garden is near it. It is the late and hard spring
frost that does the most damage, damaging blossoms and reducing
the harvest, or killing tender new growth. Peaches and apricots are
especially vulnerable to frost because they bloom early.

Beware the clear and windless night with temperature rapidly
sinking after unusually warm spring weather. Frost comes at these
times as cold air flows down from several hundred feet above the
earth. It is preceded by a loss of heat from the air near ground
level so that there is a double chilling effect.

Draping sheets, shower curtains, or other covering over plants
when frost is expected is useful if it keeps some of this ground-level
heat from escaping. To do so, the material should reach to the
ground, making a tent rather than an umbrella. We've often used
such frost protection on small or dwarf fruit trees. Ideally you
ought to support the covering with a framework so it doesn't rest
on the tree, but this is practical only with a double-dwarf or something as small, or with a young tree.

Heaters are all right for commercial orchards but few home gardeners are likely to have them. One heater is merely a five-gallon
can with a couple of inches of furnace oil in the bottom and four
compressed fireplace "logs" standing upright in it. But even this
burns for only two hours or so.

If you want to protect just one dwarf tree from a hard frost,
you'd do better to cover it with a shower-curtain tent and then
run out an extension cord with a small light bulb on the end. Hang
the light in a bucket under the tent to keep it off the ground. Use
outdoor cord, and for safety's sake, turn the light on and off at the
house end. Another method that we and many other gardeners
have used to offset frost is to turn a fine hose spray on the trees
before morning sun strikes them.

Watering

An established fruit tree, kept well mulched, will not need water
from the faucet in a home garden unless there is a long drouth or
unless it grows in a dry-summer section. If so, deep monthly water-
ings are sufficient. Here is what you need to know about water and

your fruit trees: Even a large tree has its main roots in the upper six feet of soil, and roots reach out a few feet farther than the branch spread. As a rule, water goes straight down. An inch of water on top moistens about a five-inch depth of average garden soil.

Water only if you have to, but then thoroughly. The economical way is to throw up a ridge of earth along the outer circle of the roots and run the hose within this area. A thin, stiff wire can be pushed down to determine how deep the water has gone. Since the wire will go only through moist soil, it is a good gauge.

Grapes and the berry fruits are less deep rooted than fruit trees, also dwarf apples on Malling IX rootstocks, so these are more apt to need watering. They'll ask for it by drooping their leaves; they should then be watered as soon as possible. After you and your fruit garden get used to each other, you'll find you can tell when water is needed, even if you don't know exactly how you tell.

Feeding

If you are growing fruit trees in soil fertile enough for grass, you don't have to add fertilizer to get fruit. But, adding it may get you more fruit. The best fertilizer for a fruit tree is probably stable manure, and stable manure is scarce. When we've had it, we've used it generously; when we haven't had it, we've used compost. Both give good results when spread as a mulch, which makes them doubly useful.

Fruit trees seem to get all the phosphorus and potash they need from their environment, lacking only nitrogen when they lack anything. If you are an organic gardener, you can supply nitrogen to your trees with manure or compost, or by growing a legume, such as clover or vetch, under the trees and then digging it in at the end of the season. Legumes capture air-borne nitrogen and store it in nodules on their generous root systems.

The chemicals most often recommended to supply nitrogen to fruit trees are ammonium sulphate (20 percent nitrogen) and ammonium nitrate (33 percent). You can find them at most farm-and-garden stores. Except for very acid soils, we have favored ammonium sulphate, which is slightly acid. Early in spring, apply about half a pound of ammonium sulphate, or a quarter-pound of ammonium nitrate, for each inch of tree diameter. Sprinkle it on the earth over the area the roots reach, and rake it in. Or sprinkle it on top of any mulch you are using. Rain or watering will carry it down into the ground.

Stark's apply a 45 percent nitrogen fertilizer to their orchard once a year in spring before growth starts. They allow a quarter-pound for each inch of trunk diameter.

If you prefer to feed through the leaves, apply a foliar fertilizer three times: first when all the flower petals have fallen; again ten days later; then ten days after that. Stark's nitrogen fertilizer can be dissolved in water and sprayed on the leaves, but don't do so with ammonium sulphate or ammonium nitrate, or take it for granted that *any* chemical fertilizer can be so handled. Leaves can absorb only certain kinds of chemicals; they can be damaged by high concentrations even of these.

Compared with flowers and vegetables, the amount of fertilizer given a fruit tree may seem too small. Don't give it another thought. A tree makes most of its own living, growing over a long season and searching out its food by means of a mattress of roots. You can overfertilize a fruit tree just as you can oversalt a pot of soup. The effects on a tree will be to produce too succulent leaf and twig growth at the expense of fruit, and possibly cause winter killing. In fact, if your fruit trees are growing well and giving you good crops, reduce by half the amount of fertilizer we suggested, or omit it entirely.

Compost

Since compost is both fertilizer and mulch, and also adds humus when dug into the soil, a word on how to make it may be in order. We start by building a bottomless box the size of a coldframe, 3 feet wide and 6 feet long; we make it of planks 12 inches wide and 2 inches thick. Then we make another just like it to set on top of the first, giving us a bin about 2 feet high. You can make yours still higher, up to 6 feet, but we like low compost piles.

We put one of these boxes, or frames, on the ground in a shady place convenient to the vegetable garden because that is where we get most of the raw material for compost. We draw a line on the soil, around the inside of the box, and remove the box while we dig this area to a depth of 8 to 10 inches, piling the soil nearby.

We then set the box over this hole, and begin building the compost. We do so by putting in a 6-inch layer of clean garden and kitchen waste, such as lettuce trimmings, pea vines and pods, potato plant tops and potato peelings, radish tops, banana skins, leaves, and lawn clippings. As this accumulates, we chop it up with a sharp spade. Moldy or diseased or woody plants are not good and neither is grease or meat, though coffee grounds, which are a little oily, can be used.

To hasten decomposition, we sprinkle this 6-inch layer with just enough dry commercial fertilizer to cover it. You may prefer to use a product called Adco, or you can make your own mixture: 2 pounds superphosphate, 6 pounds ground limestone, 7 pounds ammonium sulphate. Farm-and-garden stores carry these materials. Organic gardeners add no chemicals, but approve wood ashes and manures, which work, but more slowly than chemicals. On top of the fertilizer, we spread a 2-inch layer of some of the soil that we dug out of the bottom of the bin. Then we water the whole pile down, soaking it well.

As we accumulate garden waste, we repeat this process, setting the second box in place when the pile is high enough to need it. When we get to the top we finish with a layer of soil. We keep the pile moist, and we spade it up once or twice over a couple of months. We have used compost made in this way as soon as two months after finishing the pile but we often leave it alone for four to six months. It comes out looking like woods' earth, dark and pleasant-smelling. By removing the top box after the pile is partly used, we get at the compost lower down more easily.

We often add a few buckets of old compost to the pile as we build it, in the belief this acts as a sort of yeast. If you can, keep three compost piles going—one you're building up, one in the process of decomposing, and one that is ready for the garden.

Weeds

What about weed-killers in a home fruit garden? We're talking about the selective herbicides that began with the introduction of 2,4-D in 1944. Certainly they can save a world of hoeing and pulling. When we apply them we handle them like dynamite, particularly if we're spraying them. The wind has a habit of coming to life just as you aim a sprayer at the weeds, and whoosh! the herbaceous border twenty feet away meets its doom. If yours is a neighborhood of small yards set cheek by jowl, this can cause words.

Also to consider with these weed-killers is their potency in microscopic amounts. When 2,4-D (dichlorophenoxyacetic acid) was new on the market a nurseryman who knows better now employed it on some weeds, rinsed out his spray tank, and put fungicide on some tomato plants. Their leaves curled and thickened, turned yellow, and the plants died. The rinsing had left the merest trace of 2,4-D in the tank but, even so diluted, it was deadly to the tomatoes. Yet the same sort of rinsing had left residues of *other* spray solutions that were poisonous to certain plants but which did no harm in such small amounts.

The safe policy is to reserve a separate sprayer for herbicides. The same applies to any vessel you mix the solution in. For spot control of persistent weeds, we keep a plastic bottle filled with herbicide. The cap has a small hole in the top, so that a squeeze on the bottle sends a water-pistol stream at an individual weed, and very accurately. Also, there now are granular forms of weed-killers that can be sprinkled on dry; there is no problem of drift with them, of course, or of sprayer contamination.

A strong solution of table salt was once the weed-killer some gardeners relied on, and it is effective though not as much so as the new products. Dissolve a pound of salt in a gallon of hot water and sprinkle it on at once. Boiling water alone is fairly discouraging to a weed.

For a small fruit garden we think the best weed-killer is a hoe. Buy a new file and put a chisel edge on the hoe blade. If you don't care for hoeing, a sharp tool makes it bearable; if you like hoeing, it makes it sport. And don't forget to mulch—where mulch is, weeds are far less likely to grow.

Thinning

An old Dutch friend used to plead with her skinny but productive milk cow, "Lizzie, p-l-e-a-s-e keep some for yourself." The average healthy fruit tree is like Lizzie. It wants to make fruit and make fruit and make fruit. Left to itself, it will do what a neglected plum tree on property adjoining ours does every year—crack its branches with the weight of fruit. This is one reason for thinning fruit. Thinning means removing some of the fruit while it is still small and green. This gives more room and nourishment to what is left. For instance, every apple on a tree needs the work of fifty leaves to feed it, another reason for thinning. Still other reasons are to keep trees from bearing so heavily one year that they can't bear at all the next. Thinning also helps trees endure dry summers and cold winters.

We hope all this persuades you to thin your fruit, because we know you'll hate to do it. Most home fruit gardeners don't thin nearly hard enough or early enough. A commercial peach-grower may thin down to about eight hundred the eighteen hundred peaches a big healthy tree will set, and his eight hundred will amount to something. If you want proof, don't thin one limb of a tree. You'll find that the thinned ones will end up by giving you more actual pounds of fruit per foot of limb—as well as top-grade quality.

To a degree, your trees will thin themselves by losing some young fruits in what is called the June drop. This may be enough, though it seldom is. Check to see how far apart the remaining fruits are. A general rule is one fruit every twelve inches along the branch, but this is almost too general. Here are more specific spacings; the wider ones are for the larger varieties:

> Apples and pears 6 to 8 inches
> Peaches and nectarines 4 to 5 inches
> Large plums and apricots 3 to 4 inches
> Small plums, cherries, quinces, or nuts need no thinning.
> Thin grapes by removing small and poor-looking bunches early in the season.

You can thin with pruning shears but the fast way is with your fingers. To remove peaches, nectarines, and apricots, give them a twist. For apples, pears, and plums, hold the stem with thumb and index finger and rub off the fruit with your middle finger, leaving the stem on the branch. Thin most heavily through the upper part of a tree.

If thinning seems like a lot of work or if you don't have time to do it, you can buy a spray that may take care of it, or most of it *if applied at exactly the right time*. Ask for a chemical thinner at a garden-supply store, and *follow directions to the letter*. Sevin is a good one. But we think this is better for the commercial grower than for the home gardener, unless you have large trees or a big planting. Hand thinning gives you the chance to check on the fruit and to remove any runty, diseased, or otherwise unlovely specimens.

Enemies

Bird-lovers are always saying that the favor birds do gardeners by eating insects entitles them to a share of the harvest. The trouble is that birds don't take a share; they try to take it all. Also we might mention toads and bats as being great insect-eaters without making any claim on the harvest. But we aren't consistent, because we build feeders and put nuts and suet out for the birds.

For some reason, birds are much less trouble some years than others. The most popular fruits with them are cherries and grapes, the least popular are nuts. Damage to apples and pears usually amounts to a few pecks, a more serious matter for commercial growers than for home gardeners. Some home gardeners have been finding that the yellow cherry called 'Gold' fools birds; they keep waiting for it to turn red. But after a few seasons they get smarter.

What can you do to keep birds from taking more than a share of your fruit? The best protection is to throw a net over a fruit tree as harvest approaches. This is possible with dwarf trees and with strawberries, grapes, and brambles, and it is just about foolproof. You can use fishnet, or a netting sold solely for fruit trees. One gardener built a cage of rabbit wire around each of two big fig trees. We have also used such cage gardens and can recommend them.

Another form of protection consists of tying paper bags around individual fruits. This is useful on a limited scale to protect a few superb pears, peaches, bunches of grapes, and the like. Brown paper bags can affect flavor, so use white ones.

Covering with netting or cages is no solution for a large tree, such as a sweet cherry, where the fruit is too small for bagging to be practical. And sweet cherries are terribly popular with birds, as noted. The best protection for a sweet cherry tree is a mulberry nearby. Birds actually prefer mulberries to cherries, and the fruit ripens at about the same time. We've had mulberry trees but we can't say we like them, as the fruit is very staining and you can't keep a place cleaned up while the fruit is ripe.

Other ways, more or less successful, of doing something about birds involve frightening them. Or trying to.

NOISE.   This has been popular in England for centuries. Shouting and banging on metal was once the way. Today electronic devices, explosives, and auto horns are employed by commercial growers. Obviously none of these work very well for home gardeners unless the neighbors are deaf.

SCARECROWS.   You can stuff a suit and sit a dummy near your fruit trees or even up in a tree, and the birds will stay away for a while. The same goes for strips of aluminum foil hung in the tree, or foil pie tins. But soon the birds come back. However, if you put your scarecrow out as late as possible, just as the fruit is approaching ripeness, the birds may stay away long enough to matter.

CATS.   If you can get a cat to work with you, birds will bother your fruit less. Some gardeners have built a platform in a fruit tree for the cat and some have put a wire cage in the tree with the cat inside. Every cat we've known would fight like a tiger if you tried to put it in a cage in a tree, and none would have considered sitting on a platform unless he thought of it first. If you have a cat, we suggest you let the cat handle the birds-in-the-tree situation in his own way. A cat can be a real protection to strawberries and the other small fruits. Some gardeners put a collar on the cat and leash it among the strawberries but, again, we have yet to meet a cat that would put up with this. Nor have we ever found it necessary.

Squirrels can be as bad as birds about robbing fruit and nut trees. This is being brought sharply home to us at this very moment. The little plum tree we spoke of as needing thinning is being thinned to the bare wood by a squirrel, now that the fruit is ripening.

You can keep squirrels away from fruit by putting sheet-metal sleeves or funnels around trunks during the ripening season. But these will do no good if squirrels can jump overhead from other

trees, and this is something to remember when you are choosing
a site for your fruit and nuts. A slingshot is usually a good chaser
for squirrels. A jet from a hose is something else they don't care for.

What about the old, old tree?

To be coolly practical about it, most old fruit trees aren't worth
saving. Worth it, that is, from a money standpoint. Saving them
is slow work and the returns in fruit may not repay your trouble
and cost. But let's face it—some people (we, for instance) can
hardly bear to cut down a tree, especially a fruit tree. Furthermore,
the old tree may have an aesthetic appeal, may look just right
where it is. Or it may be screening a poor view, or conferring privacy, or giving welcome shade.

Helen Van Pelt Wilson, one of the country's well-known authorities on flower gardening, so admires the rugged dignity of her
ancient apple that she has planted beneath it what she calls an
apple-tree garden. Here the tree is the massive central element in
a setting of narcissus, bleeding hearts, mertensia, and ferns. When
the tree is in blossom, the spring picture is a lovely sight.

To begin with, we'll assume you want fruit from the veteran
tree you're going to save. If you want the tree just for blossoms and
form, you'll find the fruit a nuisance as, indeed, Mrs. Wilson does,
though this does not deter her. However, fruit won't be top quality
if the tree is overmature, and though there are sprays to stop fruit
from forming, they aren't a hundred percent sure. We'll go into
this in a minute.

But if you do want fruit, no matter if it isn't the best, your work
will consist of cleaning up the tree and feeding it. Scrape loose
bark off the trunk and larger limbs. Then rake up the scrapings and
other trash, and burn them.

Early in spring, before growth has started, apply a dormant oil
spray or lime-sulphur. And before you spray, scrub the trunk and
larger limbs with a wad of burlap dipped in the spray solution.
This treatment will give good control of scale. Finish up by soaking the soil around the tree with the spray solution. (But for a big
tree, better call in a professional tree-man who will have proper
equipment.)

Next prune off all dead limbs and diseased or rotting ones, and
chisel out any bad places in the trunk down to sound wood. Burn

the punky stuff or have it hauled off; save the sound wood for the workbench and fireplace. It makes a fine, slow-burning, aromatic fire.

Treat cut surfaces with shellac or a tree paint, and cover any holes you have dug in the trunk. Seal these with a commercial tree-filler. It is sold at garden stores and is better than cement as it makes a tighter seal.

You now want to open the tree to air and sun by cutting back cluttered vertical limbs to outward-growing branches, and by removing crossing limbs and any that are poorly shaped and too close together. Also take off water sprouts (the young growth arising vertically from other limbs; sometimes useful as replacement wood, and always an indication of vigor). What you are after is a strong and simple shape. To avoid shock, do about a quarter of the severe prunning the first year, the rest over the next three years.

Finally, spade up the soil under the tree, in a circle two to three feet beyond the spread of the branches. Sprinkle fifteen pounds of ammonium sulphate or about ten pounds of ammonium nitrate on the dug surface and rake it in. You'll need less than this of a higher analysis fertilizer; Stark's orchard fertilizer, for instance, 45 percent nitrogen, would be spread at a rate of about seven pounds per tree. Whatever fertilizer you use, the tree should get about three pounds of actual nitrogen.

Later in the spring, spread a mulch. Follow the spray program for the species as the season goes along if your old tree wants to fruit, and it probably will. Also, spraying will help it keep a good leaf cover.

If the tree isn't too ancient, you may want to graft on some other varieties of its species. This is called top-working, and the method is explained in Chapter nineteen.

To prevent fruiting

Now—about the old tree that you *don't* want to fruit.

A great deal of work has been done toward finding out how to keep fruit trees from fruiting when the fruit is a nuisance but the trees are attractive. Three types of compounds have been tried with some success: hormones, caustics, and liquid plastics. The hormone types are the ones most adaptable to home conditions. They are sold under several trade names (Amid-thin, Sta-Fast.

Fruitone-N, Apple-Set). All these employ naphthyleneacetic acid or a derivative, which in horticultural shorthand is NAA.

If you decide to try one of these fruiting preventers, do it with the knowledge that this is not an exact or cut-and-dried procedure, and you may succeed only moderately. The weather, the timing, the coverage, and the tree itself are all variables. Also, the only fruit trees that so far have responded to the treatments are apple and crabapple. However, the hormone type of de-fruiting spray isn't dangerous to use or poisonous.

The insecticide Sevin, which itself is used as a fruit thinner, is sometimes combined with NAA in the spray. Here are the suggested programs, through the kindness of one of the more active researchers in this field, Glen P. Lumis of Michigan State University.

> To make 1 gallon of spray:
> Apple trees: NAA 15-30 parts per million (1 tablespoon of stock solution—see below)
>   and
>   Sevin 50% wettable powder, 2 tablespoons.
> Crabapple trees: NAA 20-60 parts per million (1-3 tablespoons of stock solution—see below).

In each case the spray is applied when trees are in full bloom. In making a very dilute solution with a highly concentrated chemical, a simple way is to first make a stock solution with ¼ teaspoonful of the chemical to ½ pint (1 cup) of water. Then make your spray by putting 1 tablespoonful of this stock solution into 1 gallon of water to get a concentration of approximately 20 parts per million. Two tablespoonfuls of stock solution to the gallon of water would give you 40 parts per million, and so forth.

Mr. Lumis suggests you try the spray on a small branch at least a week before you expect to spray the whole tree, to see how it reacts. A little leaf wilting isn't serious, but some gardeners have had leaves badly damaged from sprays. When spraying the whole tree, Mr. Lumis advises, "Thoroughly cover all the leaves, because the hormone is absorbed by the leaves." You may need to call in a professional tree-man to handle a large tree properly.

To find out more

To learn more about fruit gardening and solve problems that may be unique in your area, you can tap these three good sources of knowledge:

1. GARDENERS.   Other home fruit gardeners in your neighborhood or area are prime sources of information on what fruits do well there, what pests are troublesome, and so on. Rely on their experience—though not necessarily on their methods.

2. OFFICIAL SOURCES.   The one most likely to be helpful is the agricultural extension service of your state university. Look in your local telephone directory under the name of your state for a listing. This varies from state to state and may be designated Extension Service, Agricultural Service, Horticultural Service, University of—, and so on. If there is no listing for your town, write to your university or state college for information or for direct answers to your questions.

The United States Department of Agriculture has about 4000 publications on farm and garden subjects. Only a few are of interest to home fruit gardeners. To get those you may find useful, state your needs in a letter to:

> United States Department of Agriculture
> Office of Information
> Washington, D. C.

Many publications from state and national sources are free, and none costs much.

3. SUPPLIERS.   The nursery that sells you fruit trees will also answer your questions about growing them and will send you printed information. Suppliers of fertilizer, insecticides, garden equipment, and so on, also have departments to take care of customers' questions. Just write the company at the address given on the label of its product, and your letter will arrive at the right desk. Some-

times there is a small charge for more elaborate booklets, but most
material is free.

Home gardeners interested in older and less usual varieties may
like to know about a man whose hobby this has been, and who
found himself obliged to get into the nursery business as a result.
He is Robert A. Nitschke of Birmingham, Michigan.

Pest Control is Easy Now

"Nice vegetable garden you've got there," we told the man. It was a terrace garden, an ornament to the yard. There were string-straight rows of endive, carrots, Swiss chard, and celery. A square bed of lettuce interplanted with radishes was at one end of the rows and, at the other, a block of young broccoli bordered with parsley. There were chives along the stone retaining wall in front, and the ferny delicacy of asparagus hedged the back. The owner of this productive little beauty was cultivating it.

"I've always wanted a few fruit trees, too," he said, "but. . . ."

"Well?" one of us said. We could see a place for five or six dwarf trees in the back, an open spot.

"Oh, well!" the man said. "Vegetables, yes. But I haven't got time to look after a *fruit* garden."

Now, how did he ever get that idea? We've had many vegetable gardens in many different climates, and the smallest one was in a wire cage and no bigger than a bathroom. But even that tiny garden took at least twice as much looking after as a dozen dwarf fruit trees.

Let's be realistic. Most of the time a fruit tree looks after itself. When you get right down to it, what most people mean when they say they don't have time to tend to fruit trees, is, "All that spraying!"

The new combinations

Twenty years ago those people were right. Today they're wrong. Here's the reason in three words—New Combination Sprays. Since how we discovered the flaw in this thrifty approach. A home fruit garden needs such small spray quantities that the various items often go stale or lumpy, or corrode their containers, long before you can use them up. Then they clog your sprayer and jam your duster.

Now let's look at the other side of the coin. A combination spray will take care of one mature dwarf fruit tree for one entire season for thirty-five cents—say the value of two pounds of its fruit. It works out like this: The tree will require about six sprayings, using a quart of solution or less each time. This comes to one and one-half gallons. One pound of combination material makes more than ten times that much spray and costs $3.50. The combination in dust form comes to the same cost per tree for a season's protection.

The $3.50 is the price of Stark's combination spray, but most nurseries and garden centers carry some sort of combination formula, and prices range from about $2.50 up. A popular combination is malathion-methoxychlor-captan. Stark's include these three and add two more, the fungicide zineb and an insecticide, TDE, which is a less toxic derivative of DDT.

Mix-it-yourself

We know, of course, that there is a type of gardener who *likes* to fiddle around with separate chemicals. And there is something to his point of view in the sense of accomplishment. The pest controls we list can be bought separately and used separately, following the dilution directions on the labels. You can also make your own combination spray. Here is the formula for the popular malathion-methoxchlor-captan combination, with the addition of kelthane for better control of mites. Kelthane can be omitted if mites are not bad, since malathion is also effective against them.

> 2 tablespoons malathion   (25% wettable powder)
> 3 tablespoons methoxychlor (50% wettable powder)
> 3 tablespoons captan   (50% wettable powder)
> 3 tablespoons kelthane   (18% wettable powder)

> Mix into a paste with 1 cup of water in a Mason jar (or quart pitcher). Fill the container with water, stir well, and pour the solution into a bucket or your

sprayer tank. Add 3 more quarts of water. Stir well
and apply at once.

Don't add anything to this formula, and don't change the
amounts given here. Slight alteration might not be harmful, but
if it is, your trees will be the losers.

The non-chemical approach

For the organic fruit gardener we have sympathy even if we don't
have high hopes. He distrusts chemicals and thinks that wetting a
tree with them is unnatural. It is, but so is taking aspirin for a
headache. We've seen unsprayed fruit trees crippled by insects and
disease; we've also seen unsprayed ones bear big crops of clean
fruit. Even though there are more than a hundred insects that attack fruit trees, not to mention viruses and fungi, none may be a
problem to you. It depends on season and locality. If you are the
only one growing fruit in your vicinity, there's a chance no harmful insects will search you out. Like tourists, insects are apt to rush
for obvious attractions, which for insects are commercial orchards.

Also, there are good insects—ladybugs, praying mantises, and
dragonflies are some—that eat harmful ones. These, plus varieties
of fruits resistant to some diseases, plus trees kept in vigorous good
health, can help the organic gardener, or any other, to get better
fruit. Pruning that keeps trees from overcrowding tops with
branches also helps to control disease, since sunlight and air discourage fungi and bacteria.

Another type of organic gardener prefers homemade sprays, such
as water in which crushed tomato leaves have been soaked, to kill
aphids. Soapy water is employed for the same purpose, or a brisk
jet of plain water, to wash off and drown insects. Water in which
puréed raw onion pulp has been soaked is also used, after strain-
ing, principally on aphids. To discourage borers, tree trunks are
painted with a paste of wood ashes and water, or with whitewash.

An old defense against codling moth, which causes wormy apples, was to scrape loose bark off trunks in spring and scrub them
with soapy water to get rid of cocoons under the loose bark. Another was to wrap a band of burlap around the trunk as a trap for
the larvae, which were then crushed by hand. Curculio beetles,
which cause wormy cherries, plums, nectarines, and sometimes

peaches, were and can still be shaken from a tree onto sheets on the ground, usually by jarring the tree with a rubber-headed maul. The Damson plum trees on our farm were planted in the chicken yard for this reason—so the birds could pounce on the beetles when they dropped to the ground.

Just a few days ago a friend, an intelligent woman, told us proudly of her peach tree. It seems the tree hadn't ever matured more than two peaches per season. This spring when she saw "all those ugly curled leaves it always has," she lost her temper, pulled them all off, and gave the tree a pep talk. And, she told us happily, the tree had responded with "two dozen nice peaches." Two dozen peaches. We couldn't help thinking of the two or three or four *bushels* of nice peaches she could have gathered if she had merely mixed a few tablespoons of a combination spray in a gallon of water early this spring and showered the tree with it. That healthy bath would have cleaned out the fungus that causes peach-leaf curl, and the tree would have used all its leaves to manufacture hundreds of peaches, and would have felt like a new tree in the bargain. (See the peach chapter, under Peach Troubles, for emergency measures when no *dormant* spray has been used.)

But no matter which line of control you take, organic or chemical, garden sanitation is one of the best ways to keep down trouble. Insects and fungi prosper in diseased leaves and fruit, in rotten or infected wood, and in weeds. This includes the weeds next door, so the problem is also one of human relations. Here, soft words and a share of your harvest may go a long way.

Systemics

If you care to become independently wealthy, invent something that can be fed to a fruit tree as fertilizer is, and that will repel fungi and kill harmful insects, bacteria, and viruses, but won't hurt good insects or the people who eat the fruit—or, of course, the tree. Your product will be a systemic control for diseases and pests.

A few limited-use systemic insecticides, such as cygon and meta-systox R, are already being tried for control of mites and aphids on some ornamentals, such as roses. The rose bush absorbs the material through its roots, along with food and water, and any insect that sucks the sap is poisoned. The bush is protected for about two months with a single treatment, and rain can't wash the systemic away.

We mention systemics here because, although they are in only very limited use with fruit trees at present, they are the logical pest controls of tomorrow. Three that have been used to kill sucking insects on fruit trees, applied up to within four weeks of harvest in commercial plantings, are meta-systox, rogor, and ekatin.

In general

In the chapters on each fruit we give a simple, basic program using a combination spray. (Read *dust* for *spray* if you prefer a duster.) You can follow these programs without studying either the pests or your climatic pattern. The sprays know what to do, and your trees will tell you by their spring and early summer stages of growth when to spray them. It is the early stages that are critical. As the season goes on and wood and leaves are less succulent, insects are less troublesome.

The insecticides in the combinations will take care of the bugs without your giving them another thought, but keep this in mind as to fungicides: They are preventives. If it rains, you may need to spray again. However, it takes a heavy rain to wash them off. As with an automobile, a sprayed tree doesn't get washed very thoroughly by rain. After the rain you can still see spots on the car—and the tree still has spray deposit on it, too.

Providing that rain doesn't wash off a spray, how long is one spraying effective? For ten days to two weeks. In no case should you spray while blossoms are open. You'll kill the bees and hurt pollination.

In the programs that we suggest, you may be surprised to find that no dormant spray is called for except for peaches and nectarines, where nothing else will control leaf curl. Recent experiments indicate that dormant sprays are impractical for home fruit gardens. They are apt to discolor painted walls, and they come at a time inconveniently early in the season. Omitting them has hardly affected the good quality of fruit.

You will see the merit of keeping a fruit-garden record, as recommended in Chapter three, when you try to time spray applications.

For instance, if a spray is most effective applied five weeks before fruit ripens, your own record of when fruit began to ripen in other seasons is the best possible guide.

Equipment for pest control

>   Sprayer or duster
>   Set of kitchen measuring spoons
>   Buckets
>   Wooden stirring sticks
>   Detergent or household ammonia to clean equipment

We like the trombone sprayer with a weighted hose you drop into a bucket of solution. In this way the bucket is your tank. It is easily cleaned, is replaceable at any hardware store, and you can keep the solution stirred by jiggling the weight. We also prefer plastic buckets, which are cheap, light, and easy to pour from.

Our next choice for a sprayer is the knapsack type. If you need something larger than either of these, there are several on the market, some power-driven. There are also some good hose-end sprayers if your water pressure is at least twenty pounds per square inch, which it probably is. Our liking for the trombone sprayer is partly due to our having lived most of the time in the country where water pressure was not high enough to run a hose-end sprayer.

Whichever sprayer you select, make sure it is of noncorrosive material (usually brass or bronze for working parts exposed to solutions), and that you can buy parts for it later—valves, washers, strainers, packing, nozzle. If you can't, don't buy it.

A widely known West Coast garden consultant, Gordon Baker Lloyd, sums up sprayers this way: "Generally the more you pay for your sprayer, the better job it will do and the longer it will last. Cheap sprayers are pieces of junk, and may be able to put on plant food over a given area, but are of little value for accurate measurement of chemicals for pest control." The measurement reference is specifically for hose-end sprayers, but the point of quality is valid for all. The hose-end sprayer is a handy implement, easy to clean and easier to work than the pump type.

Here is the way to use a powder form of spray in a hose-end or any other sprayer in the words of Jim Law, a Stark expert on the subject: "Pre-mix the powder into a slurry paste and then add the necessary water to come up with the gallons needed. [Your paste should be thick, as if you were mixing a little cornstarch with water to thicken a liquid.] It will be necessary as you apply this to shake the spray bottle every few moments. Handled this way, the hose-end sprayer does an excellent job on fruit trees."

As you probably know, a hose-end sprayer has a jar to hold a concentrated solution of your spray. Measure out the amount of powder needed for the number of gallons wanted, put it in the jar, add a little water to make the slurry paste, and then bring the water level up to the mark on the jar that calls for the number of gallons of spray you want. When you fasten the sprayer to your hose and turn it on, the sprayer feeds out just enough of the concentrated solution in the jar to make the proper dilution with the water as it sprays onto your trees.

Most spray materials are measured by the tablespoon. Level the spoonful with a straightedge.

> 3 teaspoons make 1 tablespoon.
> 16 tablespoons make 1 cup.
> 2 cups make 1 pint.

A rule of thumb is to consider a level tablespoonful as half an ounce. For home-garden quantities, this is close enough unless the chemicals being measured are as light and fluffy as sifted flour. Most are not. If you have any doubts, weigh them on a postage scale and write down for permanent reference how many tablespoons it takes to make an ounce.

If you'd rather use a duster than a sprayer, you can omit all the other equipment on our list. Although we prefer to spray our fruit trees, dusting does have the advantages of speed and convenience, and you don't have to clean the duster or empty it between uses. The type that throws out a continuous narrow stream of dust as you turn a crank is worth the ten dollars or so it costs. Tie a damp handkerchief over your nose to avoid breathing the dust when handling or applying it—especially if your sinuses make as much fuss about such things as ours do.

How to spray
Before you mix the solution, *read the label* on the package. Then read it again. Measure the ingredients and the water as exactly as

you reasonably can. There is a little leeway, of course, about 5 percent either way.

Spray only until leaves start to drip. Try to cover all leaves on both sides, and spray the wood, too. The ideal time for spraying is an overcast windless morning with the temperature pleasantly mild and the humidity low. If there is wind, spray in short bursts to reduce drift. As you spray, keep the chemicals in solution by shaking the sprayer tank now and then to agitate the mixture.

Don't stand where the spray will hit you, and try not to breathe it or get it on your skin. Wash your hands as soon as you are through. It is possible the danger of some insecticides in residual amounts has been overestimated; the Nutrition Foundation, a research organization set up by food and related manufacturers at about the time DDT was coming on the market has so indicated. Nevertheless, in concentrations, such as a packaged spray material, chemicals may hurt you if inhaled, swallowed, or left on the skin.

Dwarf trees are a boon when you are spraying. In fact, you can even dip aphid-infested shoots into a can of spray solution, or paint it on if there are only a few aphids. An old substitute for a sprayer was a whiskbroom dipped in solution, to shower the leaves with a swish.

If you don't use up all the spray solution you mix, don't save it or mix it later with fresh solution. Run it down the drain or dump it in a hole dug for the purpose, away from food plants. Use the same hole or the trash can for empty pesticide containers.

Keep spray chemicals sealed tight, the labels on, and of course out of the reach of children. Clean your sprayer by spraying detergent solution and then plain water through it. Or fill the tank, if it has one, with water to which you add half a cup of household ammonia; let stand overnight; then empty and rinse with plain water. Store sprayers out of sun and dust, and in a position that lets them drain dry.

Finally, try not to spray fruit within three weeks of harvest. If you must do so, the insecticide malathion is safe to use within a day or two of harvest, and so is the fungicide captan. Always wash fruit well before eating it.

The good old days

What about the good old days, when you could grow fruit without pests ever bothering it? Listen:

The Roman naturalist, Pliny, The Elder, wrote (about 77 A.D.) that worms were common to all trees, and were unusually fond of pears and apples. He was talking about the larvae of the codling moth, the same moth we have today.

In 1243 A.D. a Moorish writer detailed the ravages of caterpillars on date palms and suggested spraying them with a solution of myrrh and vinegar, or smoking them out with sulphur and henna.

Here, on blights, is an early eighteenth-century English botanist, Richard Bradley: "Plants of all degrees are subject to Blights, which are so variously communicated to them that sometimes a whole tree will perish by that Distemper; now and then a few leaves or Blossoms only, and perhaps a branch or two will be shriveled or scorched by it. . . ." A few years before this had been written, the fruit trees of New England had been close to extermination due to insects, probably locusts.

Just like certain human ills known for hundreds or for thousands of years, fruit pests were familiar—and *taken for granted because there was no cure for them.* That is why they were seldom even mentioned. The Bible cites worms, blasting (blights), and mildews; also the devouring locusts.

As a matter of fact, at the dawn of man's farming in the Stone Age, the pests were there, waiting. Apples have been found among the remains of prehistoric Swiss lake communities, sliced in half with polished stone knives for preservation by drying. And some of these apples had worms. That's right—the codling moth was there.

How to Prune
Your Fruit Trees
6

Why prune a fruit tree at all? Wild fruit trees bear fruit without pruning. This is why: We prune fruit trees to improve the harvest. That covers everything—better shaped trees, stronger frameworks, better pest control, and more fruit of better color and finer flavor.

We admit at the start that quite a few home fruit gardeners who don't ever prune their trees get a lot of pretty good fruit just the same. Many others who do a terrible job of pruning also get a lot of pretty good fruit. These aren't arguments against finding out how to prune a fruit tree the right way, but it may be a comfort to you if you're nervous about pruning. Just do the best you can and you'll get along all right.

Remember that what is important about pruning is a tree's response to it. You'll learn more about pruning by pruning than in any other way.

The basic bud

When you cut off the end of a branch, the branch reacts by growing. The growth comes from a bud. Once you realize this, you know quite a lot about pruning. This bud is a tiny promissory note on a tree—a compact tip of tissue that is waiting for the chance to grow into a flower or a leafy stem.

Let's say that one branch of your apple tree has grown too long and you cut it back. If you do it right, you'll make the cut about a quarter-inch above a leaf bud that is pointing in the general direction you want the limb to grow. That bud is called a *lateral* or

BUDS. *Top left: Peach buds, two plump buds on each side of the slender one are fruit buds; the other a leaf bud. Top right: Plum fruit spurs. Below: Pear-tree spur; larger buds at ends are fruit buds, small ones, leaf buds.*

axillary bud because it forms at the axil of a leaf where the leaf stalk is joined to a branch.

If you'll look at the tip of the branch you just cut off, you'll see a bud there, too. That one is a *terminal bud* and its job was to lengthen the branch. The difference between lateral buds and terminal buds is their location. In fact, your pruning has just promoted a lateral bud to a terminal bud's job.

There is one other kind of bud, called *adventitious*, because it shows up in odd places and just about anywhere. The shoots that sometimes spring up from a tree stump come from adventitious buds.

Since you always want to prune back to a *leaf bud* because the other kind, a *flower bud*, won't grow into a new branch, how do you tell which is which? Easy. The flower bud is always plumper. As one horticulturist friend put it, "The flower bud looks pregnant."

Tools

Most pruning can be done with a hand-pruner. Professionals use a knife but home gardeners almost always prefer shears, either the snap-cut or scissors type. A long-handled lopping shears is useful, and so is a pole-pruner if you have tall trees. You can saw limbs with a saw from your tool box, but a pruning saw means less work. We prefer a 21-inch bow saw in a narrow V-shaped frame. It cuts fast and you can twist the blade to get at cramped branches.

If you are cutting out diseased wood, disinfect your tools between cuts. Dip the blades into a solution of half-and-half water and a laundry bleach, such as Clorox.

Small wounds need no protection but treat any that are more than three inches across. You can use shellac, or one of the water-soluble tree paints, or a liquid plastic sealer. Your purpose is to keep the wood from decaying while the wound is healing over.

Techniques

Always make a clean cut when you prune. This means not leaving the bark ragged around the edge. The exposed cross section of wood should be smooth and flat. You can trim up a rough cut with a knife or chisel. Keep your pruning tools sharp and you won't need to do much trimming afterward.

PRUNERS. A *pole pruner, some with saw blade on the end, easily reaches tall branches; long-handled pruners or lopping shears remove branches up to an inch and a half thick; for smaller cuts, use hand-prunners—snap-cut type at top, or scissors type below. The latter makes a cleaner cut.*

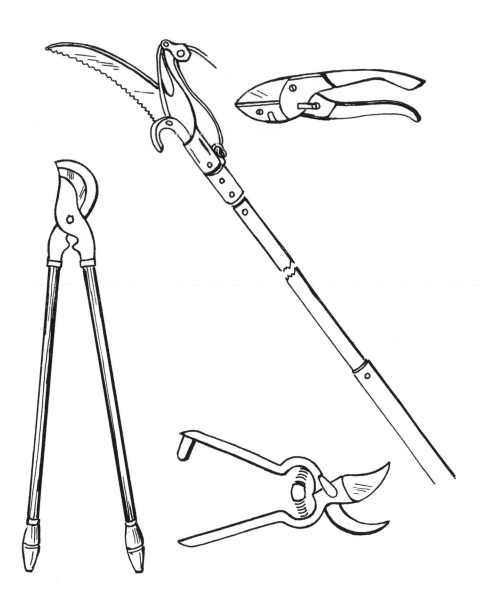

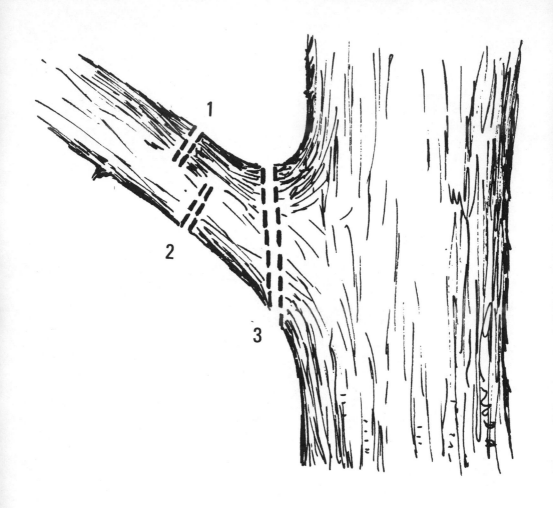

PRUNING LARGE LIMBS. No. 1 cut keeps limb from tearing bark when No. 2 cut severs the long limb. No. 3 cut removes stub cleanly at the trunk line. To keep out rot, cover larger than 3-inch-diameter cuts with tree paint.

If you are taking off a limb entirely, cut where it joins the trunk. Treat the wound if it is three inches across or larger. Where limbs are very crowded, you perhaps cannot cut back to the trunk and must leave a stub. Then make a slanting cut to shed rain, treat the wound, and keep an eye on it to see that healing takes place. A second treatment is sometimes needed to keep heartwood from rotting.

Don't use hand-pruners on a limb so big that you need lopping shears or a saw. To make cutting easier, press the limb away from the blade as you cut. This relieves the pressure of wood on the blade.

If you use a pruning knife, take off branches by cutting up from the bottom, holding the blade close to trunk. Bend the branch away from the knife as you cut, and pull the knife through in one smooth motion.

When to prune?

According to old sayings, the time to prune is when the knife is sharp; summer pruning will give more fruit, winter pruning, more wood.

Summer pruning as practiced in Europe, particularly with the Lorette System, has generally been found unsuitable for the American climate. The most common problem here has been winter killing of late-growing, tender shoots that followed summer pruning. An exception is with espaliered trees, as explained in the next chapter.

So far as dead branches are concerned, prune them off any time, and take out diseased branches at once. As for annual pruning, most fruit gardeners get best results by doing it in early spring before trees start to grow but after danger of severe cold is past.

Fruit-Tree Form

Pruning trees for form is given in the chapters on each fruit. There are many and shifting opinions on how trees should be shaped by pruning. However, the niceties are matters of interest mainly to commercial growers, who must take mechanical equipment and intensive land use into consideration.

The only pruning trees need before they start bearing is pruning to build a strong framework of wide-angled branches that will be able to carry a heavy load of fruit. Think of it this way: A mature dwarf apple tree, not much taller than a man, may bear a load of apples that weighs as much as *two men*. With either dwarfs or standards, do as little pre-bearing pruning as you can and still grow a strong attractive tree. Overpruning a young tree weakens it and can delay normal fruiting for three to four years.

Some experienced fruit-men take an even more restrained approach to early pruning. They shorten rather than remove some of the larger unwanted branches. These shortened branches are then cut back at the base the following year (or they are kept to develop future fruit spurs), unless by that time any has sprouted into something that looks better than an original framework branch. In that case the original one is removed or shortened; the later one is kept. To give yourself freedom of choice, when you shorten such a branch, be sure to make the cut to a leaf bud that points in a direction you may want the branch to grow.

To get the benefit of wide experience, we asked Stark's for their ideas on how a home gardener ought to shape his fruit trees. Here is their advice:

> Peach and nectarine trees, and Japanese plums, dwarf and standard, should be grown in the open-center or vase shape, which is their natural habit of growth. All other *dwarfs* will probably do better when grown in the pyramid form, somewhat like a Christmas tree, with a central trunk supporting strong framework branches. The reason for this is that vase-shaped fruit trees will shade each other's lower limbs when they are grown close together, as they are in most home gardens. Lack of sun due to crowding harms the tree and reduces the crop.
>
> In shaping young trees, the first two to four years are critical. After that, form is established and the tree is strong enough to maintain it. Besides thinning out weak limbs, you can help develop good form during the first few years by removing, while they are still small, fruits formed far out on a limb. This prevents them from spreading a tree by their weight. Trees are said to "umbrella-over" if they are so spread.

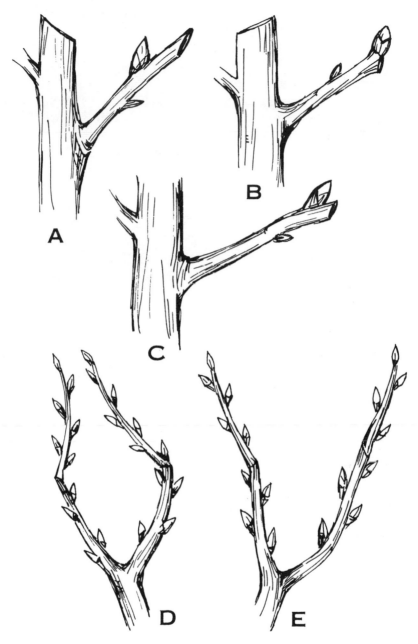

PRUNING TO A BUD. A. *Wrong, stub too long, will die back to bud, which may then die too.* B. *Wrong, stub too short, cut is so near bud it may dry out.* C. *Correct cut.* PRUNING FOR GROWTH DIRECTION. D. *Bad, result of pruning to inside buds.* E. *Good, pruning to outside buds produced open growth.*

Pyramid form

To train a tree to the pyramid or central-leader form, select framework branches well spaced around a central trunk. This central trunk is the dominant unit. For well-balanced growth, framework branches should be spaced up and down a trunk, as well as around it. When a tree is mature, there may be as many as a dozen such framework branches. To induce branching, each year prune back the top of a trunk (the central leader), cutting back to a well-placed bud or shoot.

As the tree grows, framework branches sprout secondary framework branches. Keep the best of them; prune off the rest, along with other branches growing from the trunk. The easy way is to prune as growth starts. You can then rub it off with your fingers. If you'd rather wait and see what the branches look like, prune with tools in late winter while your tree is dormant.

It sometimes happens that few or no secondary branches sprout from the framework the first year. In this case, wait for the dormant season. Then prune back the framework branches to about two feet or so. Such pruning forces wood into branching.

Following this secondary branching from the main framework limbs, the tree will be well along to establishing its form. From this point on your pruning can be confined to maintaining that form by thinning out weak and crossing limbs and relieving the tree of any dead or diseased wood.

Modified-leader form

This is a strong and good variation of the pyramid form. The difference in handling is this: After the tree has established a pyramid form, in two or three seasons for a dwarf, hold this shape with only three to five framework branches, and prune back the top of the trunk to an outward-growing branch (a lateral). This will open up the tree somewhat and stop further vertical growth.

Vase shape

In this form, also called the open-center type, about three framework branches are permitted to rise from a short trunk. As the illustration shows, the branches can be closer together at the trunk than framework branches of pyramid or modified-leader trees. The

PYRAMID FORM. *Above: Pyramid-shaped tree pruned at planting time. Below: Pyramid-shaped tree one year after planting.*

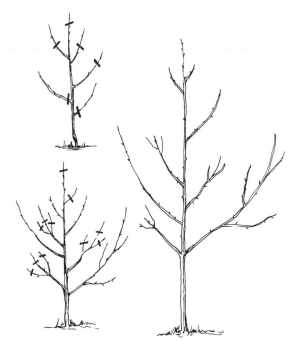

MODIFIED-LEADER FORM. *Top: Modified-leader-shaped tree pruned at planting time. Below: Modified-leader-shaped tree one year after planting before and after pruning.*

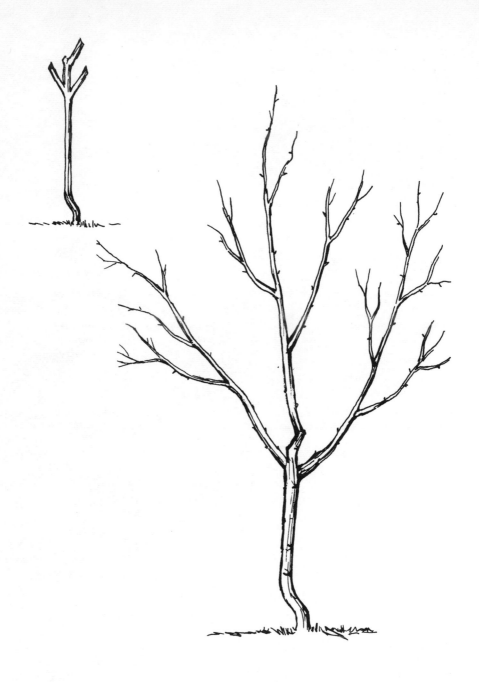

VASE SHAPE. *Top: Vase-shaped tree, with three framework limbs, pruned at planting time. Below: Vase-shaped tree, with three framework limbs, one year after planting.*

framework of the vase-shaped tree points upward at strong wide angles, to suggest the outlines of a vase.

Secondary framework branches growing from the three main frameworks should be mostly on the outside of a tree, to increase the vase effect. This is not for the looks of the tree but to let sun into the center where it promotes health and fruit production. Peaches, nectarines, sour cherries, and Japanese plums do well in the vase shape. Trees grown this way should have limbs thinned out and remaining limbs headed back every year. Pruning should be fairly heavy to force growth of fruit buds.

Spur-type trees

These can be trained either to pyramid or modified-leader form. The pyramid is best for close planting, that is, 10 to 12 feet apart.

Spur-type trees have an urge to form fruit spurs sooner than they should—when their strength should be going into making framework wood. To prevent growth of too many fruit spurs, give trees extra fertilizer and water during their first two or three years. Also, shorten upper framework branches. This encourages woody growth and lets light into the interior of the tree.

The weight of the first crop will help open up a tree. From then on, little annual pruning is needed. What is required consists of cutting out branches that grow too nearly vertical or that make narrow angles, and removing all but one of the excess extensions that come from the tips of framework limbs. Shorten the remaining extension, a little. Try not to sacrifice any spurs as you prune because fruit will be borne upon them.

For the modified-leader form, cut back the top of the trunk (the central leader) to a strong outward-growing branch when the tree is about three years old. Other pruning is the same as for the pyramid form.

Trunk

Compared to that of a shade tree, the trunk of a fruit tree from the ground level to the first limb is very short. And not everyone realizes that the height of this trunk never changes from the day you plant the tree till it dies. If you drove a nail into the trunk a foot from the ground, it would still be a foot from the ground twenty years later.

A tree gets taller by growing new wood at the tips of limbs. You determine the height of the trunk from the ground to the lowest limb simply by the height of the limb you keep as the lowest one. This point is called the head of the tree, a confusing term since *head* ordinarily means the top of something. However, that's orchard language, so when you hear trees called low-headed or high-headed, the distance referred to is from the ground to the lowest limb. Too low a head is a nuisance in culture. What you want is a head about eighteen inches high—low enough to shade the trunk from hot summer sun but high enough for convenience in mulching, cultivating, mowing of grass, checking for borers, and so on. (Most nut trees are an exception, and are headed much higher.)

Here's a tip: A low-headed tree bears fruit sooner than a high-headed one. Years ago, fruit trees were customarily headed six or eight feet high to permit easier plowing of orchards. Then trees that would have fruited in ten years if they had been headed low, often took fifteen years.

What's the angle?

You are told to save for framework branches those joining the trunk at good wide angles. What *is* a good wide angle?

It is an angle about halfway between vertical and horizontal. Look at a clock. At exactly 10 o'clock, let the minute hand stand for part of a tree trunk where a limb, represented by the hour hand, joins it. This is a good wide angle, about 60 degrees. At exactly 2 o'clock the hands are at the same angle for a limb joining the trunk on the other side of the tree.

To a carpenter's eye such an angle is too wide for the weight it must carry, but trees are different from buildings. Wide-angled limbs also have merits beside strength. They do not crowd other wood when the tree is older and the big limbs are much bigger around. While you are shaping the tree in its early years, if a limb is growing at too narrow an angle but you have no other limbs to choose from, cut the limb back to an outward-growing bud. Then let the bud grow into an extension of the limb.

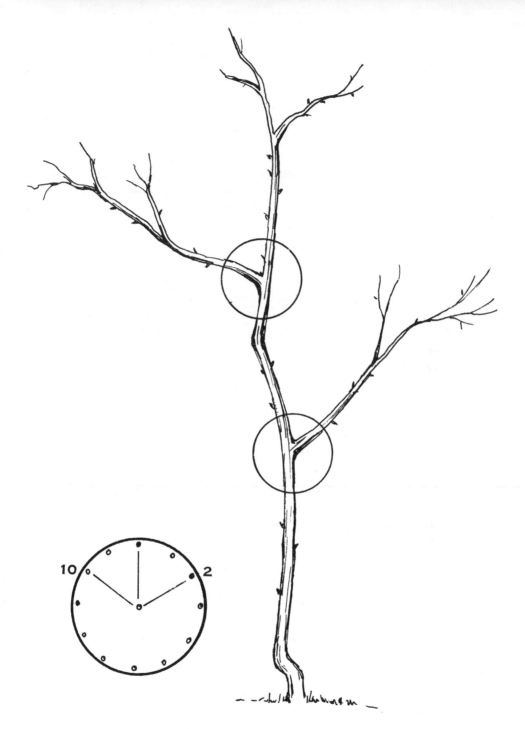

WIDE ANGLES. *Framework limbs should join the trunk at good wide angles, such as the 60-degree angles shown here—the same angles made by the hands of a clock at 10 o'clock and 2 o'clock.*

The Case for Light Pruning

Once a fruit tree begins to bear, it should need little pruning. Peaches, nectarines, Japanese plums, and, to some extent, sour cherries and apricots are lusty growers and need more pruning than other fruit trees—but even they should be given as little as will do the job. Diseased or damaged limbs must be cut out of any tree. Aside from this, pruning should be confined to thinning out weak and poorly placed wood. A too-vigorous limb can be cut back to an outward-growing lateral branch on it.

Light pruning builds stockier trees. It produces strong root systems. It encourages a tree to grow fruit instead of wood. And it lets a tree bear earlier.

A fruit tree is a factory. Leaves manufacture carbohydrates, one of the basic foods, from carbon dioxide in air and water in soil. A tree makes growth and fruit by using the carbohydrates and the minerals the roots draw from the soil. This is why heavy pruning will cause a tree to grow new wood and leaves instead of fruit. The tree is putting first things first, trying desperately to replace its manufacturing units—the leaves it has lost as limbs were pruned.

More than ninety years ago that master gardener, Peter Henderson, advised the amateur fruit grower not to prune at all if he wasn't sure he should. Here he is on the simplest kind of pruning, pinching back.

> Much pruning may be done by the use of the thumb and finger: this is termed pinching, and is practiced upon young shoots while they are yet soft. This most useful form of pruning allows us to control the form of a plant with the greatest ease . . . and may render nearly, if not quite all, pruning of ripened wood unnecessary. If a vigorous shoot has its end or "growing point" pinched out it will cease to elongate, but will throw out branches below.

Though it was not known in Peter Henderson's day, this tip-pinching has a hormonal reaction on the branch, which is what encourages it to fruit. During the growing season you can also eliminate any branch-to-be where you don't need another branch, just by rubbing off the shoot as it appears.

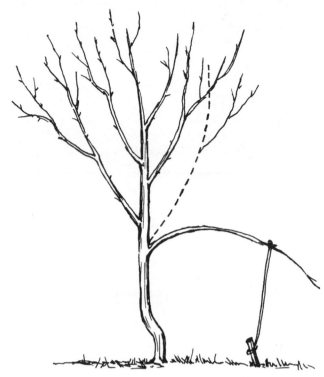

PRUNING SUBSTITUTE. *Bend down some flexible branches, not over two inches thick, that grow too upright or too strong but are wanted for fruit-bearing. Tie with rope fastened to a peg in the ground, to screw eyes in the trunk, or to weights.*

Bending

A substitute for some pruning is the bending down of branches, much as is done in some espaliering to induce fruiting. Do it this way:

Spread the branches by bending down the upright ones until they are horizontal or even lower. Hold them in position with cords tied to branch tips and fastened to pegs in the ground or to screw eyes in the lower trunk. Or hang weights on the cords. Only bend limbs up to two inches thick. Thicker ones are not flexible enough.

Bending also has a hormonal reaction, and causes a tree to form fruit buds. These will produce fruit the following year. Once a fruit tree starts producing, it stops growing so much and tends to keep on bearing. New shoots that spring up on the tied-down branches can in turn be tied down in the next dormant season, if you wish. Some growers prefer this method to annual pruning.

Cords can be removed once branches have accepted their new positions.

This bending technique has been elaborated, chiefly in the Orient, by weaving branches into a kind of untrellised espalier form, and by tying knots in supple branches, even in trunks of very young trees.

Keep a Picture Record

A fine way to discover the results of your pruning is to take a snapshot every year of each tree and from the same location.

Growth slips up on you. Without a picture taken five years ago to prove it, you get to thinking that your peach tree has always been nine feet tall, and pretty loppy, too, if you haven't been shortening the annual shoot growth. You forget what the three hefty framework branches looked like when you were selecting them in their spindly youth.

A simple snapshot record will also show you your mistakes, and you learn more from mistakes than from successes. Take a picture before you prune and another one after during the first few years when you are shaping a tree. This is the important period, the one you'll get the most out of when reviewing the tree's development through photographs—for the benefit of other trees in the future, too. It is also the time when taking pictures is simplified by the small size of the tree, for you'll probably need a backdrop to show the profile of the tree clearly. This can be a sheet stretched behind the tree. We have preferred wallboard or plywood, but whatever you use should be light colored and smooth.

If you have a camera with a fast lens, here's what you can do if you find yourself without an artificial background, particularly if your camera is a miniature with a short focal-length lens, say of fifty millimeters: Open the lens to the widest aperture for the light conditions and the speed of your shutter. With a moderately fast black-and-white film, this might be 3.5 at one five-hundredth of a second on a fair but sunless day. Focus sharply on the center of the tree and take the picture as close to the tree as you can and still get most of it in. Your wide-open lens and close-up shooting should fuzz the background enough to avoid clutter. Color slides or prints are for harvest shots; you don't need color for your pruning record.

A good accessory to stand beside the tree is a measuring pole with feet marked off in alternate black and white sections. A person can also serve in this capacity by standing near the tree, but if you use a child, consider that the child grows along with the tree each year. In later pictures, the same child may make the tree look as if it isn't trying very hard.

Date each print and keep it in your fruit-record file.

Espaliers—
or How to Grow
a Picture

7

The prospect of growing fruit trees in our friends' yard looked pretty hopeless. Edith Westwick had the front of the place loaded with peonies, irises, and chrysanthemums, to name a few, a mere few. And the back yard was chockful of roses and day-lilies, asters, marigolds, clematis—you name it, Edith grew it. Not that she wanted to be selfish; it was just that there simply wasn't one single solitary tiny. . . . "Maybe here, Bill?" she said doubtfully. She was gazing at an ex-pansy border along the west side of the house. Wilt had finished off the pansies. The bed was all of a foot wide and ten feet long. "Strawberries?" Edith murmured.

"Well, O.K.," Bill Westwick said. He didn't plant strawberries. He planted a pear tree. In four years it had grown to be quite a tree—eight feet wide, six feet high, and two inches thick. An espalier. It was the best looking thing in the yard, except Edith.

The little tree reminded people of a candelabra—a candelabra of blossoms in spring, and glowing with handsome gold and red fruit at harvest time, like a lush Della Robbia faience on the wall. It was, as nearly all espaliers are, a dwarf tree.

Bill Westwick's espaliered pear tree was more than pretty—it was productive. By the time it was bearing normal crops, this tree that looked like a picture on the house wall was giving the family every fall a heaping hundred pounds of the best pears they'd ever eaten. The fruit-bearing ability of the espaliered tree is something American gardeners don't know much about. They think of an espaliered tree as purely decorative.

The fact is, espaliering as practiced in Europe, where it was started more than three hundred years ago, is a practical way of growing a great deal of fruit on a little bit of land. For this purpose less elaborate forms of the espalier (Americanized as ess-POL-yur) are usually favored.

Some espaliered trees have lived for phenomenally long periods. The peach tree is considered so short lived that espaliering seems almost a waste of time, but it really isn't. In the nineteenth century in France an espaliered peach tree was reported to have been growing for ninety-three years in perfect health and vigor. In England, peaches are grown against walls for the sake of the warmth there.

Espalier Types

There are dozens of forms for espaliers and dozens of variations on them, so feel free to experiment. Here are some of the basic forms that imaginative gardeners have worked out over the years, in little home orchards, on monastery walls, or around the palaces of monarchs.

VERTICAL CORDON. These cordons look like poles bearing twigs—and fruit in season. Each pole is simply the trunk of the tree, about 10 feet tall, with short branches coming out only to left and right. The trunk is formed over a period of three or four years. Prune it back to a bud each dormant season; when you plant the tree, cut it back to a foot or less above the graft, making the cut just above a bud on the left or right side. If you select a right-hand bud the first year, cut back the trunk to a left-hand one the next year; alternate each year to keep the trunk growing upward in a fairly straight direction. Leaves and fruit spurs are borne on small branches up and down the trunk.

Pears can be grown in this form more easily than other fruits because of their naturally upright form. Some apples take to it also. Don't try it with cherries, plums, or peaches.

The vertical cordon is an effective decoration for a wall, and usually several cordons are grown side by side. They can be planted quite close, even two feet apart. They are supported, as are most espaliers, by being tied to parallel wires or wooden strips set be-

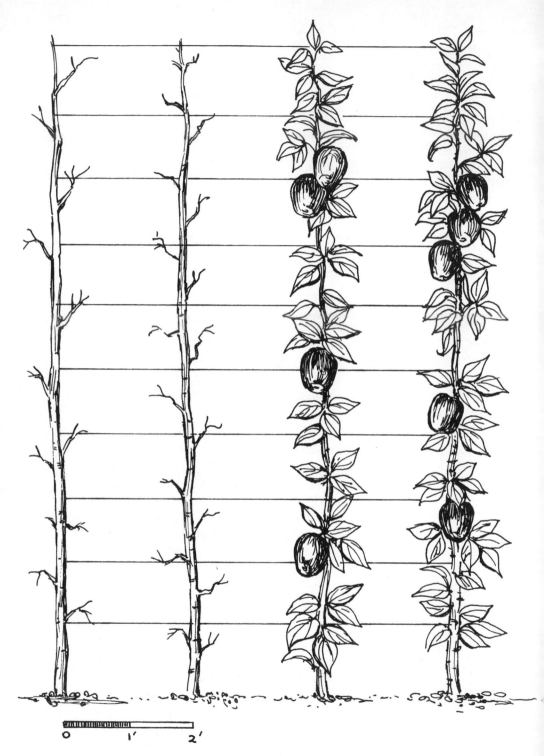

VERTICAL CORDON ESPALIER

hind them. Or you can tie each vertical cordon to a stake of its own. Height can be controlled by pinching out growing tips when they get to the place where you want to hold them permanently.

OBLIQUE CORDONS.   This half-vertical form is favored by commercial growers in Europe. It also is attractive when grown in series against a wall, and it makes an interesting narrow hedge, a yard divider, a path border, and such, when grown in the open. As with the vertical cordon, it is supported by parallel wires or strips.

You plant an oblique cordon at an angle, very much as if you were heeling it in, and with the convex curve of the graft union on top so as to discourage shoot growth from the rootstock. There will be less danger of sunscald on the trunk if the tree does not point north. Tie the trunk to a support, such as a bamboo pole; and tie the pole to the wires for easier training.

Against a wall, the oblique cordon is allowed to branch in only two directions, up and down; grown in the open, it is often allowed more freedom, especially by commercial growers. The shoots coming from the upper side of the trunk tend to grow more vigorously than others. If you wish, you can let the tree throw out horizontal branches along the wires from its underside.

The topmost support wire can be 6 feet high for convenience. When the tips of the trees reach it, just train them along the wire.

OBLIQUE CORDON
ESPALIER

HORIZONTAL CORDON.   Usually grown about 18 inches from the ground, though it can be higher, this espalier looks more vine than tree. It is supported on a single wire and is often grown beside a path as a low edger. It is a popular form for this purpose.

At the end of the first growing season, fasten the lower trunk to a post at two or three points. Then gently bend the tree, and fasten it to a horizontal wire stretched from the post to another post some 6 feet away. This is just the length the tree will grow; if you want to edge one side of a 30-foot path, you will need five trees. Sometimes they are grafted to each other by stripping a piece of bark from each where they meet—the tip of one resting on top of the bend of another—and tying them firmly together with strips of rubber bands. They will grow together in about a month.

Though there are exceptions, Horizontal Cordons are likely to bear well. Bending branches toward the horizontal is a well-known

Top: HORIZONTAL CORDON ESPALIER. *Below:* BELGIAN FENCE ESPALIER

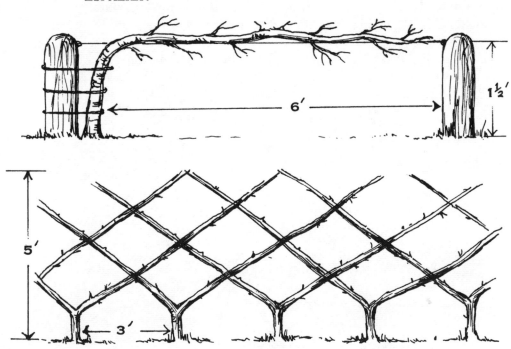

way to encourage fruit. Apples do better as Horizontal Cordons
than other fruits. Spur-type apples in double-dwarf size are exceptionally good for any kind of espaliering due to their extensive
spur formation, which gives heavy sets of fruit.

It is best to keep most vertical shoots rubbed off of Horizontal
Cordons. It is natural for them to develop, but they destroy the
form of your espalier if they get out of hand. The place for most
shoots, leaves, and fruit spurs is on the sides of a Horizontal Cordon and on the lower surface, not the upper one.

You can grow a Horizontal Cordon shaped like a squatty letter
T simply by pruning back the tree at planting time to a point just
below the level of the wire. Then train two shoots along the wire
in opposite directions. Rub off other shoots from the lower trunk,
and keep vertical growth cut back.

BELGIAN FENCE.   Also called a Two-armed Palmette or Single-Y,
this is a way of growing a very attractive living wall in your garden.
Trees are planted 2 to 3 feet apart and cut off about a foot above
the graft union to induce branching. Each tree is allowed to grow
one branch on each side, extending upward at a 45-degree angle.
Branches are tied to stakes during training, and the stakes are tied
to the parallel wires or trellis in back. Three such wires are strung,
the lowest a foot from the ground, the middle wire 3 feet above
ground, and the top wire 5 feet above. Trees are held at the 5-foot
height, which amounts to about a 6-foot length for each diagonal
arm.

Crisscrossing arms produce an effective diamond pattern. Tips
can be tied to the top wire when they reach it. The Belgian Fence
espalier has a reputation for producing a good deal of fruit in its
early years.

TIERED ESPALIER.   An attractive shape, this espalier is often used
to decorate a low wall. At planting time the tree is cut back to
about 18 inches, and this induces branching. Two shoots are selected for the lower arms, or tiers, one on each side and just below
the first wire, which is about 14 inches from the ground. The first
season, to encourage wood growth, let these branches grow up at
about 45-degree angles, and let a central shoot extend the trunk
upward.

The second spring, prune the trunk back to just below the second wire, which is placed a foot above the first one. This induces branching for the second set of tiers and for another extension of the trunk. As the second set of tiers sprouts, let them grow up for this season at 45-degree angles, but tie the first set to the lowest wire.

The third spring, repeat this procedure to form the top tier.

Other pruning should be done as for all espaliers; this is explained farther on in this chapter. If several Tiered Espaliers are grown side by side, tips of touching tier branches can be grafted to each other by tying them, as with the Horizontal Cordon. This is not only attractive, but if one tree should be girdled by mice or rabbits, it would not die, since it would be nourished by the trees to which it was grafted.

SINGLE-U. This simple form of espalier is especially good for training a peach or nectarine. It gives such a tree room to make its characteristic lush growth of fruiting shoots all the way up and down the two vertical branches. It is also a popular way of training pears and apples.

To form the Single-U, the tip of the young tree is cut back a foot or so from the ground, and two shoots that grow from buds on each side are trained out to become the arms. Let these arms grow up at 45-degree angles the first season to induce strong vegetative growth. At the close of this season, bring both arms gently down to the horizontal, bend up the ends vertically at the proper places, and tie them to the trellis. For peaches, the bend should be about a foot from the center of the trunk for each arm. As the two vertical branches grow upward they will then be 2 feet apart. One foot is enough for apples and pears, which are more compact growers.

Shoots that appear on the short lower trunk are rubbed off, and so is any shoot that tries to extend the trunk itself. The verticals are encouraged to grow upward and to throw out side shoots by pruning them back in the dormant season until they reach the height you want. Thereafter, hold them at this height with dormant pruning. The annual pruning back during training is especially important with pears and apples, which are not so inclined to throw out side shoots as are peaches and nectarines.

SINGLE-U ESPALIER

The Single-U has a good name for coming into bearing early in life, and it is more manageable than some other forms.

SINGLE-Y. Because of their lustier growth, peach and nectarine trees are often trained in Y-form, which gives more space for their lateral shoots. The only difference in training, as compared with the U-form, is that the two arms rise directly from the trunk at 45-degree angles. In fact, this is the first-season appearance of the Single-U.

DOUBLE-U CANDELBRA. This espalier form is started the same way as the Single-U, by cutting back the tip of the young tree to produce growth of a lateral branch on each side. These branches, after growing upward for a season, are tied to the horizontal but bent up at the tips. At the start of the second season, these tips are pruned back to induce branching. In the case of a peach tree, tips are bent upward at a point about 30 inches from the center of the trunk for each arm. For apples and pears, make it 15 inches.

At the start of the third season, select two shoots that grew from each arm during the second season. Tie them to the horizontal that extends out from each arm. For peaches, bend the tip of each one upward 12 inches from the vertical; this makes each pair of upright branches 2 feet apart when mature. The measurement between the inner verticals of each pair will be 3 feet. For apples and pears the distances are half these. Now prune back each of the four verticals to force shoot growth during this third season.

At the start of the fourth season, retain the best upward-growing shoot on each of the four verticals; prune each back to a bud that will keep it growing strongly upward. Prune off other shoots to stubs of three or four buds. The stubs will grow leaves to nourish the tree and will provide places for fruit buds to form.

Continue to extend the verticals upward by pruning the same way each dormant season until the form is completed.

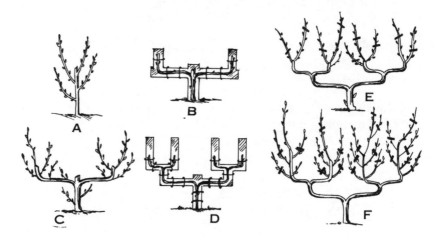

DOUBLE-U CANDELABRA TRAINING IN FOUR STAGES. A. *Growth made by the end of the first season, following the planting-time pruning back. B. The tree is dormant-pruned and fastened to a temporary trellis of wood strips held to the permanent wire trellis behind it. (Bamboo poles can be used for the temporary trellis.) C. Growth made by the end of the second year, ready for pruning and retying. D. The tree is dormant-pruned and refastened to a new temporary wooden trellis. E. Growth made by the end of the third year, ready for dormant pruning and refastening to a temporary trellis. F. Growth made by the end of the fourth year, ready for dormant pruning and refastening to a temporary trellis. Training is usually completed during the sixth year. After P. Champagnat.*

SINGLE-Y ESPALIER. *A good form for peaches and nectarines. Cut back the young tree a foot from ground level at planting time; train two side shoots at 45-degree angles from each side, to become the fruiting arms; keep all other branch-forming shoots rubbed off. Do not permit formation of another central leader. Above: A mature peach tree before spring pruning. Shoots rising from the two arms are from the previous season's growth. Those marked A are to be pruned off entirely, being the overgrown branches, so-called "bull growth." Those marked B are to be shortened to stubs with two or three buds each; this season they will grow wood to bear next year's peaches. Shorten all other shoots by only a few inches or leave them alone to bear this season's fruit. Below: The pruned tree. Grape-growers will recognize this pruning as similar to that for grape vines.*

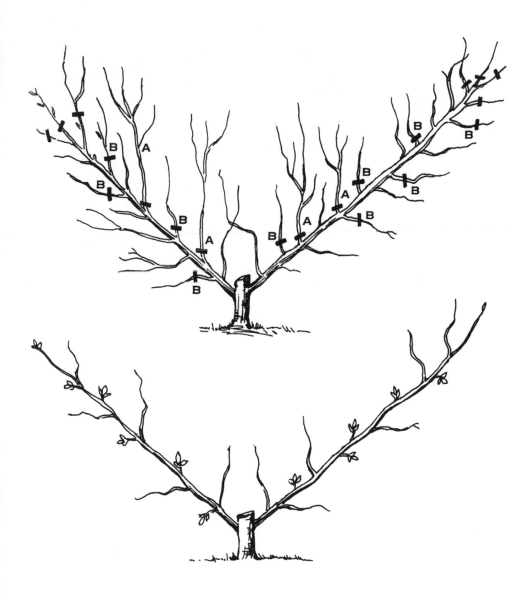

ARCHED CORDON. This curving variation of the other espaliers makes an attractive fence to enclose a patio or to screen off a garden service area. Trees are planted as for Oblique Cordons, and are then bent over (arched) when they reach a height of about 5 feet. This is best done the second season. To hold arched trees in place, tie each to the lower wire. This can be placed about 18 inches from the ground. If a tree is too stiff to be fully arched, first bend it halfway; then bend it the rest of the way the next year.

The second tier of arches is made with shoots springing from the tops of the arches. Bend these to the left instead of to the right, as in the first arching. Your purpose is to obtain a better curve

The third tier is formed the same way from shoots that arise from the second tier. These third shoots are bent to the right, in the direction of the original arches.

Heavy spurring will take place on the arches. Each year at dormant pruning, cut back to the top wire any upright shoots you allowed to grow the previous season—or arch them, to form renewals for the old arches. There will sometimes be vigorous lateral growth, front and back. Pinch out the terminal buds of this growth two or three times during the season; this will cause each shoot to form fruit spurs.

The Arched Cordon requires a good deal of pruning and pinching back to keep down the vigorous growth of vertical shoots and some of the excess lateral ones. Fruit production is good. In fact, the form was originated for this purpose in France.

FAN PALMETTE. This shape is the least formal of all espaliers. It appeals particularly to gardeners who have a minimum of time or who like their trees less stylized. The design is the natural one of a tree, but flat, like a flower pressed in a book. Any buds that would form limbs growing to the front or the back are pinched off while they are still buds or shoots, but fruit spurs are allowed to form at will along the branches.

It takes about three years to develop an apple into a Fan Palmette. Set the lowest supporting wire 18 inches above the ground; space the other four wires a foot apart. At planting time, prune back the trunk to just above the bottom wire. This forces shoot growth from buds below. Using three shoots, you can train two as

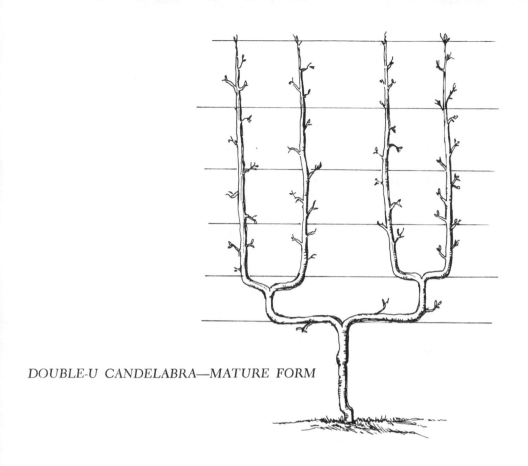

DOUBLE-U CANDELABRA—MATURE FORM

Below left: ARCHED CORDONS, *after Jean Bretandeau. Below right: FAN*
PALMETTE ESPALIER.

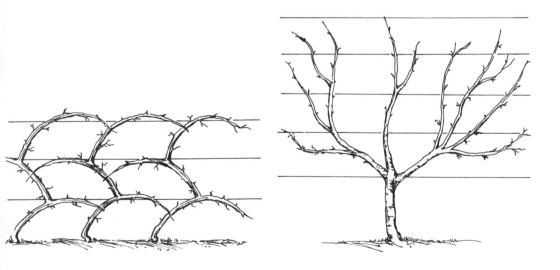

branches and the third as an extension of the trunk. Rub off any other shoots that develop on the trunk below the bottom wire. When the three branches you are retaining have grown about a foot, tie them loosely to the wires, allowing them to grow at the angles they prefer. Prune any wrong-pointing shoots on these branches, cutting them back to two or three buds to encourage them to form fruit spurs.

At dormant pruning time, just before the start of the second growing season, prune away a third to a half of the growth made by the upper trunk and each limb during the first season. This will force branching and give you a choice of limbs with which to form the pattern the second season.

One more such pruning at the start of the third season will complete the branching of the side limbs. At this time it will not be necessary to prune back the upper trunk. This should be held to a minimum of branching.

A peach or nectarine tree also takes well to the Fan Palmette, and can be developed in two years.

Techniques of Espaliering

When you grow an espaliered tree, handle it a little differently from your other fruit trees. These differences, plus a few special techniques are now explained.

What species of fruit trees?

You can espalier any fruit tree, and grape vines are ordinarily grown in this form, but best is a dwarf tree. Young-bearing varieties of dwarf apples or pears are most likely to satisfy you. These are fairly compact in growth, and once they develop fruiting spurs, the spurs last for years.

For pears, use those dwarfed on 'French Provence' rootstock. With apples, we suggest one of the spur-type dwarfs, called double-dwarfs. The spur-type tree is by nature a small tree, and when further dwarfed with a dwarfing stem-piece, it becomes an exceptionally good little tree for espaliering, richly endowed with bearing ability. Next best is an apple on Malling IX rootstock, the most dwarfing of the Mallings.

After apples and pears, a peach or nectarine has possibilities provided you can accommodate the vigorous shoot growth. But they have a shorter life than pears and apples.

Plums are sometimes espaliered. Damsons and the European Domesticas are more adaptable to restricted forms than the vigorous Japanese plums.

Cherries do not yield enough crop to make them favored for espaliering, though they can make a pretty design.

What age trees?

Year-old whips—single-stem, unbranched trees—are often preferred for espalier training, but you can also use a branched tree. This is what a nursery will send you unless you ask for a whip. If a branched tree has limbs at the right places for training, you may gain a little time.

However, for Vertical, Oblique, and Horizontal Cordons, select whips, not branched trees.

Trellising

Nearly every form of espalier needs support, and it is supplied by a simple trellis. Three strands of 14-gauge, galvanized wire strung between posts make a good trellis. Space wires about a foot apart. You can use strips of wood or bamboo poles instead of wire. A combination of wire for horizontal supports and wood for vertical ones is good during the training period. Even if you should grow an espalier against your house, support it with a trellis, and fasten the trellis to the house with expansion bolts or brackets, allowing 6 to 12 inches of clearance between trellis and wall. Fastening the tree directly to the house isn't good for either, and makes it awkward for you to work.

On which side of the house should you plant? If summer temperatures don't get into the high nineties, you can plant next a south wall where reflected heat will help ripen the fruit, as in England. But in hot-summer regions, this location will sunburn both tree and fruit, and also damage the tree. In such a climate, a west or southwest wall is better. An east or southeast wall is good but exposes the tree to more danger of bud injury from late spring frosts when morning sun strikes. For protection, hang a shower curtain or other covering over the tree. This is made more possible by the trellis, which can support the curtain. It should be done the night before the morning on which frost is expected, and the curtain should reach to the ground.

Fasten branches to the trellis with strips of cloth or raffia, or a commercial tie that will not bind and perhaps girdle growth as wire would. Use plenty of ties, to keep branches straight, not arched, except where arching is called for. For temporary fastening, you can use wooden spring-clip clothespins.

Wire fencing can also serve as a trellis, but don't bother with chicken or rabbit wire. Both are flimsy and homely, and woven wire isn't much better. Welded wire is the strongest and best looking.

For posts, you can use gas pipe, which lasts forever but always looks like gas pipe. We like wooden 4 by 4's. We have never found it necessary to set them in concrete if we used cypress or redwood posts.

Feeding and watering

In general, you don't need much fertilizer for fruit trees but give espaliers a good feeding of nitrogen every spring, and keep them well watered, too. If you feed them generously, they get filled with vigor and are all set to grow bigger. Then when you prune them severely in summer, this energy goes into a good crop. For its size an espalier bears a great deal of fruit—far more than it could support if it weren't for the trellis.

Pruning

You never stop pruning an espalier. After the form is established through pruning, as already described, and by training, you must then prune the constantly growing new shoots to hold the form and to encourage fruiting. Most of this pruning is done in summer, and mainly by pinching off tender shoots with your fingers. The motto of most successful espaliering gardeners is, "Keep your thumbnail sharp."

Starting in May or June each year, pinch off about half of every side shoot that gets to be a foot or more in length. Shoots will be

SUMMER PINCHING. Three stages of summer pinching on the same shoot. The pinching or pruning is made at points indicated by arrows. Above: The first pinching off of half the growth. Center: The next pinching, after new growth is a few inches long. Below: The third pinching if necessary. After Jean Bretandeau.

about as thick as a pencil and will then put out new growth. This regrowth should be pinched back later in the season to its last two leaves. A third such pinching may be necessary before growth stops. Your purpose is to make shoots form fruit spurs.

Shoots shorter than a foot are not pinched back, except the regrowths just mentioned; these are pinched back after they have grown 6 inches or less. You never remove fruit spurs on trees that bear them, either—which means all the fruit trees covered in this book except peaches and nectarines. Spurs usually form in great profusion between vigorous shoots.

In summer pinching, let terminal shoots alone. These are the shoots growing from the *ends* of the main branches.

In spring of each year, prune away the previous season's growth of terminal twigs on mature espaliers. This maintains the espalier's form and size. If you decide you want branches a little longer, prune off less of the terminal twigs.

Peaches and nectarines are handled a little differently from other fruits, being more vigorous and not growing spurs on which to bear fruit. Pruning back shoots on them is not done to make them grow spurs, but to keep them from getting out of bounds. The single-Y illustrations show how this is done—shortening some shoots to two buds to grow next year's fruiting wood, removing over-vigorous shoots entirely, and shortening slightly shoots that are to bear fruit during the current season. As with the other fruits, terminal shoots are shortened at spring pruning time on a mature tree.

Carried out faithfully and well on a mature espaliered tree that is vigorous and well nourished, this kind of pruning produces so much fruit that you'll have to thin the crop drastically and early. Do this thinning when the fruit has begun to plump up. Thin enough to have a little space between fruits when they are mature. They are apt to be larger than on non-espaliered trees, so take that into account.

Training

Of all fruit-tree culture, that of the espalier is the most intricate, probably because the French worked out many of the techniques and found satisfaction in the refinements they produced. These techniques are each intended to make a fruit tree do what you want it to—usually something the tree had no intention of doing. There's no question there is a subtle and deep satisfaction in this most controlled form of practical fruit-growing, a peculiar sense of power. When you espalier, you definitely *design* a tree. And you'll discover that an espalier in your yard will steal the show every time even from a spectacular ornamental.

Here, now, are some of the training tactics that you may find it interesting to try:

To induce fruiting

BEND BRANCHES DOWN so that the tips are below the horizontal. If branches are springy, they can be bent so that tips point straight down. Tie bent-down branches in place. Bending produces a hormonal reaction that favors fruit development.

BARK-RINGING often makes reluctant trees bear fruit. Make two shallow knife cuts, a quarter-inch apart, around the trunk. Carefully remove the strip of bark between the cuts. Take care not to damage the cambium layer under the bark—it is quite delicate. Cover the wound with adhesive tape.

If this sounds drastic and you prefer to do something milder, cut out a half-ring on one side of the trunk, and another half-ring on the opposite side, but an inch or so lower. Cover both cuts with adhesive tape. Or score the trunk halfway up with a single knife cut made all way around, cutting through, but not removing any, bark. This cut need not be taped.

The time for bark-ringing is two to three weeks after blooming ends.

ROOT PRUNING is another way to more or less frighten a tree into bearing fruit since (though this is not a scientific explanation) a plant seems to respond to what appears to be a threat to its life by hurrying into reproducing the race via seeds, of which fruit is the carrier. For a small tree about five years old, dig a semicircular trench 2 to 3 feet out from the trunk.

For older trees, make the trench farther out, but not so far as the spread of the branches. Dig the trench the width of your spade and 1 to 2 feet deep. Chop off any roots you find. A harsher treatment is to dig a complete circular trench around the tree and to cut off the tap root too, by digging across and underneath. We've always felt this was harsher than we cared to be.

To encourage growth

IN A BUD. Make a horizontal notch in the branch *above* the bud

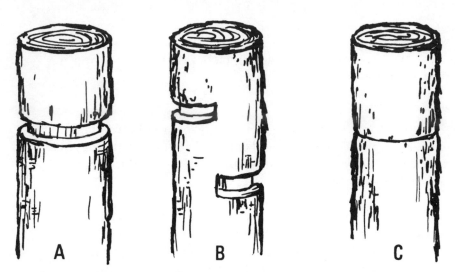

BARK RINGING TO INDUCE FRUITING. A. *Entire ring removed, most drastic treatment. B. Two half-rings removed, less drastic. C. A single scoring cut through the bark, least drastic.*

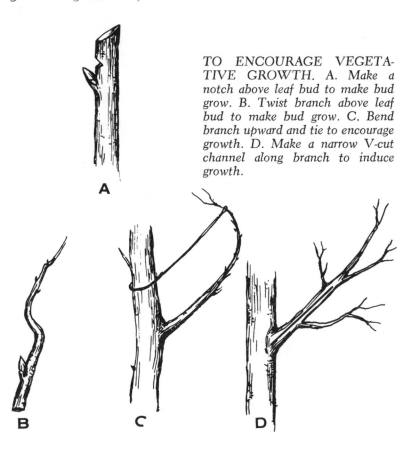

TO ENCOURAGE VEGETATIVE GROWTH. A. *Make a notch above leaf bud to make bud grow. B. Twist branch above leaf bud to make bud grow. C. Bend branch upward and tie to encourage growth. D. Make a narrow V-cut channel along branch to induce growth.*

with two nicks of a sharp knife; remove the small wedge of wood. This decreases the sap flow into the wood *beyond* the bud, and the bud itself gets more nourishment.

Or to make a bud grow, twist the end of the twig that holds the bud if the twig is succulent enough to be twisted. This slows the flow of sap to the tip, retaining more for the bud.

IN A BRANCH. To encourage growth in a weak but well-placed branch, make a narrow V-cut along as much of its length as you conveniently can. This speeds sap flow. Cut on the side of the branch facing wall or trellis.

Or bend a branch *upward*—the opposite of the fruit-inducing tactic of bending down, and tie it in position. It is always the highest part of the tree that gets the most sap.

To discourage growth

IN A BUD. Make a horizontal notch in the branch *below* the bud with two nicks of a sharp knife; remove the small wedge of wood. This slows the movement of sap to the bud.

IN A BRANCH. Make a notch with two knife cuts in the trunk just *below* a branch that you want to slow down; remove the wedge of wood. This hampers the movement of sap into the branch and is most effective on small young branches. At the same time that it slows vegetative growth, it encourages the development of fruit buds.

Or pinch out the tip of a branch that is growing too fast. Repeat several times in a season on a determined branch. If successful, it will slow the extension of the branch without causing it to throw out shoots, as pruning would do.

IN A TREE. To slow growth of a tree, cut out a ring of bark clear round the trunk as in the bark-ringing technique already described. The ring can be a quarter- to a half-inch wide. Instead of discarding it, replace the ring *upside down* (though not inside out, of course). The effect is to slow down movement of the sap. This slow-down lasts for about one season. Protect the replaced ring with a strip of adhesive tape. You can slow the growth of a single limb by doing the same thing to it.

Treasury of Fruits

And now for the fruits themselves. In each case, we list varieties in order of ripening, starting with the earliest, a few exceptions being made for groups, such as Delicious apples and Elberta peaches. Ripening dates are given for northern Missouri. This is a kind of average dating; ripening will be later in colder areas and earlier in warmer ones.

Recommendations follow the map of the United States Department of Agriculture Zones of Plant Hardiness. These zonal limitations are not hard and fast. Nearness to a large body of water may give you a local climate milder than that of your zone in general and location in high mountains may make your site as cold as if you lived one zone farther north.

Many varieties are mentioned but the ones for which full descriptions are given are those you can count on finding. There seemed no point in describing fruits of purely historical interest—but if you particularly want something you don't see in these lists or in nursery catalogues, we recommend our own procedure—ask your nurseryman for it. He may carry a few things he doesn't list, or suggest a nursery that does. Or he may know a reason why the kind you're looking for is wrong for your location. Or perhaps there is an improved variety of the same type and season, an offspring of the other. Varieties do get discarded or are allowed to die out sometimes, but good ones persist.

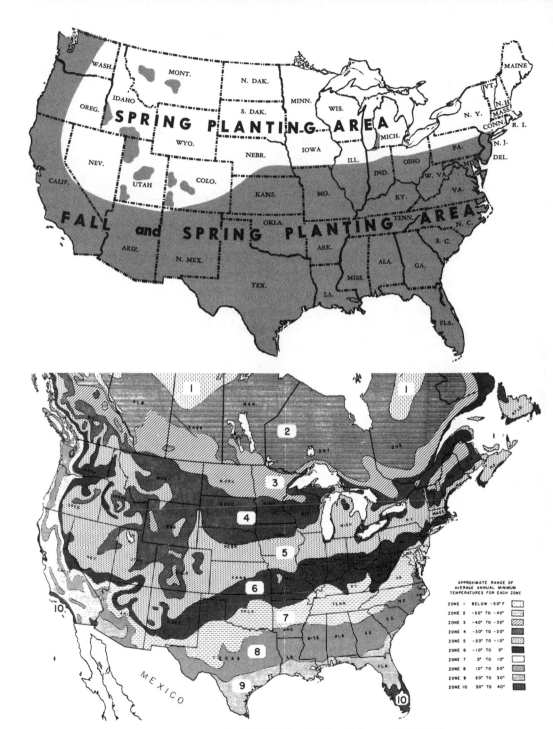

Above: SPRING AND FALL PLANTING MAP. *Below:* UNITED STATES DEPARTMENT *of* AGRICULTURE ZONES *of* PLANT HARDINESS.

A respected nineteenth-century British horticulturist and plant breeder, Thomas Andrew Knight, developed a peculiar theory in this respect, holding that every variety of fruit had a limited life expectancy. Knight declared in a paper published about 1830 that when the original tree of a variety— say an apple—petered out and died, all the trees that had been propagated from it by grafting or any other vegetative means would die soon after.

Though Knight did a great deal for horticultural science and was a founder and first president of the London Horticultural Society, and though his varietal-duration theory was accepted by many contemporaries, it was in fact nonsense. Varieties do die out from time to time, but because of a disease they cannot overcome, or from poor care, or because a better variety replaces them, but not because their ancestor, the original seedling tree, has reached the end of its life.

In some cases, it is largely the commercial grower who is on the nurseryman's mind when he offers certain varieties. Since this book is for home fruit gardeners, we do not take up your time here describing such varieties. However, if a commercial variety has some advantage for home growing, such as extreme hardiness for gardeners living in cold regions, we include it and note the point.

Cross-pollination sometimes bewilders a fruit gardener, and lack of it may be the reason a tree does not bear. In each chapter, we say if the fruit requires cross-pollinating; if it does, we suggest pollinators that will bloom at the same time. Fruits needing cross-pollinating include most apples, a few peaches and apricots, most sweet cherries, most pears, all Japanese and American plums, and most European plums.

A word about earliness in fruits. The best thing about a very early fruit is usually its earliness, and it isn't quite fair to expect it also to be supreme in taste. The late great pomologist U. P. Hedrick said of apples: "Earliness and high quality are seldom correlated . . . Nature is for the most part experimenting in July and August and her successes are nearly all registered in October." But a generation has passed since Dr. Hedrick wrote this and many new varieties have appeared. Some of the early ones are of higher quality than we had before.

Finally we'd like to put in a word for the extra refrigerator. It makes a fine small cold storage for your fresh fruit, and is also useful for holding seeds and scion wood and strawberry plants in good condition until you are ready for them. The refrigerator to use is not the automatic with fluctuating temperatures but the manually defrosted one. If you have such a refrigerator now, keep it for fruit storage if it is running all right when you buy a new one. It will be worth much more to you that way than as a trade-in.

Another good place to store fruit is in an air-conditioned room. The cellar used to be the place but many houses today don't have cold enough cellars or any cellars at all—not to mention separate fruit cellars outside the house. Some of our farm neighbors still had these a few years ago. They looked like the still older cyclone cellars that once dotted Midwest rural communities, and also served for fruit storage in that day.

The
Apple

8

No class of gardener seems to exceed the fruit grower in pride
of accomplishment, and perhaps with reason for fruit trees are attractive in any season, and in blossom glorious. They live on for
years, even pacing a man's lifetime. This is strikingly true of apple
trees, and is a reason for the apple's enduring appeal.

We have mentioned the old apple tree on our farm that we
could not think of chopping down. Our feeling is shared by everyone who sees more to a tree than a form against the sky. So we
saved the veteran and then planted an orchard of new apple trees,
about a dozen, starting with an 'Early McIntosh' and ending with
the beautiful little Christmas apple, 'Lady', to give us fragrant
abundance all through summer, fall, and winter. Apples are members of the great rose family (as are peaches, pears, and cherries,
among others) and are of the genus *Malus* and the species *domestica*.

"Flavour," an English epicure declared of apples, "depends
much upon the season, and many varieties require a really hot summer to develop their highest qualities." In Missouri, we certainly
had the hot summers. The English enthusiast also asserted that
certain late apples "have their vintage years, [and] all varieties have
their optimum moment of aroma and also of acidity." *Moment*,
mind you. Some he advised you not to pick until the instant you
are ready to eat them—as with sweet corn from the garden. The
epicure here was Edward Bunyard and the quotations are from his
appealing little book, *The Anatomy of Dessert* in which all the
desserts are home-grown fruits. In identifying the varied tastes he

found in apples, Bunyard mentioned strawberry and raspberry, nut-meats, fennel, pine, grape, quince, pear, honey, anise, pineapple, clove, and musk.

But like a pretty girl who can also cook, the apple owes its great appeal to more than flavor. Settlers of the American wilderness in the nineteenth century "suffered a lack of fresh fruits," as Richard Osborn Cummings points out in *The American and His Food*. These pioneers ate wild berries, and planted orchards as soon as they could clear land. "But most fruits were perishable and, unless preserved pound for pound with costly sugar, could be had only in dried form except during the growing season. Peaches not in-frequently were left to rot on the ground or were fed to the hogs after day-to-day appetites had been satisfied. Apples, however, could be kept for several months after the growing season and so were an exception."

By 1845, when Andrew Jackson Downing published his monu-mental *Fruits and Fruit-Trees of America*, about two thousand varieties of apples were being grown—"All the finest American and foreign varieties yet known in our gardens," Downing wrote. He was America's outstanding horticulturist and landscape architect of his time. Before he died at thirty-seven, he had found time to plan the grounds of the White House, the Capitol, and the Smith-sonian Institution.

Some readers in or near Ohio may know of a large, yellowish green apple, unattractive but toothsome, called 'Stark'. It is not one of the apples of the Stark Bro's Nurseries, but seems to have been named for Ohio's Stark County. Downing said it was a good keeper, and old Stark catalogues say it had "strong, tough branches." We mention it as an apple that originally could have been one of the famous Johnny Appleseed trees. Johnny, whose real name was John Chapman, was a contemporary of the found-ing Stark, Judge James Hart Stark, having begun his apple-planting career shortly before 1800. Johnny, who wouldn't have approved of having his old tree propagated by grafting—which he held to be a violation of nature—died the year Downing's book was pub-lished. By that time, he had spent more than forty years raising apple trees from seed and selling them to settlers in Ohio and Indiana.

As for old varieties, dedicated hobbyists sometimes try to build up a complete collection of species they fancy. With apples this is an awesome task. More than five thousand varieties are said to exist. One way to develop a collection is to get scions and do your own grafting. These are sometimes available.

Culture

Apple trees are agreeable about where they grow; they get along on most soils but they prefer a deep garden loam, well drained. They are distressed by hard and persistent wind and by extremes of heat and cold, as who isn't? Yet they are as adaptable as people in such ways, and you will find that there are varieties of apples for nearly every place throughout the United States especially under home-garden conditions. However, most of Zone 9 is an exception; we didn't even try to grow apples on the Mississippi Gulf Coast, but there is a variety now available that will grow there, and also in Florida—an Australian apple called 'Tropical Beauty'. You'll find it described in the variety list later in this chapter. The 'Winter Banana' apple also needs less chilling than some, and will grow in mild-winter climates.

Like most fruit trees, apples respond to nitrogen. Feed them in spring, if you do feed them, following the suggestions in Chapter 4 as to amounts of fertilizer. The suggestions there on mulching and other care also apply. Dwarfs, spur-types, and standard apple trees take essentially the same attention.

Pollination

Most apple trees need other varieties nearby for cross-pollination in order to set fruit. Even those that do not, such as 'Wealthy', 'Grimes Golden', 'Stark Jon-A-Red', and 'Golden Delicious', will set more and better fruit when cross-pollinated. There are only two important considerations:

A few varieties of apples are no good as cross-pollinators. Their pollen isn't fertile. The only ones you'll need to take in account here are 'Gravenstein', 'Arkansas Black', and the Winesap group—which includes 'Stayman Winesap' and relatives, such as 'Stay-mared'. In addition, 'Baldwin' and 'Northern Spy' are not good pollinators.

Trees must bloom during the same period in order to cross-pollinate each other. Since nearly all of them overlap in blossoming, this need not concern you unless you plant a very early-season tree, such as 'Lodi', and an extremely late one, such as 'Rome Beauty', and nothing else. The early apple would be just about through blooming as the late one was starting. Simply add a midseason variety to your planting. 'Golden Delicious' is an ideal pollinator, and has three different sets of blossoms each season.

Pruning

Apple trees do well when trained in the modified-leader form, though they can be grown in vase shape; as dwarfs in close plantings they are better grown in the pyramid form. (See Chapter 6, for these shaping methods. Special handling of spur-type trees is also given there.)

In general, pruning should be light for mature standard trees. Remove poorly placed limbs; shorten limbs that are growing too far in any direction, including up; thin out limbs and water sprouts in the center if they are crowded.

Most apple trees bear all their fruit on spurs, though a few varieties—'Cortland', some Winesaps, and Jonathans among them—bear some of their fruit on one-year shoots. Apple spurs are quite long-lived, old gnarled ones sometimes still blossoming when twenty years old, though not always doing well at setting fruit. Since spurs do bear for several years, you are relieved of much pruning to encourage the growth and location of new fruiting wood.

Some of the older spurs on apple trees can be pruned away each year after trees are mature. Cutting off about one old spur out of ten is a rule of thumb.

Harvesting

To get good apples, thin out the young fruits; this is partly accomplished by the June drop, when trees voluntarily shed some fruits. Look them over afterward to see that the apples remaining are six to eight inches apart. They will be much closer when mature, so thin as hard as necessary.

The ideal eating apple is a fine ripe one, but even a highly esteemed dessert apple is at a disadvantage if it hangs too long on the tree. It inclines to become mealy. These are the signs of ripening that indicate when fruit is at its prime:

COLOR.   Watch for apples to change to the ripe color—from green to yellow, for yellow apples; for red ones, a change from the basic dull green undercolor to bright yellows and reds.

SEEDS.   Until it is ripe, an apple usually has white seeds. Then they turn brown.

FEEL.   Ripeness is often heralded by the appearance of a waxy coating that makes apple polishing possible. This is a reliable sign.

TASTE.   This is the most dependable test. When the apple on the tree begins to lose its decided tartness, harvest time has come.

To pick an apple, bend it upward quickly. If it is ready, it will break cleanly and not tear the spur as it comes.

The apples you want to store should be picked a little early, just as they are getting ripe. You can store apples in a cool place, and it shouldn't be so dry that they will shrivel. In Shakespeare's day they called such specimens "apple-johns," and Falstaff complains in the first part of *King Henry IV*: "My skin hangs about me like an old lady's loose gown; I am withered like an old apple-john." As suggested before, a refrigerator is fine for storing fruit. We asked a man who is successful at this to describe his method. He is Henry Weinland of Santa Rosa, California, formerly on the faculty of the University of California and at one time farm advisor of Sonoma County. Here is how he stores 'Golden Delicious' apples from his home garden:

> We load the very best apples into plastic freezer bags, turkey size, and tie tight. Then we stack them in a refrigerator used for this storage and set to hold a temperature no lower than 32 to 34 F. Insulator cardboard keeps the apples from touching the sides of the refrigerator. The last of our 1966 apples were taken out of the refrigerator in good shape on May 15, 1967.

Mr. Weinland has kindly added a recipe for preserving any apples still in the refrigerator when you want to empty it in spring.

Mr. Weinland says the apples have a caramelized flavor, retaining most of the apple essence, and are excellent for deep apple pies and cobblers.

Apples Santa Rosa

Peel and core the apples and cut them into eighths. In a good-sized crock, alternate layers of apples and sugar, using about 2 cups of sugar to a dozen apples. Cover the filled crock, and let it stand for 48 hours. Then fill quart jars with the apples to within three-fourths of an inch of the tops; pour the remaining liquid from the crock into the jars. Seal and process in a boiling-water bath. Keep the water boiling for 5 minutes.

Leading Apple Varieties

The list that follows includes apples for all purposes; of these, perhaps a dozen rank so high as dessert fruit that they can be called connoisseurs' apples. We asked Stark's to select from them a group that would cover the season well enough to keep a family supplied. This would be for three months and, of course, longer if late apples are stored. We also asked that the varieties named be available in dwarf trees to make them practical for home gardens. Here are their preferences with Midwest ripening dates.

'Stark Summerglo'	Early August
'Starkspur Earliblaze'	Late August
'Starkrimson Delicious'	Mid-September
'Stark Jonalicious'	Late September
'Stark Splendor	Early October

These apples are the Nursery's exclusive property, so while they are understandably proud of them—and bought them because they considered them outstanding—you will not find other nurseries singling them out. All five are choicely good. Stark connoisseurs made particular mention of 'Jonalicious' as having the unique tang found in 'Cox's Orange Pippin', perhaps the most famous of English dessert apples.

We would add 'Golden Delicious'. The Starks omitted it only because its ripening date is almost the same as that of 'Stark Splendor', of which it is a parent. But another late variety would give you more apples to store as the season ended. A thrifty 'Golden Delicious' double-dwarf would be a little beauty in the yard, too. One tree in vigorous health could give you up to six bushels of fine apples, three hundred pounds, keeping the family in epicurean fruit clear into the Christmas holidays.

STARK EARLIEST. Ripening in northern Missouri a week or two after school is out in mid-June, this is a very fast apple indeed. Since it is so early, it has superiors in appearance and taste, but the medium-sized fruits are agreeably red colored and have nice flavor. It is both for eating and cooking, quite hardy, and available in dwarf and standard sizes. It grows well as far north as in Zone 4; the southern limit is Zone 8.

RED MELBA. This Canadian apple is considered an August or September ripener by most nurseries, but Stark's have a strain they supply as a dwarf that starts ripening in mid-July. 'Red Melba' has a bright red skin and white flesh, and is a large fruit. Though recommended especially for cooking, the variety enjoys a name among some fruit gardeners as ranging from good to very good for eating. Mildly tart and aromatic, it is also juicy. Zones 4 to 8.

STARKSPUR LODI. A fairly new apple, but well established as a nursery item for home gardeners, this is an improved 'Yellow Transparent' originated by the New York State Agricultural Experiment Station. It is more resistant to blight than 'Yellow Transparent'. The fruit is conical, larger than 'Yellow Transparent' and better flavored, ranking it as a very good summer dessert apple when tree ripened. 'Starkspur Lodi' makes superior applesauce, too, smooth and light green in color. The skin is bright yellow with faint brown dots and the flesh is white. Fruit ripens in mid-July or soon after in northern Missouri, but it is an August apple in more eastern and northerly sections. It is a fair keeper. Originators say the tree is inclined to bear every other year, but that rigorous thinning will make it produce annually. Most nurseries carry this as a standard; some dwarf it on Malling rootstocks. Stark's offer it as a spur-type in semidwarf and double-dwarf sizes. Zones 4 to 8.

STARK SUMMERGLO. This firm red apple with heavy skin is new on the market, recently originating in Michigan as a chance seedling of McIntosh parentage. Stark's, who now own it, consider it the top summer apple for flavor—crisp, juicy, and moderately tart. They class it as one of their apples for connoisseurs. The standard tree is vigorous and spreading, but a dwarf is available. In northern Missouri, ripening begins the first week in August and spreads over three weeks. Fruits are medium sized; severe and early thinning to 8-inch intervals is needed. The tree is a fast grower and a regular producer. Zones 5 to 8.

MCINTOSH. One of the best-known apples of the American continent, this came from Canada almost two hundred years ago, having grown as a seedling of another renowned apple, 'Fameuse', thought to be an old French variety and called the "snow apple" because of its white flesh. 'McIntosh' has always been somewhat plagued by disease, and the fruit bruises easily, so that it has been controversial among orchardists. For the home garden, 'McIntosh' is very good if given a little special attention.

Stark's offer two sub-varieties: 'Early McIntosh', ripening in early August; and 'Stark McIntosh Double-Red', ripening in early September in northern Missouri. This is of more interest to home gardeners since it is available as a dwarf. Both are recommended for Zones 3, 4, and 5. However, they will grow in Zones 6 and 7, their only fault there being a habit of dropping fruit as it ripens, which isn't a bad fault, in a dwarf tree especially, where the drop is not far. Both these McIntoshes are attractive apples, with crisp, white, slightly tart flesh. The Double-Red is larger and is a better eating apple; both are fair cookers, and neither is a good keeper.

Another sub-variety, 'Sweet McIntosh', is seen occasionally in nurseries, and some apple fanciers call it the best sweet apple. A McIntosh type called 'Red Sauce' has red flesh. It makes a naturally red sauce. Zones 3 to 5 for 'Sweet McIntosh'; 5 to 8 for 'Red Sauce'.

SUMMER CHAMPION. This August-ripening apple grows better than some do in southern states. It originated in Arkansas, has a name for resisting drouth, and is a vigorous grower. Fruit is bright red and of fair quality, keeps well, and is not easily bruised. Trees are available in standard size. 'Summer Champion' can be considered a home-garden apple if you have space for a standard tree and especially if you have problems of summer heat and drouth. Not recommended for above Zone 5 but adaptable as far south as Zone 8.

STARK SUMMER GOLD.   Available in both standard and dwarf trees, this handsome apple—blushed red over light yellow—is liked by many home gardeners for its fine quality as a dessert apple, particularly since it ripens in late August in the Midwest—long before some of the best fall and winter apples are ready. The fruit is firm and the flavor agreeably tart and full-bodied. Stark's say it keeps for months in a refrigerator. The tree is vigorous, rather spready, and a regular bearer. It is not recommended for planting north of Zone 5; the southern limit is Zone 8.

STARKSPUR EARLIBLAZE.   For home gardeners, this apple has an advantage over 'Summer Gold', which it duplicates in ripening time—the second half of August. The advantage is in the size of the trees, which are spur-type, and so come in semidwarf and double-dwarf forms. This is one on Stark's connoisseurs' list. 'Starkspur Earliblaze' is bright red with white dots; the firm flesh is of excellent quality. A splendid keeper, it is a good home-orchard apple. Severe and early thinning of the fruit is suggested. Zones 5 to 8.

WEALTHY.   This choice red apple is usually considered an early fall ripener but the strain listed by Stark's, called 'Wealthy, Double-Red', and offered in standard size, ripens in mid-August in Missouri. The original 'Wealthy' was grown in St. Paul from a seed found in Maine about 1860 by Peter M. Gideon, a famous experimenter. As you would expect, 'Wealthy' is a good cold-country apple. The fine-grained white flesh, tinted red, is juicy, lively, and slightly tart—a good eating apple. It is also a good cooker, especially when baked. Though some claim that 'Wealthy' does not keep well, it has long had a name with many others as a good to very good keeper. Keeping qualities along with size of fruit, color, and bearing capacity, are influenced by where a tree is growing, and this is the answer to a good many gardening mysteries. Zones 3 to 7.

BEACON.   A bright red widely grown apple, this starts ripening in mid-August in Missouri and you can pick it for a month, as fruits ripen in succession. If left too long on the tree, they tend to "watercore," but this is no drawback for the home gardener; in fact, it makes the fruit sweeter. Though not available from many nurseries, and then mostly in standard trees, 'Beacon' is highly regarded by some fanciers. It is also quite attractive, a quality that many other good eating apples most dismally lack. Originally from Minnesota, 'Beacon' is a hardy tree and a good keeper as a fruit. Zones 3 to 8.

STARK REDGOLD.   This big red apple, ripening in early September in Missouri, is handled exclusively by Stark's. It is an offspring of the 'Red Delicious' called 'Starking' and of 'Golden Delicious'. It originated in an old orchard of 'Golden Delicious' in Cashmere, Washington. The flavor is a blend from both parents, tangy and tart, the flesh crisp and juicy. Enjoy it fresh and in its prime through September and October; it is not recommended as a keeper except in Zone 5. It is a very good home-garden apple, additionally desirable by being offered in dwarf size as well as standard. Zones 5 to 8.

GRIMES GOLDEN.   Once called 'Grimes' Golden Pippin', this fine yellow apple came from West Virginia about 1800, originating on the farm of Thomas Grimes. He prized it for its sturdy good health and regular bearing habit, not to mention its spicy, nicely tart fruit. If 'Grimes Golden' has had a serious fault, it has been a tendency toward collar rot. The Grimes that Stark's carry is free of this. It is double-grafted, so that the trunk at ground level, where collar rot attacks, is a resistant variety on a crabapple root, a robust combination. (If you have an apple tree of any variety that is bothered with collar rot, a sanitation measure that sometimes works is to scrape away the earth from around the trunk and replace it with gravel.)

Grimes ripens about mid-September in the Midwest. It hangs

well on the tree but is not a very good keeper, so pick any fruit
to be stored while it is a little green. Grimes is somewhat tem-
peramental about site, but the only way to find out if it will thrive
for you is to plant it. Zones 5 to 8 and certain coastal apple-growing regions of California.

JONATHAN.   This grand old productive apple, known for its lively
tart flavor, used to be called 'Philip Rick', sometimes 'King Philip',
in honor of the man on whose New York state farm it was found.
It was thought to be a seedling of 'Spitzenburg' and was later
named 'Jonathan' after Jonathan Hasbrouck, who brought it to
horticultural attention.

Long-lived and an early bearer, 'Jonathan' has set a standard of
excellence for fruit quality. It is the apple supreme for apple butter, and deserves the best handling when so used. Here's the way
we made it on our farm, cooking it on a big screened porch that
was handily near the kitchen.

Kraft Farm Apple Butter

Quarter the apples and remove blossom and stem ends. Put the
quarters into a large stew pan, pour over them 1 cupful of good
apple cider, and steam until the apples are soft. Run them through
a sieve or food mill, and turn the pulp into a large, heavy roasting
pan, or the inset pan of a portable electric roaster. Set the thermo-
stat at 225 degrees. Add one stick of cinnamon, a few whole cloves,
and about a pint of cider. Cook for several hours, stirring every
half hour, and adding more cider as needed to keep the mixture
from getting too dry. Test by spoonfuls in a saucer for right flavor
and consistency. When the apple butter is done, seal in jars. No
sugar is added or needed, as cores and skin add sweetening. The
low cooking temperature almost eliminates spattering, and gives
wonderful flavor to the butter.

Stark's carry two Jonathan-type apples. One, 'Stark Jon-A-Red',
is their own strain found among some extra-red sports that 'Jonathan' produced. This is the only one so far to be given a patent.
It has the famous Jonathan flavor, a solid red skin, and is a better
keeper than the original. It is supplied in dwarf and standard sizes
and is specifically recommended for planting in the Midwest. It
ripens there the middle of September.

The other Stark Jonathan type is a chance cross from Texas of 'Stark Jon-A-Red' and 'Starking Delicious', and is called 'Stark Jonalicious'. It combines something of both flavors, as well as the piquancy of the English 'Cox's Orange Pippin'. If you go to England and fall in love with that one, 'Jonalicious' will be a very good apple for you to grow when you get back home. It is an excellent cooker as well as a superb eating apple, and one of the best keepers. It ripens just after 'Jon-A-Red', is bright red with yellow dots, and like 'Jon-A-Red', is fairly large and roundish. Supplied both as dwarf and standard. Zones 5 to 8.

The Delicious Family

Practically everybody knows what a Delicious looks like, even if he knows no other apple. It has a crown of five rounded points on the blossom end. Few other apples have such a crown, and none of these is well known. At first, this built-in trademark worked against Delicious. People thought it looked peculiar; it had to win its way through pure merit as a superb fruit. It did it so well that the Delicious varieties have become, to quote Dr. Donald V. Fisher, speaking in 1966 as president of the American Pomological Society, "the world's most important apples," with more than twenty million trees in bearing.

The original Delicious—still alive and bearing—is in Iowa. It sprouted in 1872 from a seed. The best guess as to its parentage is that it was a cross of 'Winesap' and 'Yellow Bellflower'. Stark's first saw the apple when the owner sent some of the fruit to a contest the Nursery held in 1893 in a search for good new varieties. The owner, Jesse Hiatt, had called the apple 'Hawkeye', and it proved to be every bit as good as he thought. Stark's bought the tree outright and began the grafting routine that precedes introduction of a new variety. Today there are five apples on the Stark list that carry the name Delicious, and nearly every nursery today stocks a red and a yellow Delicious.

SUPER STARKING DELICIOUS. The original Starking was a bud sport that occurred on a Delicious tree in New Jersey, producing a single limb on which the apples turned a vivid red weeks before the other apples on the tree reached full color. This made them better keepers because they could be picked earlier. The Starking now being offered, 'Super Starking Delicious', colors all the apples on the tree at about the same time, and still earlier than the original Starking—in late August or early September in the Midwest. It is ready for harvest about three weeks later. The tree is a heavy producer, capable of at least thirty bushels, which is about fifteen hundred pounds of big red apples. It is offered in standard size only. The fruit is aromatic, only slightly acid, spicily sweet, and highly favored as a dessert apple. It keeps well in storage. Zones 5 to 8 and California's colder apple-growing regions.

STARKRIMSON DELICIOUS.   This is the Super Starking in a compact, spur-type tree. Fruit has better color and is slightly larger. It reddens two weeks before ripening in mid-September in the Midwest. Other characteristics are the same as the Super Starking. 'Starkrimson Delicious' is also available in double-dwarf and semi-dwarf sizes. Zones 5 to 8 and California's colder apple-growing regions.

STARKSPUR RED DELICIOUS.   This is almost the same as 'Starkrimson Delicious', the important difference being color development in stripes that blend into a final over-all red. It is especially well adapted to higher elevations and more northern areas—in other words, to a slightly cooler climate than Starkrimson might be happy with, though the same zones are its practical limits. It is also for use in colder California apple-growing areas. Primarily intended for commercial orchards, this is supplied in semidwarf size. Zones 5 to 8.

GOLDEN DELICIOUS.   This world-famous apple, also known as 'Yellow Delicious', was discovered by Stark's in 1914; like 'Red Delicious', it was a seedling that sprouted on a farm. This time the farm was in West Virginia, and the best guess on parentage was 'Golden Reinette', a popular old European dessert apple, pollinated by 'Grimes Golden'. Consequently red and yellow Delicious apples are relatives in name only, even though 'Golden Delicious' does have the famous five-point crown, in less prominent form, and there is taste similarity.

DOUBLE-DWARF 'STARKRIMSON DELICIOUS' APPLE TREE.
Slightly taller than six-foot Paul Stark, Jr., this will be another two feet
or so higher when mature, and may bear as many as six bushels of beautiful big red apples in a single season. The double-dwarfs are a new development in home-garden fruit trees. (STARK PHOTO)

PATENT APPLICATION AND A MUTATION. *Above:* To patent a new variety, like this 'Stark Blushing Golden' apple, a picture is required that shows typical foliage and the inside and outside view of the fruit. *Below:* This red cluster appeared on a white-blossoming Starking apple tree. From the red branch, trees with all-red blossoms are grown but fruits are identical with those of the white-flowered trees. (STARK PHOTOS)

DOUBLE-DWARF 'GOLDEN DELICIOUS' APPLE TREE. Six years old and mature, this eight-foot tree is bearing a tremendous crop of one of the best-liked apples of all time. It will grow in a home garden in a space ten feet square. (STARK PHOTO)

SEMIDWARF SPUR-TYPE 'STARKRIMSON DELICIOUS' APPLE TREE. This little tree has more bearing surface because of an abundance of spurlike growths on which fruits develop. (STARK PHOTO)

'Golden Delicious' has been so successful in the market that the superintendent of the experiment farm of the University of West Virginia, Professor Edwin Gould, said of it in 1964 on the fiftieth anniversary of its discovery, "No single factor has had so great an impact on our industry as the discovery of this one variety of apple." Unlike some good commercial apples, 'Golden Delicious' is also superior for home gardens, a handsome apple of zestful flavor, pleasantly tart and rich, juicy, aromatic, and altogether excellent. It is a fine cooking apple and does not turn brown quickly when sliced.

As already noted, 'Golden Delicious' has a name for being a good pollinator. It is a regular annual bearer, starting when quite young. Even under poor conditions, though fruit may be small, trees seldom miss a crop. It keeps well, particularly if humidity is high. Store it in plastic bags and in a refrigerator, if possible. In California's lush interior valleys 'Golden Delicious' becomes a summer apple. Elsewhere it matures late, in the Midwest about October tenth, close to the average date of the first frost.

In addition to their own strain of 'Golden Delicious' in a standard tree, Stark's have it in spur-form, which they call 'Starkspur Golden Delicious'. This is, in fact, the original spur-type discovered in this famous variety, the find Stark's felt so elated at getting that they paid fifty-one thousand dollars for the tree. It is available in semidwarf and double-dwarf sizes. Zones 5 to 8 and California's apple-growing regions.

STARK BLUSHING GOLDEN. Apparently a seedling of 'Golden Delicious' with the same size and form, this has firmer flesh and a pink blush on every fruit. Originating in a commercial orchard in Illinois, it is slightly more tart than 'Golden Delicious', though rich and mild. Ripening still later—in late October in the Midwest—'Stark Blushing Golden' is a remarkable keeper, holding in cold storage until the next May or June. Zones 5 to 8.

The McIntosh Type
TROPICAL BEAUTY. This is the apple for mild-winter climates where other apples fail because of the lack of cold severe enough to break their dormancy. 'Tropical Beauty' was discovered in

Queensland, Australia, half of which is tropical. The tree has now borne fruit in southern Florida, in Hawaii, and other areas with similar mild winters. This is a big, roundish, wine-red apple, mildly tart when harvested at the right time. In the Midwest this time is late fall—from the middle to later October. In Florida, it is fall-ripening, dates varying with the area, but with ripening extending over several weeks in every case. Trees are moderately vigorous and highly productive. A peculiarity is that they need no pollination to set fruit; apples are sometimes seedless as a result. Trees grow as far north as Zone 5, though the variety is mainly intended for more southern Zones 8 and 9, where almost all other apple trees fail to thrive.

SPARTAN.   This Canadian apple, a McIntosh type, often does well where 'McIntosh' does not. 'Spartan' is a hybrid of 'McIntosh' and 'Yellow Newtown', the latter a handsome old apple of superior keeping quality, with crisp, brittle flesh. 'Spartan' combines the flavors of its parents and is noted for hardiness. It ripens in the Midwest late in September. Offered by Stark's in standard size only, it is a variety not found in most nurseries, but ranks as an apple for the epicure. Zones 3 to 8.

CORTLAND.   Another development of the New York State Agricultural Experiment Station, this is a late-ripening McIntosh type, a heavy annual cropper maturing in the Midwest in early October. The skin is dark red and somewhat striped, the size is large, and the fine-grained juicy white flesh of dessert quality does not discolor when cut. It is also a good cooking apple. Trees are sometimes available in dwarf size, though 'Cortland', a 'Ben Davis'-'McIntosh' cross, is not offered by as many nurseries as the quality of fruit justifies. It is an early bearer and quite hardy. Pick as soon as ripe, as apples hang on the tree indefinitely, gradually losing quality. The Station suggests they be picked within four or five days after the optimum picking date for 'McIntosh'. Zones 3 to 7.

ROME BEAUTY.   This old apple from Ohio used to trouble growers by not always coloring up well, a fault that was corrected when some red sports were found. The strain Stark's carry is notably red; they have it in new semidwarf spur-type trees as well as standards. Most nurseries offer some kind of red 'Rome Beauty', since it is popular and an excellent baker. It is sometimes dwarfed on Malling rootstocks. In the Midwest the apple ripens in early October. Zones 5 to 8, and the colder apple-growing regions of California.

STARK SPLENDOR. This beautiful red apple is one of those surprises that come along now and then—a seedling, of that famous and very yellow seedling, 'Golden Delicious'. Stark's found it in New Zealand and consider its future extremely bright. The yellow in its parentage is suggested by the warmth of the red color. Fruit is about the size and shape of 'Golden Delicious', with a somewhat similar sweet and rich flavor of excellent dessert quality. Ripening in early October in the Midwest, these firm, crisp, juicy apples keep best under refrigeration. Trees bear vigorously and early, are supplied in dwarf and standard sizes. Zones 5 to 8.

YORK IMPERIAL. A Pennsylvania apple, named for York County, this red fruit of good quality, in main a cooking apple, has always enjoyed a reputation as a superb keeper when gathered fully ripe. The 'York Imperial' that Stark's carry is a red variety that they call 'Stark York-A-Red'. It does well in the South. Primarily a commercial variety, it is inclined to be a biennial bearer—a point against it, of course. It is supplied in standard trees. Zones 6 to 8.

The Winesap Family

There have been many strains of the 'Winesap', another way of saying it has been justly popular for a long time. Downing called it "very good," gave it a long season, "November to May," meaning the fruit keeps all winter and spring, and said it was also known as Potpie Apple and possibly as Wine Sop. "This is not only a good Apple for the table," he stated, "but it is also one of the very finest cider fruits," which made 'Winesap' an exception from the general rule that the best cider apples are tough, piquant, and astringent, not good for eating. Probably best-known is the 'Stayman Winesap', named for its grower, Dr. J. Stayman, who raised it in Kansas from a Winesap seed planted during the Civil War.

The Winesaps now offered by nurseries are usually red sports of 'Stayman Winesap' or of one of the other members of the group. Nearly every big nursery carries one or more Winesaps, and dwarf trees are generally available. Of three that Stark's offer, one is a semi dwarf:

STARK WINESAP, DOUBLE-RED.   This is a smooth, beautiful apple with a rich, winey flavor, a good keeper even without refrigeration. It ripens in mid-October. Trees are standard size. Zones 6 to 8.

STARK SCARLET STAYMARED.   Color is brilliant red, and the apple is one of the biggest grown, with a sweet but tart taste. It ripens in mid-October and is a fair keeper. It comes in standard size only. Zones 5 to 8.

STARKSPUR WINESAP.   Available in semidwarf spur-type trees, this is not as highly colored as the Double-Red, but otherwise the two are identical. Zones 2 to 5.

These three Winesaps do well in the colder apple-growing parts of California.

Other Excellent Varieties

ARKANSAS BLACK.   Though not often listed in catalogues, this is a very good apple that has enjoyed popularity in the Northwest and in New Mexico. It is a strikingly handsome dark red, with firm, rich, golden flesh. A good keeper, too, it matures in mid-October in northern Missouri, and is a consistent and productive bearer. The 'Arkansas Black' offered by Stark's is a semidwarf spur-type. Zones 5 to 8.

NORTHERN SPY.   This old American apple began life near Rochester, New York. It is one of the last to ripen—late October in the Midwest. Unfortunately, it is also very late to come into bearing, up to fifteen years, though this did not keep it from wide acceptance. A fragrant and delicious dessert apple with a characteristically fresh flavor, it is a good keeper. Stark's offer it in a Double-Red (the original Spy is striped with red on a greenish undercolor) and in standard size only, but dwarfs on Malling rootstocks are available from some other nurseries. Zones 4, 5, and 6.

Crabapples

When we planted two Dolgo crabapples in our farm orchard, we didn't do so because we are extravagantly fond of sweet pickled crabapples; also, we can take apple jelly or leave it. We planted the trees mainly because we wanted to look at them. In bloom these crabapples are a cheerful little pomp and glory, and when they develop their miniature fruits, like jewels bobbing in the breeze, you can hardly stand to pick the pretty things. We planted the Dolgos near the pond so we could admire them when we went fishing, and we urge you to remember crabapples when you consider specimen trees for your home grounds. Put one on the lawn where you can see it the year through from inside the house—and from the sidewalk; strollers will thank you for the view, too.

HYSLOP. This crabapple is an old-time favorite for jelly, sauce, tarts, sweet pickling, and cider. Fruits are large for a crabapple, and rich dark red with heavy blue bloom. They are produced in clusters, ripening in early September in northern Missouri. 'Hyslop' is a little inclined to blight, though less so in the West. Like all crapapples, it is winter-hardy. 'Hyslop' is a standard processing variety commercially, but is also a good home-garden crabapple. Zones 3 to 8.

DOLGO. This handsome red crabapple makes exceptionally pretty jelly, and need not be used for it while green. 'Dolgo' is a most attractive tree in bloom, having white flowers, and it is a young and heavy bearer, ripening its beautiful little oval fruits in mid-August in northern Missouri. Zones 3 to 8.

STARK CARDINAL. This red crabapple is shaped somewhat like a miniature Delicious apple, and is young-bearing, often having its first crop when three years old. It was developed by Professor Richard Wellington at the New York State Experiment Station. 'Stark Cardinal' is unusually resistant to pests and disease, and ripens a month after 'Dolgo', in mid-September, making the two good companion trees for spacing a harvest. Zones 3 to 8.

Apple Troubles

Although the apple is attractive to more pests than any other fruit you'll grow, you can get control with surprisingly few sprayings or dustings.

The commonest insect scourge is the codling moth, brownish gray with a wing spread of less than an inch and a life of two weeks. It lays white eggs the size and shape of a pinhead on leaves. The eggs hatch into pink worms, which burrow into the young apples, feed for three weeks on seeds and cores, and then depart. Everybody has seen these apple worms, but few ever notice the moth.

Aphids, leaf rollers, and apple maggots are the next most common; less likely are mites and borers, the plum curculio, and bud moths. San José scale looks like ashes on the bark; under it are tiny sucking insects. Scrape the scale and you crush them, producing a yellowish ooze. You can usually scrub scale off with a wad of burlap or with a stiff brush—a simple way to defeat a bad pest.

Scab is caused by a fungus; it attacks twigs, leaves, and fruit and looks like spots of olive-green velvet.

Fire blight is a bacterial disease that causes blackened branches. In the home garden it is practical to break off the affected branches several inches below the blackened parts, and burn the wood. You can prune broken ends later for a neater look. By breaking them, you get the job done right away, which keeps the disease from spreading and avoids contaminating your pruner. To disinfect a pruner, dip it into a solution of half water and half laundry bleach. Since new growth is most vulnerable to fire blight, reduce or omit fertilizer if blight shows up.

Apple schedule with combination spray

> 1. Pre-bloom: Spray when blossom buds show pink, but before they open.
> 2. As soon as petals have fallen.

3. Ten days after No. 2.
4. Two weeks after No. 3.
(*Note:* Omit further sprays on early ripening varieties.)
5. Two weeks after No. 4.
6. Four weeks after No. 5. (Omit if pests are under control.)

Notice that no dormant spray is called for here. If used, it should be applied early in spring before growth starts.

If scale is troublesome, give the tree trunk and limbs an extra spraying two weeks after No. 5.

If borers are a problem, cut them out, use a special borer spray, or spray with DDT, malathion, or methoxychlor, three tablespoons per gallon of water. Spray the tree trunk and limbs twice at ten-day intervals in late spring or early summer—for instance, when you apply sprays No. 2 and No. 3 above. Repeat the borer spray a month later and ten days after that if needed.

The
Pear 9

If you wish to taste pears at their delectable buttery best, you must raise your own. A good pear, pleased with where it is growing and properly ripened, is one of earth's more glorious morsels. What a pity that so few people ever discover this.

The pear, *Pyrus communis*, was one of the luxuries the ancient Romans treasured, but the luxury was mostly in novelty, as pears for them apparently weren't anything like the good sorts we have now. The naturalist, Pliny the Elder, who seems here to have been drawing on personal experience, wrote, "All pears whatsoever are but a heavy meat, unless they are well boiled or baked." The early varieties disappeared along with the Roman Empire, and it wasn't until the late Middle Ages that pears became good enough to rank with apples as a choice fruit.

Long life in a tree appeals to home gardeners, and here the pear is even more notable than the apple. A pear's life on the average is about seventy-five years, and some veterans have lived to see four centuries roll by. Old Peter Stuyvesant planted a pear on his farm in New York City when it was still New Netherland, and it was there and bearing fruit when the Civil War ended, more than two hundred years later.

Though the pear was not the American pioneers' standby that the apple was, it was close behind, and there were many noble pear trees still producing fruit in the Old Northwest Territory in the late nineteenth century. Pear wood was valued for tool handles and furniture, being heavy and fine grained and looking like ebony when stained black. Pear leaves were also a frontier staple, as they make a yellow dye. The pear version of cider is called perry.

As for tree size, some trees divert from the usual compact habit of growth and become quite large. There used to be a giant in east central Illinois with a hundred-foot limb spread and a trunk four feet through, but you're not apt to grow anything like that in your back yard today. Or have to face a harvest such as the eleven thousand pounds it had one year.

The newer dwarf pears are what are apt to appeal to you. The fruit you pick from them will be a little better than from the same varieties in standard-sized trees—a little bigger, a little better colored.

Culture

Pears will grow almost any place apples will grow, and in some places where apples won't. Pears are most at home in Zones 5 to 8, the great central belt of the country, omitting the colder and the milder regions, but several pears—as 'Hood', 'Pineapple', and 'Baldwin'—grow in mild Zone 9 down into Florida, and the tolerant 'Kieffer' thrives both there and also farther north into Zone 4.

Choose a deep soil for pears if you can. They will grow on heavier soil than most fruits, but don't pick too rich a soil as it can cause rank growth, and rank growth is susceptible to fire blight. For the same reason, don't over-fertilize your pear trees. The rule of thumb is—pay attention to the look of your trees and feed them only if they are not looking thrifty. Pears are deep rooted, and in our experience they are diligent at finding their own nourishment. Though they prefer heavy loam, they'll grow on many soils. They have done well for us on sandy soils, and we have seen them flourish in clay.

As to moisture, it depends on where you are growing the trees and what varieties. Our experience has been that established pears adapt themselves to available moisture. We suggest you mulch your trees well and then water them only in long dry spells.

Like the apple, the pear needs some winter cold to break its dormancy. There are varieties that need comparatively little, but these are not among the choicest pears. As a rule, pears escape spring frosts because they bloom late, but if frost comes unusually late, it can destroy a crop, even after fruit has set. Consequently, try to avoid planting in a low spot, where cold air settles. A windy site is hard on the fruit, knocking it about, but this can be controlled by a windbreak.

Because they grow more upright than apple trees, pears can be planted closer, about 20 feet apart for most standard sizes. Plant dwarfs 10 to 12 feet apart.

Pollination

The grandmother of one of the writers had two stately pear trees in her back yard, and over a period of twenty years the only harvest was shade. No pears came, for the blossoms were never pollinated, the two trees being of the same variety. Most pears must be near another variety for cross-pollination or they won't form fruit. In our list of varieties only one, 'Duchess', is sure to pollinate its own blossoms. It will also pollinate all the others, so if you want huge fruit and a good tree in your collection, include 'Duchess' and forget pollination. Most of the others, except 'Magness', will pollinate each other. 'Bartlett' and 'Seckel' can't pollinate each other, but plant a third variety and you'll be all right. 'Starking Delicious' would be a good choice since it also comes in dwarf size and would extend the season. It is resistant to blight, as well, and wouldn't be apt to die off and leave you with no pears at all from any tree that year.

Pruning

Pear trees are grown in the same shapes as apples, even though inclined toward a more upright form. They also produce fruit on spurs as long-lived as the apple's, though shorter in length. And like some varieties of apple, some varieties of pear also produce fruit on one-year shoots. 'Bartlett' may, also 'Winter Nelis' and 'Duchess'.

Except for a trifle more attention to keeping the top of a pear tree open to sunlight—by pruning back upward-growing branches to outward-growing shoots or buds, and taking care that branches do not touch each other as this favors spread of fire blight—pears are pruned so exactly like apples that you can follow the suggestions given in the apple chapter.

Their upright habit sometimes makes pears slow to bear. To get a tardy tree into production, do this: In early summer, at about the time of full bloom or just after, with a knife make a cut clear around the trunk and just deep enough to get through the bark.

This is called scoring. For lighter treatment, you can do it on every other framework limb instead of around the trunk. Then tie down limbs to as near horizontal as they'll easily bend. These two fruit growers' secrets have turned many an idle pear tree into a good provider. (See the section, "To Induce Fruiting," in Chapter 7 for more on these tactics.)

Harvesting

One of the advantages in growing your own fruit is that you can get what you almost never see in the stores—tree-ripened beauties. Pears, however, should not be tree-ripened. There are exceptions but they are minor. Most pears must be picked *before* they are ripe, if they are to fill themselves with the delectably fruity flesh you can spoon like ice cream—juicy, spicy, velvety.

How then do you tell when it's time to pick pears? The pears will tell you. One or two will drop, and the color of all of them will begin to look more yellow than green. To test readiness, grasp a pear gently and tip up the bottom. If it is ready to come, the stem will part easily from the spur. If it doesn't, try again later, for pears picked too green will shrivel instead of ripening. 'Bartlett' and 'Kieffer' are exceptions and should be picked while it still takes a twist to get them loose, especially 'Kieffer'. The most common mistake is to let pears hang on the tree too long. The time to pick is while they are still rock-hard. If you are growing a very late variety and hard frost is predicted before the pears are quite ready, go ahead and pick them. Frost will hurt them a lot more than early picking. As you gather pears, handle them as if they were eggs, and avoid like the plague any bruising, heaping, or dropping.

To ripen them, enclose each pear in a soft wrap, such as paper toweling, and arrange them in shallow boxes, one layer deep; place in a cool room, ideally 65 to 70 degrees. Some authorities say the room should be dark, and we've always thought so, but this may just be force of habit. If you don't have a cold basement, store in the coolest room in the house.

How long pears will take to ripen depends on variety as well as on storage conditions and other factors; it may be as little as two to three days or as long as six weeks. Winter pears take longest. You can tell when pears are ripening by a certain softening near the stems. We usually test them by eating one each day after we think it's high time they were ready, and there comes a day when they all seem to be getting ripe at once.

To stretch the season, you can store pears in plastic bags in the refrigerator after they're ripe, but warm them up before eating to bring out full flavor. The English epicure, Edward Bunyard, mentioned in the apple chapter, discovered in his pears the flavors of musk, almond, grape, and honey.

Leading Pear Varieties

TYSON. This is a native American that grew on its own, like an Horatio Alger, Jr. hero; it was found on a farm near Philadelphia in 1794, growing in a hedge. It ripens early and is sometimes called Summer Seckel because of its good quality. The fruit is tapered and a little below medium size usually, though some strains of 'Tyson' have larger pears. The yellow fruits have a blush and the flesh is sweet and aromatic, smooth and tender—melting, as pear-fanciers say. Hardy and resistant to blight, 'Tyson' ripens in mid-August. It is not an easy variety to find, though well worth finding. Stark's offer it in standard-sized trees; it may occasionally be located in a discriminating regional nursery. Zones 5 to 8.

STARKRIMSON. This new variety originated as a bud sport of 'Clapp Favorite', showing up as a limb of bright red pears on a tree of yellow ones. 'Clapp' is a well-known summer pear, having appeared as a seedling in Massachusetts many years ago. It has always been a good variety when the climate suits it, and its bud sport tastes just like it—juicy, with buttery white flesh when at its best, and sweet.

As with 'Bartlett', it is well to harvest 'Starkrimson' and 'Clapp' a little sooner than other pears for the most perfect ripening. They are ready to pick in mid-August, about ten days before 'Bartlett' in the Midwest. 'Starkrimson' comes in dwarf trees and it has shown itself extremely hardy, young-bearing, and a hard worker. Zones 5, 6, and 7.

FAME. This is a big greenish yellow pear that sprouted in Arkansas in the late 1880's, probably from a seed dropped by one of the

workers on a tunnel that was being dug under the Boston Mountains in northern Arkansas. A fruit-grower in the vicinity dug the
seedling tree and planted it in his orchard to please his small
daughter. It was discovered there on a field trip by one of the
Starks of that era, Clarence, who was impressed with its good
flavor and texture, with its small core and few seeds, and with its
size. Stark's have carried it ever since, for more than seventy years.
Having discovered long ago that it did better as a dwarf, they now
offer it only in that size. 'Fame' ripens the second half of August.
Zones 5, 6, and 7.

STARKING DELICIOUS.   If fire blight has barred pear-growing where
you live, this variety may change things. *The American Fruit
Grower* wrote of it: " 'Starking Delicious' may be the pear many
fruit-growers are looking for. Its high resistance to blight makes it
a notable contribution to horticulture. Its large size, attractive
color, fine texture, and flavor make it a pear that should be the
answer to a fruit-grower's dream."

The pear is yellow, and unlike most pears, it develops into an
eating-quality fruit while still on the tree—though it improves if
given some of the usual after-harvest ripening. Pick the pears as
they turn bright yellow and ripen them for a week or ten days. The
variety can be regarded as a commercial one that also has a place
in home plantings, particularly in areas where blight is a problem.
It is available in both dwarf and standard trees, ripens in early
September, and keeps well. Zones 5 to 8.

MOONGLOW.   This is a new pear from the Beltsville, Maryland, experiment farm of the United States Department of Agriculture.
It is a big handful of a fruit that ripens about two weeks ahead of
'Bartlett', in mid-August. Smooth fleshed and mildly tart, for both
eating and cooking, it ripens about fifteen days after picking and
storing. The tree form is upright, generously spurred for good
crops, and it is resistant to blight. 'Moonglow' is available in dwarf
and standard trees. Zones 5 to 8.

BARTLETT.   Undoubtedly the best-known pear in America, 'Bartlett' came to us from England. There it is called the Williams
because it was introduced by a nurseryman of that name. He got

it from a schoolmaster who had raised it from seed, about 1770. It became 'Bartlett' over here when it was imported by Enoch Bartlett of Massachusetts, the true name having been mislaid in transit.

Pear gourmets sometimes belittle 'Bartlett', but most people like it. It is a big handsome eating and cooking pear, with a pleasant touch of acidity, a slightly musky flavor, and smooth flesh. It ripens in late August. The trees are thrifty growers and bear annually under favorable conditions but they are subject to blight. Nearly every nursery lists 'Bartlett', and Stark's carry it in dwarf and standard trees. Zones 5, 6, and 7.

MAGNESS.   Another United States Department of Agriculture development like 'Moonglow', 'Magness' is also resistant to blight. It ripens toward mid-September and is ready to eat about ten days after picking. Quality is good to very good, color a rich and ruddy yellow, the size medium-large. The pears keep well, up to three months in cold storage. 'Magness' is not yet widely carried, but Stark's supply it in dwarf and standard trees. Unfortunately it does not produce useful pollen, so it must be planted with two other varieties for all of them to bear fruit—'Moonglow' and 'Starking Delicious' would be good companions and would extend the pear season. If you have room for only two pear trees and one is 'Magness', plant 'Duchess' for the other as it will pollinate itself and 'Magness', too. Zones 5, 6, and 7.

GRAND CHAMPION.   This lavishly named pear is one of those good bud sports nurserymen are always hoping to find. In this case, it was 'Gorham' that produced a single limb of pears different enough to carry another name. 'Gorham' itself is a very promising pear that was developed at the New York Experiment Station by crossing 'Bartlett' with a small pear named 'Josephine de Malines', a straggly little tree that bore sweet little pink-fleshed fruit. 'Gorham' was introduced in 1923; it is a yellow pear of buttery white flesh with a fine musky flavor. 'Grand Champion' looks like 'Bartlett' but leans toward 'Gorham' in flavor. 'Grand Champion' has gained wide acceptance in Europe, where it is considered by many to be the perfect eating pear. It is medium-large, ripens about mid-September, and is a particularly good keeper. Zones 5, 6, and 7.

SECKEL. Some pear-lovers say that when God made 'Seckel' he made it homely so that other pears would have a chance. 'Seckel' is a yellowish, brownish, reddish runt, but its spicy, honeyed, and rich taste has been the pear standard of excellence in the United States for almost as long as the United States has existed. 'Seckel' was another of those seedlings that grew up on its own, so far as anyone knows, and like that other good seedling, 'Tyson', the original 'Seckel' appeared on a farm near Philadelphia. It was a mature tree when the Revolution broke out, and it didn't get its name until years later, when a man named Seckel bought the land it was growing on.

Sometimes called the sugar pear, it was also known as the Shakespeare. When samples were sent to England in 1819, the London Horticultural Society pronounced it "Exceeding in flavor the richest of their autumn pears." 'Seckel' forms a compact and symmetrical tree that bears regularly and laughs at blight. It is also longlived and a generous producer. Almost every nursery carries it, as you'd expect. It wants a rich soil and is a slower grower than many varieties. Some nurseries offer it in both standard and dwarf trees. 'Seckel' ripens in mid-September. Zones 5, 6, and 7 and coolerwinter sections of Zone 8.

DUCHESS. Her full name is 'Duchesse d'Angoulême', and she has been known to grow fruits that weigh a pound and a quarter— big, greenish yellow pears full of juice and delicious melting white flesh. 'Duchess' was found in a French forest, and has been a favored pear for more than a century. It bears quite early in life, and regularly, and—rare with pears—is self-pollinating. This is a variety that not only takes to dwarfing but usually does better as a dwarf. It starts ripening in September and is a good keeper. Zones 5, 6, and 7.

BEURRE BOSC. This is an excellent old fruit that has the agreeable habit of needing little thinning. Bosc is a large, long-necked pear, bronzy yellow, the white flesh rich and aromatic, buttery in texture. The trees are regular bearers and productive, though apt to grow slowly. Fruit ripens in middle or later September. Bosc can sometimes be found in dwarf trees. Zones 5, 6, and 7.

ANJOU.   This is an old French pear, the full name being 'Beurre d'Anjou'. The large fruits are greenish with some russeting, the flesh quite white with a brisk flavor. It is a good pear, though not so good as the best, but it is an outstanding keeper if handled right. Pick 'Anjou' in late September in the Midwest, just before it drops, and store it in a cool place. Even under less than ideal storage, 'Anjou' will keep a good while.

Some fruit gardeners find that it skips a crop some years, but for most it is an annual bearer. The tree is well shaped and is hardy, resisting blight, but it may be a little slow to reach bearing age in standard trees. Zones 5, 6, and 7.

COMICE.   A connoisseur's pear and none too easy to find at nurseries since the trees are not awfully vigorous, 'Comice' is the one to grow if you live in a good pear-growing area. The variety does especially well in the higher mountain sections of California and the Northwest—but also in some western coastal districts, and it has survived in Massachusetts. 'Comice' is a big pear, prettily blushed, of French origin, delicious eating when ripened as suggested for 'Anjou'. 'Comice' is the pear you often see in commercial gift packs, sometimes called the Royal Riviera. Pick it in late September in the Midwest. Zones 5 to 8.

KIEFFER.   Poor old 'Kieffer' is usually mentioned by gourmets of the fruit bowl only with contempt. It is a hefty winter-cooking pear, not usually attractive or nicely shaped, with a sturdy skin and flesh that even when well ripened has some grit cells. We knew 'Kieffer' in Missouri, and had an orchard of a related variety on the Mississippi Gulf Coast where you were lucky to grow any pears. Old nursery catalogues were noted for chatty frankness, and one remarked of 'Kieffer': "Excellent for canning—thousands of cans are annually sold, labeled 'Bartlett'."

As a matter of fact, 'Kieffer', picked when it should be—before leaves start to fall and while fruits are still quite hard—and then ripened well, is very agreeable to eat fresh. The flesh is smooth then and has few grit cells. Many nurseries offer 'Kieffer' because it grows willingly in so many areas, and is tolerant of fire blight. It is ready to pick in mid-October in Missouri. This is a good variety to use as a stock on which to bud other kinds of pears. With an older 'Kieffer' tree, you can get the same results by top-working it, as explained in Chapter nineteen. Zones 4 to 9.

Pear Troubles

Several insects that attack apples also attack pears, so the same sprays or dusts control both and make it a good idea to plant pears and apples together in your fruit garden. San José scale and codling moth have been described in the apple chapter. Psylla is a tiny sucking insect; it makes a sticky secretion on which a blackish fungus shows up, which is how you discover the presence of the psylla. Pear mites and pear slugs occasionally cause damage, but often pears are not troubled at all by insects.

A scab that looks like apple scab sometimes appears, and fire blight may attack a susceptible variety of pear. Treat it as with apples, breaking off affected branches as soon as you see them, being sure to break them off a few inches below the blighted (scorched-looking) part. Burn such wood promptly.

Pear schedule with a combination spray

1. Pre-bloom: Spray when blossom buds show pink, but before they open.
2. As soon as petals have fallen.
3. Ten days after No. 2.
4. Two weeks after No. 3.

Note: Omit further sprays on early varieties.

5. Two weeks after No. 4.
6. Four weeks after No. 5. (Omit if pests are under control.)

If scale is troublesome an extra spraying of trunk and limbs can be made two weeks after Spray No. 5. See that other sprayings also wet trunk and limbs well.

If borers are a problem, use a special spray for borers, cut them out, or spray tree trunk and limbs with DDT, malathion, or methoxychlor, 3 tablespoons per gallon of water. Spray twice at ten-day intervals in late spring or early summer—for instance, at the time you apply sprays No. 2 and 3 above. Repeat borer spray a month later and ten days after that if needed.

The
Peach

10

When one takes in hand a great ruddy-streaked, golden peach, wrapped in blushing velvet, tinted by the sun lavishly as the West is at fall of day, its rich flesh dripping with lusciousness, with that bittersweet and honey-tart flavor which belongs to all the other delicious things of life, one is tempted for a moment to think that if America has done no more for the world's pleasure, it would have done enough in this.

Here, in the buxom prose of the century's youth, is the peach, the quotation from a 1911 nursery catalogue. The writer—who is crediting America with the improvement, not the origin, of *Prunus persica*—is unknown to us, but peaches are still making people feel about them as he did—ecstatic. These are tree-ripened peaches, we should add, picked with tenderness and understanding and at the climax of their maturity, which is just short of eating-ripe, neither a day before nor a day after.

It is this particularity of the peach, even in demanding special care in harvesting, that makes it a prima donna of the fruit garden, and this extends to pest control and to pruning. All in all the peach is anything but a happy-go-lucky, anything-will-do member of your garden. The fact is, a fruit has to be very, very good for a gardener to take such extra care—and the peach is.

Culture

Ideally, give the peach well-drained soil, such as a sandy loam. Actually, trees will get along nicely on any reasonably good garden soil, and we have grown them in soil so largely clay that a hole dug in it would hold water like a jug, or almost. If your soil happens to be heavy, you'll be glad to know that the dwarf peaches will like it. This is particularly true of peaches dwarfed on 'St. Julien' rootstocks—in other words, all dwarfs except 'Bonanza' and 'Stark Starlet'.

More important than soil is exposure to late frosts if you live where this is a danger to blossoms, for the peach is in a hurry to get started each spring. The safeguard is to plant on a site sloping to the north. There sun will not warm the tree as soon as a south slope, and this will hold back blossoming a little. Few of us have a choice in these matters. You plant where you can, but check the variety list for peaches that are late to blossom or resistant to cold if cold is a problem. *Resistant* does not mean *immune*, of course. All gardening is somewhat of a gamble.

Here the new tiny genetic dwarf peaches, such as 'Stark Starlet', score heavily. They can be protected from late frosts, as described in Chapter 4, as can other dwarf peaches to a much greater extent than standard trees.

The peach, delicate though it may be to spring frosts, yet wants a certain amount of cold in winter. For most peaches, 15 degrees below zero is too cold. Though trees will survive, fruit buds will be killed and no peaches will form the following summer. Exceptions are the varieties 'Reliance', 'Sunapee', and 'Sure-Crop'. 'Reliance' is outstanding in this respect, and has borne fruit after a winter when temperatures dropped to 28 degrees below zero.

There are also varieties now that need much less cold in winter to break their dormancy—'Southland' is one—and recent studies indicate that fog can substitute for cold to some extent. In Florida the 'Jewel' is a popular peach, as are several of the Demko hybrids developed by Dr. Charles Demko of Altoona, Florida. One of these, 'Hawkins Spanish', is so long-lived it has been reported as bearing well when over sixty years old.

Like most fruit trees, peaches need little fertilizer and, if given too much, may run to leaves and wood rather than to fruit.

Normally the peach is a young-bearer, setting a crop the second year in your garden and coming into full production the fourth year or so. You can then expect good crops for about another ten years. A healthy tree will live longer than this and may have sufficiently good crops to justify keeping it.

Pollination

The majority of peaches are self-pollinating, so a tree planted alone
will usually set fruit. The most noted exceptions are 'J. H. Hale'
and some of its relatives. Three varieties listed here are not self-
pollinating: 'Golden Elberta Cling', 'Honeydew Hale', 'RedGold'.
Neither is 'Hal-Berta Giant'. Any of the others listed will pollinate
them.

Pruning

Peach trees are grown in the vase shape, described in Chapter six.
When pruning peaches, keep in mind that they are vigorous growers and bear fruit fairly far out on their slender shoots—on the
section of wood that grew the year before. This new wood may be
as long as three feet; it is easily identified by its reddish color and
glossy look. The older wood behind it is dull grayish brown, and
the bark where the newer wood starts is slightly wrinkled.

Once you have established the form of your tree and it has
started to bear, annual pruning will consist largely of shortening
by half or more new wood on the end of each shoot. This will reduce the number of fruits formed, but these will be of better quality, though additional thinning will be needed. Also remove some
older shoots entirely to let sunlight into the interior of the tree and
encourage new growth there. Cut back to outward-growing wood
any too-vertical shoots.

Some pruning can be avoided by keeping an eye on trees during
the growing season and pinching out unwanted shoots when they
are an inch or so long, usually from the center of the tree. It is
also a time-saver to halt growth of a wrong-pointing shoot by
pinching off the tip when the shoot is about as long as your fore-
arm. After it has borne fruit, you may want to remove it entirely.
Peach fruit buds are not borne on spurs except in a few cases, but
lie rather flat along the outer ends of the branches and look somewhat like leaf buds. But fruit buds are plumper and become furry
like a pussy willow; they are usually in pairs with a leaf bud between them. Leaf buds are small and pointed, and occasionally
one of them becomes a flower bud. A few flower buds also occur
on thin stiff twigs in the interior of the tree.

You prune dwarf peach trees more lightly but in the same way
you prune standards, except for the tiny genetic dwarfs, such as

'Bonanza' and 'Stark Starlet'. With these, very little pruning is needed.

Harvesting

The time to pick garden peaches is when they are firm tree-ripe, which is to say before they are quite ready to eat. You will find you can sense this time after you get to know a variety. The way to tell by feel is not to press with your finger but to take hold of a peach on the tree gently and give it a little twist. It will come loose if it is ready. If it is a white-fleshed peach, the greenish skin will have turned yellow-white; a yellow-fleshed peach will have an orange tint, in some varieties a red glow.

Having picked the peach, handle it with care and put it in a cool place, such as an air-conditioned room between 70 and 80 degrees, to finish ripening. It will be ready in twenty-four hours. You can then enjoy it at once or store it in the refrigerator.

If sweet pickled peaches are popular in your family, the 'Sure-Crop' is a variety to consider. One of the writers has memories of a favorite aunt who came to the family farm for a three-week visit each year at harvest time to make her famous pickled peaches.

Aunt May's Eighteen-Day Sweet Pickled Peaches

Fully ripe, peeled clingstones were put into a twenty-gallon crock. Aunt May then combined cider vinegar, sugar, stick cinnamon, and whole cloves, and brought all to a rolling boil. This liquid was poured over the peaches. The next morning it was drained off, again brought to a full boil, and poured over the peaches. This was repeated each day until the eighteen days were up. As it went on, the aroma of the bubbling nectar permeated the entire farmstead; nieces, nephews, and their small friends kept appearing in the kitchen, each holding a saucer into which Aunt May happily spooned a peach and some of the golden syrup. Needless to add, by the time the eighteenth day had come, this wonderful and generous cook had perhaps barely enough sweet pickled peaches left in the crock to fill a couple of half-gallon jars—which she re-signedly stored away for Thanksgiving and Christmas dinners.

Leading Peach Varieties

EARLY WHITE GIANT.   Ripening in the Midwest with the early to-matoes soon after the Fourth of July, this is a big white-fleshed freestone, the skin red with white splashes. Primarily a home-garden peach, it is supplied in dwarf as well as standard sizes by Stark's, who have their own strain. Thinning to about 8 inches apart on the branch is advisable, as compared to the 4- to 5-inch space usually needed for peaches. This variety is a heavy bearer. Zones 5 to 8.

EARLIGLO.   This yellow-fleshed freestone peach follows 'Early White Giant' by a week or so, and is also a large fruit if given heavy and early thinning. In that case, you can expect peaches up to 3 inches in diameter. 'Earliglo' is red over a yellow ground, juicy, firm, and mild. It came from Canada and is a mutation of another popular peach, 'Redhaven'. 'Earliglo' has a name for hardiness in colder areas. Available only in standard size from Stark's own strain, it is a variety not often seen on nursery lists. Zones 5 to 8.

STARKING DELICIOUS.   Ripening in mid-July with 'Earliglo', this peach is a bud mutation of the 'Burbank July Elberta', and has close to the same excellent eating quality with the added advantage of ripening two to three weeks sooner. Everything considered —earliness, flavor, its unusually good quality in dwarf form—this is one of the very best for home gardens. It is a yellow-fleshed red peach, freestone when fully ripe. Thin to 8-inch intervals for peaches that will measure about 10 inches around. Zones 5 to 8, but it also does well in cooler parts of Zone 9 and West Coast peach areas.

SUNHAVEN.   Another of the very early group, this close-to-fuzzless freestone peach is yellow with a red blush. It has yellow flesh of good quality that resists browning, making it useful for freezing. It ripens along with 'Starking Delicious'. Like all peaches with Haven in the name, this is a development of Michigan State University's South Haven Horticultural Experiment Station, which has done a great deal of work with peaches. 'Sunhaven' is available in standard size from Stark's. Specimens have survived temperatures of 19 degrees below zero, though suffering some bud damage. Zones 5 to 8.

SURE-CROP. This early cling peach has special value where late frosts often kill blossoms, as it has high resistance to cold. Stark's have a special strain and consider it the hardiest of the white-fleshed peaches. 'Sure-Crop' ripens in mid-July along with the two just mentioned, the skin an attractive pinkish red. It also makes good sweet-pickled fruit, and the peaches are large. Standard trees are available. Zones 5 to 8.

STARK STARLET. This is something unusual in peaches—a dwarf that is intensely dwarfed by nature, is quite ornamental, yet works at its job of fruit production—fine, delicious peaches, starting early in its life. Like the good little 'Bonanza' dwarf, bred and introduced by Armstrong Nurseries, 'Starlet' also often bears the second year after planting, on trees not so tall as a child in first grade. The peaches are yellow-fleshed freestones, the skin bright red on a golden undercolor, the flavor sweet, rich, and delicious. Even when full grown, these sturdy little trees are tiny, no more than 6 feet high, and they *can* be held at 4 to 5 feet with a minimum of pruning. Of all dwarf trees, they are most at home in planters, and, since the foliage is unusually heavy due to short leaf spaces on the compact branches, the trees make most attractive ornamentals for home grounds. Fruit ripens in mid-July in the Midwest. Zones 5 to 8.

REDHAVEN. Hardier than 'Elberta', this new and popular yellow-fleshed freestone ripens late in July in the Midwest. Fruits are medium to large and of good quality. An all-over red, 'Redhaven' colors before ripening and needs early thinning for good size. The tree is extraordinarily resistant to cold. Most large nurseries carry this and many offer it as a dwarf. Zones 5 to 8, and also West Coast peach areas.

GOLDEN JUBILEE. Considered one of the best early peaches, this oval, extra-large, juicy freestone is a development of the New Jersey Agricultural Experiment Station. It is hardy, vigorous, and a consistent producer, rather spreading as a standard, but also available in dwarf size. Skin is a deep yellow with orange tinge, and the flesh is yellow. With the added advantage of blooming late, 'Golden Jubilee' is a good home-garden variety. Handle the fruit tenderly, as it is quick to bruise. Zones 5 to 8 and West Coast peach areas.

RELIANCE.   If cold winters are your peach problem, consider this variety—just about the winter-hardiest of all. The well-named 'Reliance' has even fruited after going through winters of 28 degrees below zero. Sweet and mild, attractive and of very good quality, 'Reliance' is a medium-large, yellow-fleshed freestone with dark-shaded red skin. Trees are vigorous and productive. Zones 5 to 8.

SOUTHLAND.   As the name implies, this is popular in southern peach-growing areas where winters are too mild for most peaches. 'Southland' needs less chilling than many varieties do. (About 750 hours of temperatures no higher than 40 degrees above zero will suit it.) 'Southland' was developed by the United States Department of Agriculture and was introduced right after World War II. It is a round, yellow-fleshed freestone, the skin yellow with a red blush, the fruit large when thinned early. It also keeps well. Despite its adaptability to the South, this variety, which ripens in early August in the Midwest, does well farther north than most peaches—to Zone 4.

REDGOLD.   A hybrid with 'Hal-Berta Giant' as one parent, this is a handsome new peach with unusually good resistance to brown rot and leaf spot. This should recommend it to home gardeners. Moderately hardy and productive, RedGold's bright red skin underlaid with yellow is nearly fuzzless. The flesh is yellow streaked with red, is freestone, and of good quality. 'RedGold' needs cross-pollination to fruit. Use any other peach with it except 'Golden Elberta Cling', 'Honeydew Hale', 'J. H. Hale', and 'Hal-Berta Giant'. Zones 5 to 8.

FAIRHAVEN.   This commercial peach has possibilities for the home garden in some problem areas, since it is an unusually vigorous tree that will set a crop when other varieties may not. Supplied in standard-sized trees, 'Fairhaven' ripens large, firm fruit in early August in the Midwest. It is a yellow-fleshed freestone, of good quality. Zones 5 to 8.

The Elbertas

Like the Delicious in apples, Elberta in peaches is the one name nearly everybody knows—or everybody in the United States, for both are native Americans. The original 'Elberta' came from Georgia about a hundred years ago and soon became so popular with peach-growers that it was dubbed Queen of Peaches. In some places it is called the Queen Peach, also the Alberta.

'Elberta' is a big yellow-fleshed freestone, with an attractive yellow skin blushed red. It is tender, juicy, and good, but many epicures of the orchard look down upon it as second-rate compared with, say, 'Belle of Georgia' or 'Burbank July Elberta'. Although 'Elberta' is first of all a market peach, it is also excellent in the home garden when tree-ripened, and it has the merit of being a willing worker. It is now being replaced in commercial plantings by 'Jefferson' and 'Redskin'.

Several peaches with Elberta in the name are offered by nurseries, some in dwarf trees. Stark's offer four, listed here in ripening order.

BURBANK JULY ELBERTA. This is an Elberta in name only, a round peach, finer-grained and juicier and generally superior to 'Elberta' in quality. One of several hundred experimental plants that Luther Burbank was testing on his Sebastopol, California, farm at the time of his death in 1926, this is the only peach of importance that he developed. It is so splendid that Stark's consider it and its bud mutation, 'Starking Delicious', the two best peaches they have ever grown for home gardens. The fruit is yellow-fleshed and freestone with a small pit, popular with commercial growers because it does not bruise easily. The tree is a quite early bearer, regular and productive.

Home gardeners in areas where peaches have been a chancy crop may find 'Burbank July Elberta' a surer producer than most. Sometimes called Kim Elberta, it ripens fruit in early August in the Midwest. Stark's supply the tree in dwarf and standard sizes and recommend them for Zones 5 to 8, also cooler parts of Zone 9 and northern and central California peach areas.

EARLY ELBERTA.   In the 1890's the Stark nursery made a practice of sending, as gift trees to some of their peach customers in colder areas, Elberta seedlings, because seedlings were hardier than budded peach trees. One of the seedlings turned out to be a week earlier in ripening than 'Elberta' and was also a very tasty peach. It was named 'Early Elberta' by the customer who had received the seedling tree. The Nursery sells this original strain today as 'Stark Early Elberta'. Other nurseries handle other strains, and it is also called Golden Elberta. It is a yellow-fleshed freestone that looks much like 'Elberta'. It can be considered a market variety that home gardeners may find useful for its keeping qualities and ripening time—the middle of August in the Midwest—and for canning, since it is the best freestone canning peach on the market. Zones 5 to 8.

GOLDEN ELBERTA CLING.   Stark's first peach with this name was a seedling of 'Elberta' raised in the home nursery—Louisiana, Missouri. The variety currently offered, 'Golden Elberta Cling', resembles 'Early Elberta' and is raised particularly for canning, ripening early in September in the Midwest. This peach needs cross-pollination to set fruit. Use any other variety except 'RedGold', 'Honeydew Hale', 'J. H. Hale', or 'Hal-Berta Giant'. Zones 5 to 8.

ELBERTA QUEEN.   This is 'Elberta' in a little larger size, with better flavor and richer color, ripening over a period from late August through early September. Trees are supplied in dwarf and standard sizes. Zones 5 to 8.

Other Good Varieties

MERRILL HALE.   If you live in peach-growing country of the Midwest and want one big peach tree that will give you a lot of fruit for eating, canning, and freezing in early August, this is a good one, though developed for commercial growers. Fruit is very large, attractive, yellow-fleshed, and freestone, of excellent quality. It was developed by California hybridizer Grant Merrill, who has an international reputation for breeding new fruits. Standard-sized trees are available, and no cross-pollination is needed. Zones 5 to 8.

MADISON. We include this peach because the blossoms are frost-resistant, an asset if late spring frosts are a problem where you live. The fruit is attractive and close to fuzzless, the flesh a rich yellow, mild and good. A freestone, it ripens in early August. Zones 5 to 8.

GLOHAVEN. An all-purpose freestone peach, this is one of the best in the Haven series from Michigan—well flavored, a glowing red, large and round, the yellow flesh resistant to browning. The tree is hardy and bears heavily. Fruit ripens in early August. Zones 5 to 8.

SUNAPEE. Since this originated in New Hampshire, you'd expect it to be winter-hardy and it is, able to bear a good crop after a winter that will keep many other peach trees from fruiting. Too tender for shipping, 'Sunapee' is a garden peach, medium to large, juicy and good, a yellow-fleshed freestone. Zones 5 to 8.

LORING. This excellent peach was developed by Director Paul Sheperd of the Mountain Grove, Missouri, Fruit Experiment Station. It is one to try if your winters are too mild for some peaches to succeed. 'Loring' is also hardy in colder country, and is quite resistant to bacterial leaf spot. The pretty oval fruits are yellow-fleshed freestone, fine-grained and juicy, ripe in mid-August. Zones 5 to 8.

JEFFERSON. Now and then a commercial variety is also very good for the home garden, and this is so here. 'Jefferson' is new, so good that it is one that is replacing 'Elberta' in orchard plantings. A freestone with bright-colored skin and well-flavored flesh of fine texture, it is also excellent for freezing and canning. Blossoms are resistant to late spring frosts, and the tree is a vigorous producer of big crops. Fruit ripens in late August in the Midwest. Zones 5 to 8.

BELLE OF GEORGIA.   Peach fanciers have been known to grow misty eyed in praise of old Belle's creamy white flesh, thought by some to be the best of its type ever grown. A large and delicately colored fruit, freestone to semicling, Belle is happily resistant to bruising. The trees are hardy and blossoms are frost-resistant. A late August ripener, you can get Belle in dwarf form at some nurseries. Zones 5 to 8.

HONEYDEW HALE.   Like 'Merrill Hale', this is a commercial peach that still has some home-garden advantages. It arose as a bud sport on a 'J. H. Hale' tree—in the same way nectarines sometimes show up—and it is almost as fuzzless. The big white-fleshed fruits each have a single pie-slice-shaped yellow segment under the suture, the creaselike indentation in a peach, and they are juicy and of good quality. Because 'Honeydew Hale' is an excellent shipper, even when picked ripe, it is also an excellent keeper for the home gardener, holding for a week or two in a cool place and for a month in the refrigerator. The crop comes in late August. Exclusive with Stark's, 'Honeydew Hale' needs cross-pollination. Use any other peach except 'Golden Elberta Cling', 'RedGold', 'J. H. Hale', or 'Hal-Berta Giant'.

REDSKIN.   The skin is red, as the name implies, and the freestone flesh is yellow clear to the pit and of such good quality that even though this is a commercial peach (a reliable shipper), it is recommended here for the home garden. 'Redskin' is a hybrid offspring of 'J. H. Hale' and 'Elberta'. Along with 'Jefferson', it is replacing old 'Elberta' in commercial plantings. You'll need to thin 'Redskin' to get the extra-large fruit the tree is capable of producing, although it gives very respectable-sized peaches even when loaded. Ripening time in the Midwest is late August. Trees are quite hardy, and blossom buds can take a good deal of springtime cold. 'Redskin' is an all-purpose peach, a dessert fruit for eating fresh, a canning and freezing peach as well. Zones 5 to 8.

LATEGOLD.   A hybrid of 'Hal-Berta Giant' and 'Elberta', this big peach ripens in early September, a yellow-fleshed freestone of good quality. It is young-bearing and hardy, not primarily a home-garden variety but so used when its ripening time is the desirable one. Zones 5 to 8.

LATEGLO. Similar in quality and appearance to 'Lategold', but ripening even later—in mid-September, after Jonathan apples— this is rated by Stark's the best late-ripening peach they have tested. 'Lateglo' is also a commercial variety, but worth consider-ing for home gardens as a late peach and for dependable perform-ance, as well as quality. Despite lateness, 'Lateglo' keeps its fine flavor and sweetness intact. Standard trees are available, and they take up a little more space than the average peach tree. Zones 5 to 8.

Flowering Peaches

We haven't said anything about flowering trees because we are talking primarily about fruit trees for fruit. However, one of the delights of having your own fruit trees is their beauty, and though most flowering fruit trees bear fruit fit only for the birds, there are two flowering peaches on the market that also give good fruit. They would be a wise choice for specimen trees if you wanted a kind of happy compromise. Though the fruit is not the superb quality you can get from some other peach trees, it is attractive and welcome.

SATURN has showy rose-pink flowers that go to two inches or more across if the tree is pruned heavily for fruiting purposes. The Arm-strong Nurseries, who own both the varieties we describe here, recommend pruning after blooming for best flowering, though branches can be cut earlier for bouquets. The after-bloom pruning serves as fruit thinning also. Trees are vigorous, need only mod-erately cold winters, and produce red-blushed yellow fruits, mildly tart, of good quality, ripening in the Midwest in mid-August. Zones 5 to 8.

DOUBLE DELIGHT has a more coral-pink bloom than 'Saturn', is a more compact tree, and needs a little more cold to break its dormancy. It ripens fruit either a few days ahead of 'Saturn' or a few days after, and the peaches are perhaps a little sweeter. Zones 5 to 8.

Peach Troubles

San José scale sometimes attacks the peach along with the apple, but more of the peach troubles are shared only by the other stone fruits—nectarine, apricot, plum, and cherry. The plum curculio is a beetle that causes worms in fruit; her mark is a small crescent cut on the skin, looking somewhat like a tiny pair of lips. Peaches are not apt to be attacked unless plums are growing nearby.

The larvae of the Oriental fruit moth may bore into fruit or tender twig tips, causing tips to die back. The larvae are small pink worms in the fruit. Aphids and mites sometimes bother the peach, but borers are most likely to give trouble. They commonly attack at the base of the trunk and at various places on limbs, indicating their presence by gum and borings. They can be cut out or controlled with sprays. The peach-twig borer attacks twigs. Cut them off before the borer moves on to the fruits.

Several viruses and fungi may attack peach trees, but the most likely trouble is leaf-curl, caused by a fungus and appearing in early spring, when leaves pucker and twist, lose their green color, and fall. Both this disease and brown rot—dark spots on ripening fruits —are controlled by the combination spray program below. If you don't use a spray in time to get such control, and you find peach leaves curling in spring, try these stopgaps: If only a few leaves are affected, pull them off and burn them; if most leaves are affected, give the tree an emergency feeding at the rate of 2 ounces of pure nitrogen for each inch of trunk diameter. This would translate into 10 ounces of ammonium sulphate or 6 ounces of ammonium nitrate per inch of trunk diameter.

Peach schedule with combination spray

> 1. Dormant spray to control leaf curl. Spray before any buds show green, in late winter or very early spring.

    Note: Stark's combination spray is effective here, but not the homemade combination given in Chapter five. Instead, apply ferbam, 2 tablespoons per gallon of water.

    2. As soon as petals have fallen.

    3. Ten days after No. 2. (If Oriental fruit moths are in your area, add 1 tablespoon of Sevin per gallon to this and to later sprays.)

    4. One week after No. 3.

    5. Two weeks after No. 4.

    Note: Omit further sprays on early ripening varieties.

    6. Six weeks after No. 5.

Note: In wet seasons, avoid brown rot with two or three sprays of captan—1½ tablespoons per gallon of water—at weekly intervals, starting two to three weeks before harvest. Captan can safely be sprayed on fruit as late as a day before picking.

If borers are a problem, use a special borer spray, cut them out, or spray trunk and limbs with DDT, malathion, or methoxychlor, 3 tablespoons per gallon of water. Apply July 1, August 1, and September 1 in Zones 3 to 6. Apply June 15, July 15, and August 15 in Zones 7, 8, and 9.

The
Nectarine

11

If a peach tree and a nectarine tree were growing side by side, you couldn't tell which was which until you saw the fruit. So far as botanists have been able to see, peaches and nectarines are exactly the same species, *Prunus persica.* Plant a peach seed and what comes up may be a nectarine tree. And vice versa. Sometimes a single branch on a peach tree will bear nectarines—a bud mutation, it is called. Yet a nectarine, often called simply a fuzzless peach, tastes different—more tangy and aromatic, less rich than a choice peach, often sweeter and juicier. But, again like a peach, it may be cling or freestone, white-fleshed or yellow. The nectarine is by no means a new fruit. It appeared in English horticultural literature more than three hundred years ago, and the great American pomologist, Dr. U. P. Hedrick, thought the ancient Romans had nectarines.

Nectarine trees have traditionally been less hardy than peach trees and more prone to disease. Until a few years ago, you seldom found them growing either in home gardens or commercial orchards except on the West Coast. Today, though most eastern and Midwest nurseries list only one or two varieties, nectarines have been vastly improved. The New Jersey Agricultural Experiment Station has worked on them, and so have such private fruit breeders as Grant Merrill of Exeter and Fred Anderson of Merced, both in California. They have had the needs of the commercial grower in mind, but some of the new nectarines have also turned out to be excellent home-garden performers, producing big juicy fruits that may weigh a pound apiece. With such help, and with trees

'JON-A-RED' APPLE TREE IN BLOOM. A big standard fruit tree in flower is a gladsome sight, especially in a home garden. This is an all-red-skinned mutation of the original 'Jonathan', does best in the Midwest, ripening its attractive fruit in September. (STARK PHOTO)

AN ESPALIERED APPLE TREE. Apples are well suited to this form due to their compact habit of fruiting on short spurs and their adaptability to such restricted growth; an espaliered apple, peach, or pear makes one of the most attractive living designs you can put on a house wall. For espalier training, use dwarf trees. (GENEREUX PHOTO)

LUSCIOUS GOLDEN PEARS. A modern dwarf pear tree that needs only a 10- by 10-foot space will bear delicious fruit for forty years or longer. (GROFFMAN PHOTO)

BIG PEACHES FROM DWARF TREES. *Above:* These fine, big, yellow-fleshed freestone peaches grow on naturally dwarf trees so small they will thrive in planters. *Below:* This brand-new variety, 'Stark Starlet,' also makes an ornamental row planting for the garden or specimen for the terrace or patio. (STARK PHOTOS)

that are hardy and healthy, no wonder this superb fruit is becoming familiar in home gardens.

Nectarines that were growing on our Missouri farm when we bought it had come from peach seeds planted years before and, frankly, were more stone than flesh, as seedlings often are. But their flavor was spectacularly good. One summer in peach-canning time an elderly great-aunt who was visiting us took a notion to peel half a bushel of our nectarine windfalls. The resulting preserves so outclassed our good peach preserves that we held them strictly for ice-cream topping and voluptuary friends.

As to culture—pruning, spraying, and so on—nectarines take exactly the same care as peaches, with possibly an extra pre-harvest spray or dust to prevent brown rot. Plant a few of the new nectarines along with your peaches, and start enjoying the wonderful difference.

Leading Nectarine Varieties

These are all good home-garden varieties with about a six-week spread in ripening time.

EARLY FLAME. A bud sport of 'Flaming Gold', described below, this is a ruddy red fruit with beautiful golden yellow flesh, a semi-freestone. It ripens in late July and keeps well. It is offered in standard trees by Stark's, who own it. Zones 5 to 8.

STARK SUNGLO. Developed by breeder Fred Anderson, this fine-flavored nectarine is one of the largest, going to fourteen ounces. Fruits are round and bright red on a rich yellow background; they are juicy and sweet, of superb dessert quality. Ripening in the Midwest in early August, the trees have proven hardy in all peach zones from 5 to 8, and have even set fruit in some seasons when peaches were frozen out, following very low winter temperatures and spring frosts. Fruits ripen over about two weeks, and store well in a refrigerator. Standard trees are of medium vigor and productiveness. For maximum quality, thin fruit early, and apply one or two extra captan sprays to control brown rot. Zones 5 to 8.

STARK DELICIOUS.   This variety, also developed by Fred Anderson, has been widely tested for hardiness in peach-growing regions of the East and Midwest with good results to date. It is an early bearer, trees often fruiting the second year in the home garden. The Delicious has a bright red skin and freestone yellow flesh of good quality. The great big handsome fruits, with thinning and good culture, will weigh a pound apiece. An exceptionally good keeper, this ripens in early August, and comes in standard size. Zones 5 to 8.

FLAMING GOLD.   Like the 'Burbank July Elberta' peach, this nectarine, ripe in mid-August, is another of Luther Burbank's fruits that he had under development on his experiment farm at the time of his death. It is still the finest flavored of all nectarines. Burbank produced 'Flaming Gold' by crossing the 'Muir' peach (named for the naturalist John Muir, in whose garden it grew from a seed) with a nectarine called 'New White', which had a white skin as well as white flesh. The flesh of 'Flaming Gold' is brilliant yellow, firm, rich, pleasantly tart, and freestone. The skin is deep yellow and crimson. Trees are standard size. Zones 5 to 8.

FUZZLESS-BERTA.   Much prettier than its name, this nectarine's brilliant red fruit is ripe in early September, just in time to go into school lunch boxes or on late picnics. The flavor is rich and sweet, and the yellow flesh is freestone. Trees are standard size and have proven generally hardy in their planting range. Zones 5 to 8.

The
Apricot

12

Until fairly recently in history, apricots were called "apricocks" in England and the United States, and before that they were called in England "the hastie peche" because they ripened early. China has had the fruit for at least five thousand years, but in the western world, apricots have been cultivated for only a few hundred years, arriving in England during the reign of Henry VIII. The botanical name is *Prunus armeniaca*.

One of the best-known varieties in this country for home gardens is 'Moorpark', though in recent years others have been crowding it out. 'Moorpark' came to us from England; it is a bright orange-colored fruit of rich and luscious flavor. Unless you grow your own apricots, you aren't apt to know what a good fresh one tastes like, and while the West Coast has the bulk of favorable apricot country, home gardeners can usually grow the fruit wherever peaches grow.

Apricots can be raised from seed almost as successfully as peaches, if you don't mind waiting four to six years for fruit. What you'll get will be a new variety—and it may be good or poor. In England, so many varieties came about as seedlings that no one can now be positive if certain old kinds exist.

As specimen trees for the lawn and as shade trees, apricots have a good deal to recommend them. So used, they should be pruned more lightly than we specify a little farther on in this chapter, and allowed to grow taller than you might want them to grow in the fruit garden. Either the vase or modified-leader shape is suitable.

The trees are beautiful in bloom and in fruit, and the fruit itself is highly attractive.

Culture
Like peaches, apricots get along on various soils, except wet ones. Also like peaches, they need some cold winter weather, and tend to bloom so early that late frosts may kill the young fruit. Plant them in a non-sheltered spot to hold back early bloom. An open slope dipping to the north is good. In this and other respects, care for them as you do peaches.

Pollination
Fortunately most apricot trees that you can buy will set fruit without cross-pollination. Three exceptions are 'Riland', 'Perfection', and 'Reeves', mainly grown on the West Coast; also two new varieties developed for colder regions—'Moongold' and 'Sungold'. Plant the last two together for cross-pollination. Any other apricot will pollinate the first three.

Pruning
Prune the apricot tree to vase shape, as described in Chapter six. Because it is so vigorous, it can be pruned harder than most other trees that bear fruit on spurs. With apricots, spurs produce fruit for about three years, so the object of pruning is to make the tree form new spurs. Letting in sunlight does this. Remove older branches that bend down or grow too willowy. Or cut them back to points where they grow upward.

Trees can be held at the height you want by cutting back vertical branches to lateral ones at the desired height. Trees sometimes grow too densely in the center, and no fruit is borne on the inside wood as a result. To correct this, remove entirely some branches rather than merely shortening them.

Harvesting
The first step toward a good harvest is severe thinning of green young fruits, for apricots bear so prodigally that if left to themselves they overdo it and have to take a rest every other year. Furthermore, the fruit during the bearing year in that case will be small and inferior.

In addition to fruit-bearing spurs, the apricot also bears part of its crop on paired blossom buds with a leaf bud in between, like peaches. Thin so that no fruit will be close enough to another to touch it when fully grown. This means thinning to 3 to 4 inches apart when fruits are no larger than an inch in diameter—about the width of a twenty-five-cent piece.

Connoisseurs of the apricot differ as to when fruit should be picked. Some claim it is most delectable when fully tree ripened; others maintain that it will grow sweeter ("sugar up") if picked before tree-ripe and allowed to rest in a cool room for a few days. Try both ways and make up your own mind.

To pick apricots, take hold of the fruit and give it a little twist. If it is ripe enough to pick, the stem will come loose. You can pick fruits as they ripen over a period of about three weeks. For cooking, pick them before they are dead ripe. Apricots will keep for about three weeks in a cool place. They should be handled gently, even though they resist bruising fairly well.

Commercially, apricots to be dried are first exposed to the fumes of burning sulphur for about six hours, but at home you can dry them in the oven without this preliminary treatment and get a pretty good product. Pick them ripe, split and stone them, and spread them on racks, cupside up. Set the oven for 190 degrees or a little lower. Keep the oven door open while fruit is drying. In a low-humidity climate, you can dry apricots outdoors in the sun, protected from insects by netting.

Leading apricot varieties

In the apricot districts of California and Arizona, the 'Royal' and 'Blenheim' varieties are widely planted and have been popular for generations. The newer 'Wenatchee' is especially adapted to Washington and Oregon. For the rest of the country, the old English variety 'Moorpark' is offered by several nurseries. So are 'Moongold' and 'Sungold', both developments of the University of Minnesota, introduced in 1961, and able to take temperatures to 25 degrees below zero.

Most nurseries offer apricots in standard trees; only a few dwarfs are on the market. Stark's used to offer up to a dozen varieties; they now offer three that they consider especially good for home gardens, though none is a dwarf. However, apricot trees do not grow very large, and standards are normally planted about 20 feet apart in home gardens.

STARK EARLI-ORANGE.   An orange-fleshed freestone, this ripens in the latter part of June. Fruits have a bright red blush on an orange-colored skin. The hardy trees are fairly large. For best flavor from this variety, let fruit hang on the tree until fully ripe. Zones 5 to 8.

WILSON DELICIOUS.   A large-fruited, yellow-fleshed freestone, this ripens early in July in the Midwest. Trees bear young and well. 'Wilson' is an all-purpose apricot, with a rich sprightly flavor, too tender for shipping fresh, but delicious to eat and to cook, freeze, or dry. Zones 5 to 8.

HUNGARIAN ROSE.   This variety is considered by most connoisseurs we know to be the finest flavored of all apricots, especially when picked fully ripe. The trees are not quite so hardy nor so prolific as 'Earli-Orange' or 'Wilson Delicious', but they bear good crops, ripening in mid-July. Zones 5 to 8.

Apricot Troubles

Surprisingly, this luscious fruit isn't a great favorite with insects. If it is attacked at all, it will be by the same ones that attack peaches and plums—plum curculio, borers, San José scale, and codling moth.

The disease most apt to occur is brown rot, as with peaches and plums.

Apricot schedule with combination spray

>   1. Spray as soon as petals have fallen.
>   2. Ten days after No. 1.
>   3. One week after No. 2.
>   4. Two weeks after No. 3.

In wet seasons, avoid brown rot by an additional spraying with 1½ tablespoons of captan per gallon of water at weekly intervals, starting two to three weeks before harvest. Captan can safely be sprayed on fruit as late as a day before picking.

If borers are a problem, use a special borer spray, or cut borers out with a knife, or spray trunk and limbs with DDT, malathion, or methoxychlor, 3 tablespoonfuls per gallon of water, twice, at ten-day intervals in late spring or early summer—for instance, at the times you apply sprays No. 1 and No. 2 above. Repeat this spray a month later and ten days after that if needed.

Cherries   13

We still had the last of the winter apples in the stone-walled fruit cellar of our Missouri farmhouse when we started picking cherries each spring off the two old Montmorency trees that were growing just outside the cellar door and inside the yard fence. They were closer to the house than any of the other fruit trees because the farm wife who had planted them there a generation before probably knew she'd have to keep an eye on cherry-loving birds. It is this extreme earliness of the cherry that is one of the good things about the fruit, the first to ripen coming along while it is still May in the Midwest—only five to six weeks after the average date of the last killing frost.

Cherries have always been one of the most popular home-garden fruits, and why not? The trees are beauties, like bouquets in bloom, they aren't fussy, they give you fruit quickly and every year from the first year on. And cherry preserves are delicious, cherry pies wonderful.

As you probably know, there are three types: sour cherries, *Prunus cerasus*; sweet cherries, *P. avium*; and Duke cherries, which are hybrids of the other two.

SOUR CHERRIES.   Of the three, sour cherries are the easiest to grow and the most undemanding as to climate. And "sour" is misleading. Most sour cherries are correctly called tart (pie cherries, nurserymen call them), but a tree-ripened Montmorency is also delicious and sweet for eating fresh.

Sour cherry trees are smaller than sweet cherries, and some varieties can be found in dwarf, 8 feet tall, or semidwarf sizes, 9 to 12 feet tall. They are also more tolerant of chilling, needing less winter cold than sweet cherries to break their dormancy. Sour cherries will also go through hotter summers and will put up with fog if they have to. They are amiable trees.

Most sour cherries won't grow south of Zone 7, but there is a new one, 'North Star', that is adapted to higher elevations of Zone 8. Since sour cherries bloom late, they don't often lose buds to spring frosts.

SWEET CHERRIES.   Prima donnas next to the sours, sweet cherries don't care for blistering summers. In fact, the trees sunburn. Neither do they want fog in the growing season, or much humidity. Actually there is some leeway. It depends partly on the spot where the tree is growing, the variety, and even the individual specimen. The Washington, D. C., area has hot and humid summers, and in a yard next to ours there, a sweet cherry tree taller than the two-story house it grew beside had great groaning loads of fruit. It was also an excellent shade tree, as sweet cherries usually are.

Contrary to a general impression, winter cold does not bother sweet cherries if it isn't too severe. However, a sweet cherry may die of the same cold that the tender-seeming peach would endure. But there are exceptions to this, as we have noted in the variety list that follows.

DUKE CHERRIES.   In general the Dukes have sour-cherry looks in their fruit but a much milder taste. Trees are more like the sweets, and Dukes need approximately the same kind of climate as sweet cherries. Dukes are good cherries and many gardeners like them, but to be practical, you have trouble finding Duke trees today. They were much more popular before sour cherries became sweeter and sweet ones became hardier in new or improved old varieties.

Culture

At the start of its life with you, the cherry needs special attention. Be tender with it at this time, most particularly with the roots. Keep them covered from sun and wind with a wet cloth until you plant the little tree, and it is well to mingle a bucketful of damp peatmoss with the soil you put around the roots.

We have seen cherries thrive in a wide variety of soils. Like all fruits they do well on the kind of soil that grows a good garden. Good drainage is important for sweet cherries. Sour cherries are a little less particular, but if you plant either in a downright swampy spot it will die.

You can plant dwarf cherries 10 feet apart. Standard-sized sours need about 20 feet, and sweets take 25 to 30 feet.

Deep cultivation isn't good for cherries, especially for the sours, which are shallow rooted. For this reason, mulching is an especially good practice. It also helps a tree get through the first two years when water needs are more critical than later. During this time, water every two to three weeks in drouthy periods.

Fertilize your cherry trees only if they are making weak growth. Nitrogen is what they'll need. A mature dwarf can be given up to a pound of ammonium nitrate; a mature standard sour cherry can use up to three pounds; and a mature sweet cherry can use as much as ten pounds if it is a large old tree. (Ammonium nitrate is 33 percent pure nitrogen; adjust the amounts accordingly if you use some other nitrogenous fertilizer.)

Pollination

All sour cherries pollinate themselves, so you can plant just one tree and get fruit.

Sweet cherries are selective about pollinators; you cannot plant just any two varieties together and be sure of getting fruit. To keep it simple, we give for each variety listed below its best pollinators. Of course, you can plant any other varieties with it without affecting pollination. Can a sour cherry pollinate a sweet cherry? Yes, it can, but the joker here is that their blooming times do not overlap enough for dependable fruit setting.

Duke cherries must be cross-pollinated to set fruit, and any other Duke or any sweet or sour cherry blooming at the same time will do.

One other point: Ideally, plant a dwarf tree to pollinate a dwarf, and a standard tree to pollinate a standard.

Pruning

Sweet cherry trees are naturally inclined to the pyramid form and should be so trained, as described in Chapter six. Sour cherries adapt themselves to the vase shape, though dwarfs of both are better grown as pyramids in a closely spaced planting. Standard trees of both types are usually headed low, with the first framework limb about two feet from the ground.

The only problem you are apt to encounter in shaping your trees will be with the sweet cherry's tendency to produce upright rather than outward-growing branches, particularly 'Lambert' and 'Black Tartarian'. The remedy is to cut back these upright branches without mercy to a twig or bud pointing out in the right direction. After about three seasons of this pruning, you should have a tree of satisfactory form.

Sweet cherries bear fruit on spurs that last for ten years or more, so prune trees lightly to avoid removing productive wood. Sour cherries fruit on spurs occurring on wood two to five years old. Pruning here should also be light—mainly the removal of crowded wood in the tree's interior and a shortening of too-long fruiting branches.

Harvesting

These tender and juicy fruits should never be picked until they are dead ripe. A sweet cherry becomes noticeably firm when it reaches this point; a sour cherry is ripe when it parts easily from the stem. But unless you want cherries for cooking, pick them with stems attached. This is not only a more agreeable way, but you'll get higher quality and a better keeping product.

You can pile cherries in a bucket or basket without damage. Any surplus can be held in the refrigerator. Soft-fleshed cherries will keep in this way for about a week, firm ones for two to three weeks.

Leading Sour Cherries

EARLY RICHMOND.　Known by many names, this old European red sour cherry is the true Kentish cherry. It is earlier than 'Montmorency', and has continued to be popular in spite of Montmorency's wider appeal and the fact that it can't thrive in too hot an area. 'Early Richmond' is hardy and very productive, and has the good habit of possessing a stone that clings so desperately to the stem, you can remove it by pulling the stem out. For this reason the fruit has been popular for drying in the sun. Let it get full ripe for this treatment. The flavor is rich and tart, whether fresh or dried. The tree comes into bearing young, and ripens fruit late in May. Several nurseries offer it, mostly in standard trees. Zones 4 to 7.

This is self-pollinating.

MONTMORENCY. The most popular sour cherry, this has many strains and sub-varieties, and is offered by almost all nurseries. Color ranges from light to dark red, and the yellow flesh is tart and good—an eating-out-of-hand cherry if you grow it yourself and pick it tree-ripe. Fruit is large and resistant to cracking when there is much rain at fruiting time. Trees are young-bearing and hardy. Bloom comes late and so escapes some late frosts, and fruit ripens in early June. Years ago Stark's offered five different Montmorencies; today, like most nurseries, they offer one, and that in standard trees. They consider it the best 'Montmorency' of all that they have tested over the years. It ripens in early June. Zones 4 to 7.

All Montmorencies are self-pollinating.

METEOR. This semidwarf originated with the Minnesota Experiment Station and is an attractive little tree, 10 to 12 feet high, pretty enough for an ornamental. The light red fruits are tart and large, and there are lots of them. It is a cooking and freezing cherry and ripens in June. It stands cold particularly well. Zones 4 to 7.

It is self-pollinating.

NORTH STAR. Also from the Minnesota Experiment Station, this dwarf tree grows to 8 feet and bears good crops of big, deep red cherries, tart and juicy. The juice is red and they make a delicious— and delicious-looking—cherry pie. Ripening in mid-June, the variety will grow farther south than most sours. Zone 4 to higher parts of 8.

This is self-pollinating.

Since it is a natural dwarf, 'North Star' serves as a trunk section for dwarfing other varieties of cherries. For the rootstock in these cases, Stark's use a wild cherry, the mahaleb.

SUDA HARDY. Pomologists call this a Morello type of sour cherry, the Morellos being dark and sour and yielding red juice. They are pretty strictly cooking cherries. 'Meteor' and 'North Star' are also of this type. Suda is probably a seedling of English Morello, the best known of the group; the original Suda tree grew in a garden in the town of Louisiana, Missouri. This location seems to have given Stark's a kind of tacit patent on it, for though the variety appeared long before the Plant Patent Act was passed, no other nursery carries it. Offered in standard trees, which are smaller than other standards, Suda is a young and regular bearer and is long-lived. Fruit ripens late—early July. Trees are quite hardy to cold. Only Zones 4 and 5.

It is self-pollinating.

Leading Sweet Cherries

VISTA. One of the early sweet cherries, this is larger than most others of its season, and colors up a good red. It ripens in early June and is used for eating fresh, cooking, and freezing. The trees are standards but not large, and are quite productive and hardy. Zones 5, 6, and 7.

Pollinate with any other sweet cherry listed here.

STARKING HARDY GIANT. A sweet cherry that can survive 30 degrees below zero and bear fruit the next season is quite a sweet cherry, and this one has done it. It comes from Wisconsin, is dark red, the fruit borne in clusters, and is one of the biggest of the sweets. It is also crack-resistant. If it has a fault, it may be the small one of lacking tartness for some tastes when cooked. It ripens in early June. Zones 5, 6, and 7.

Pollinate with any other sweet cherry listed here.

BLACK TARTARIAN. This old and well-known black sweet cherry came to us from Russia via England early in the nineteenth century; it has long been a favorite. The fruit is somewhat small and soft. 'Black Tartarian' is both a home-garden and a commercial cherry. In some areas, however, it lacks vigor and hardiness, and is a so-so producer. Most nurseries carry it, some in dwarf trees. Stark's used to but have dropped it in favor of such other dark reds, as 'Van'. 'Black Tartarian' ripens in early June. Zones 5 to 7.

One of its notable advantages is self-fruitfulness; it can set a crop when growing alone.

EMPEROR FRANCIS.   Borne on a medium-sized standard tree, this good sweet cherry may be the tree for you if you live in Zone 5, 6, or 7 and have had trouble getting sweet cherries to bear. 'Emperor Francis' is more tolerant of wet weather at fruiting time, in mid-June and just before, than most varieties. In fact, it can stand many kinds of adverse weather and growing conditions, and is a very good and cheerful cherry indeed. It is highly esteemed for eating fresh, and is also used for canning and for making maraschino cherries. Zones 5, 6, and 7.

Pollinate with any other sweet cherry listed here.

VAN.   Quite hardy and very productive, this sweet red cherry looks and tastes like the excellent 'Bing', and all the cherries on the tree ripen at the same time. This suggests it is a commercial variety, and it is. However, it is also a good home-garden type and is available in dwarf as well as standard trees from Stark's, one of the few nurseries listing it. 'Van' came from western Canada. It ripens in mid-June and has delicious red flesh. Trees bear early in life and heavily. Zones 5, 6, and 7.

Pollinate with any other sweet cherry listed here.

NAPOLEON.   Also known as Royal Ann, this red-blushed yellow cherry is the one you often see as a canned product. Maraschino cherries are often Napoleons, too. It is a good cherry for eating fresh and a good home-garden as well as commercial cherry, though the trees are apt to be choosy about growing conditions. 'Napoleon' is moderately vigorous, fairly hardy, and productive. Most nurseries offer it, usually in standard trees. It ripens in Mid-June. Zones 5, 6, and 7.

Pollinate with 'Van', 'Starking Hardy Giant', or 'Stark Gold'. Next best: 'Vista', 'Schmidt's Bigarreau', or 'Black Tartarian'.

BING. This came from Oregon, where it is a popular commercial cherry, a big, very dark red fruit, firm and juicy and delicious. It is also a good garden variety if you like a crop that ripens all the fruit at the same time, and if you don't have much rain just before harvest—which is the middle of June in the Midwest. 'Bing' is one of the varieties that crack if there is more rain than they care for. It is a fine fresh fruit, and also cans and freezes well. Usually offered in standard trees, it is adapted for sweet-cherry areas in Zones 5, 6, and 7.

Pollinate with 'Van'. Next best: 'Starking Hardy Giant', 'Stark Gold', 'Vista', 'Schmidt's Bigarreau', or 'Black Tartarian'.

LAMBERT. To sweet-cherry fanciers, this is one of the finest. It came from Oregon and is a large, heart-shaped, red cherry so dark it is almost black when ripe. The flesh is firm and meaty, of excellent flavor. 'Lambert' does have one fault, a tendency to crack in very wet seasons. Nevertheless, commercial growers like 'Lambert' for it is an eye-catcher, and the cherries are sometimes as big as small plums. It is also a home-garden variety and will take colder weather than some other sweet cherries. It is not carried by many nurseries despite its fine quality of fruit, big crops, and rugged good health of tree. In the Midwest, it ripens in mid-June. Zones 4 to 7.

Pollinate with 'Van', 'Starking Hardy Giant', or 'Stark Gold'. Next best: 'Vista', 'Schmidt's Bigarreau', or 'Black Tartarian'.

SCHMIDT'S BIGARREAU. The name Bigarreau is a type name applied to firm-fleshed sweet cherries; there are all sorts of varieties with Bigarreau in the name. This one, 'Schmidt's Bigarreau', is a big black sweet cherry borne in clusters. The tree is a strong grower and hardy, quite popular in the East and Midwest. Fruit ripens about mid-June. It is tender and fine-grained, good for eating fresh and for cooking. It does not crack easily in rainy weather. Most nurseries offer this, and some supply dwarf trees. Zones 5, 6, and 7.

Pollinate with any other sweet cherry listed here.

WINDSOR. Sometimes called Black Oxheart, 'Windsor' is one of the hardiest sweet cherries, a vigorous and rapid upright grower.

It originated in Canada, and the hardiness extends to the fruit buds. The cherries are a dull dark red outside and pink inside, substantial and firm, very good. Size is medium to large. This commercial cherry is also a home-garden variety. It ripens in mid-June or a bit later, and is a dessert cherry, good fresh or cooked, and for canning, too. Zones 5, 6, and 7.

Pollinate with any other sweet cherry listed here.

STARK GOLD.   Originating in Nebraska, where it took temperatures to 30 below, this medium-sized cherry is the hardiest yellow sweet cherry on the market. The flesh is also yellow, almost translucent, with a spicy flavor. 'Stark Gold' ripens in late June and will hang on the tree about ten days longer. This is fine until the birds get used to the color and realize the cherries are ripe even though they aren't red. 'Stark Gold' is good for eating fresh and for cooking and freezing. It is available in dwarf and standard trees. Zones 5, 6, and 7.

Pollinate dwarf trees with 'Van'; standards with any other sweet cherry listed here.

Cherry Troubles

Along with insects that attack some of the other fruits—mainly San José scale (mostly on sweet cherries), plum curculio, mites, aphids, and slugs—the cherry sometimes is troubled by a fruit fly that causes maggots in the fruit, and with a fruit worm, the larva of a moth.

Diseases include some viruses, but virus-free trees are offered by most progressive nurseries.

Brown rot may occur, as in peaches; black knot, as on plums, is cut out of the wood with a knife. Certain varieties of cherries are troubled in bad seasons with leaf spots or blights, rusts, and mildews; and yellow leaf sometimes occurs, as with plums.

Despite these possible problems, most insects and diseases of cherries are easily controlled with three or four sprayings or dustings with one of the new combinations.

Cherry schedule with combination spray

1. Spray as soon as petals have fallen.
2. Ten days after No. 1.
3. One week after No. 2.
4. Two weeks after No. 3. (Omit this spray on early varieties.)

Note: In wet seasons, avoid brown rot by spraying with captan, a tablespoon and a half per gallon of water, at weekly intervals starting two to three weeks before harvest. Captan can safely be sprayed on fruit as late as a day before picking. In such wet seasons, cherry leaf spot may occur, so apply the combination spray immediately after harvest to insure healthy trees for next year's crop, and repeat in two weeks if wet weather continues.

If borers are a problem, apply a special borer spray, or cut the borers out with a knife, or spray with DDT, malathion, or methoxychlor, 3 tablespoons per gallon of water, twice at ten-day intervals in late spring or early summer—for instance, at the times you apply sprays No. 1 and No. 2 above. Repeat borer spray a month later and ten days after that if needed. Delay this second spraying until after harvest, however, for the earliest varieties.

Plums and Prunes   14

Plums are so good that the name has passed into the language as a synonym for something special—a prize, a bonus, a coveted appointment. This sounds as if plums are rare, or hard to grow, but actually they thrive throughout the temperate zones and survive some pretty intemperate weather. Furthermore, the trees are fairly small so that they fit neatly into gardens and landscape plans.

In addition to the ornamental plums, some of which bear small edible fruits, there are four groups of food plums. The genus is *Prunus*, the same as apricots, peaches, and cherries. The four groups comprise two European species, one Japanese, and the Americans, and you'll find all of them growing in the United States. In fact, the plum—which is quite an old fruit, almost as venerable as the apple—has so many forms that it is a difficult location where *some* plum won't grow and be happy.

Probably there are wild native plums in your area. There are about thirty species of them, the leading one, *Prunus americana*. This grows pretty generally over all the country east of the Rockies, bearing gay little red or yellow fruits, small by commercial standards, and tart, but good. We had two such trees on our Missouri farm, the red ones, and besides bearing acceptable fruit for eating fresh and for cooking, the trees were a froth of lovely blossoms each spring. Keep this in mind when locating your plum trees, as all plums are perfect beauties in bloom and should be enjoyed.

Prunus americana is as hardy as a weed and will grow where European plums droop and Japanese ones expire. Another native plum common in the Midwest is *P. hortulana*; to the South, *P.*

munsoniana is important. The little beach plum, *P. maritima*, grows on sand dunes of the East Coast and is treasured by many a resident. North to Canada the native plum is *P. nigra*. Native plums have been much used in breeding, so that their blood is helping acclimate new hybrids to special geographic conditions.

Most people know Damson and Green Gage plums. The Damson especially has made itself at home here, but it is European, belonging to the *P. insititia* species. The Green Gage is the best-known member of the other European species, *P. domestica*. In the European group are some of the best plums on earth, and here also are the plums that are sweet enough to make dried prunes. Not everyone knows that a prune starts life as plum, or that a fresh prune looks like a plum, tastes like a plum, and *is* a plum. (Despairing of making everyone understand this, nurserymen are sometimes led to call prunes plum-prunes.)

The old way of making prunes in France, which once had a monopoly on prune-making, involved a fearful amount of handwork. After careful harvesting, fresh prunes were laid on wicker sieves in the sun for days until they softened. They then went through five heatings in ovens of different temperatures and humidities, interrupted by a turning of each prune on the sieve, and by an operation called rounding in which each prune had the stone loosened by gentle pressure between thumb and finger.

Japanese plums (which came from China in the first place), *P. triflora* or *P. salicina*, will grow in some regions where the Europeans won't, as in areas of the South and Southwest. However, they are usually more hurt by cold than the Europeans—particularly the Damsons, which shrug off sub-zero chill in the way of apples. In general, you can grow Japanese plums where you can grow peaches, and European plums where you can grow pears. Hybrids may grow where one of the parents could not survive.

Luther Burbank did more for Japanese plums than anyone else, and this was the most important aspect of his work with fruits. The best-known Japanese types today are those he introduced, and the one he named 'Santa Rosa' after the California town, where he spent his horticultural working life, is still the state's leading variety. But he didn't limit his breeding to Japanese plums. His method was always to make a great many crosses between varieties and, where possible between species, and he used every plum he could get. One of his developments, the 'Alhambra', was called with some wonder by the great Dutch botanist Hugo de Vries, a "seven-fold" combination, the ancestry including Japanese, European, various American, and even ornamental plums.

To identify type, some use this rule of thumb: Japanese plums are red, European are bluish. There are too many exceptions to this to make it dependable, even though most Japanese plums *are* red and most Europeans *are* blue. Damsons are always blue to purple, and native American plums are mainly red, with some yellows. Between Japanese and European types, leaves offer a clue, Japanese plum leaves being glossy green, and European, dull green. But along with exceptions, there are the hybrid varieties to muddle things.

Culture

Plant your plum trees on a slope if you can, preferably a north slope. Japanese plums bloom early and so are vulnerable to late spring frosts. European plums bloom late but a north slope also suits them, particularly where summers are hot. The American species are the least demanding and will get along almost anywhere.

Given a choice, Europeans and Damsons would prefer a medium-heavy loam. Japanese and American plums are ideally suited to a lighter soil, sandy or gravelly. A good compromise is a medium-textured and well-drained garden soil. On this all plums will thrive.

In the home fruit garden, plan to fertilize your plum trees. Give them nitrogen in spring, at this rate for mature trees if you use ammonium nitrate, which is 33 percent pure nitrogen:

> Japanese plums .... 3 to 5 pounds
> European and Damson plums .... 2 to 6 pounds
> American species plums .... 1 to 2 pounds

Plums are hard-working trees and need water, and a mulch is the best way to hold moisture in the soil. Young trees may need water in dry spells, but once trees are established, a good thick mulch should make watering unnecessary. If you live in an arid region and must irrigate, do so for plums during their blooming and fruiting seasons.

Most European and Damson plums need some winter chilling to break their dormancy. Most Japanese plums get along with a minimum and will grow as far south as Florida. Native species are available only where they do well.

Pollination

Plums vary a good deal in pollination requirements; furthermore, some varieties of some species will pollinate each other and some won't. Since the varieties we list include more than one species, as well as some very mixcd-up hybrids, we give the pollinators for each variety that needs cross-pollination. As usual, varieties are listed in ripening order rather than by species or groups.

Pruning

All plums bear fruit on spurs. When you prune, it is important to know where the spurs are, especially with European plums because they bear less heavily than Japanese and can be pruned into non-fruiting. Whatever species you grow, the form usually preferred is the vase shape that lets more sun into the interior.

JAPANESE PLUMS.　Most take the vase shape naturally, and some, 'Burbank' and 'Red Ace', for instance, may even need to have some lateral branches pruned away in order to throw strength into more upright growth for the sake of the tree's form. A few of the Japanese, however, are inclined to upright growth; with these, it may be a good idea to prune some upright branches back to outward-pointing buds or to lateral branches for a better spread. 'Wickson', 'Kelsey', and 'Santa Rosa' are all of this nature. Japanese plums bear fruit spurs generally *throughout* the tree and so abundantly that there is small danger of your reducing the crop by pruning off spurs. These spurs are also long-lived, bearing fruit for five seasons or more.

Annual pruning is a matter of cutting out surplus wood—water sprouts and new shoots in places where they aren't wanted—and removing some older fruiting wood no longer very productive. Trees grow so vigorously that there will be no lack of replacement wood for what you take out, and a good deal of taking out will be needed. Fruit thinning is also an annual need, so much so that a piece of rubber hose on a pole is usually used to knock off surplus fruit while it is still young. Thin fruit 2 to 4 inches apart.

NATIVE AMERICAN PLUMS.   These are pruned much like the Japanese, but need thinning only if the set of fruit is quite heavy.

EUROPEAN AND DAMSON PLUMS.   These trees grow rather slowly so your choice of framework limbs will be more limited than with Japanese plums. The Europeans are generally upright growers. To open them up, it is often necessary to prune some vertical branches back to outward-pointing buds or branches. This is likely to be needed with the varieties, 'President', 'Pond', and 'Giant'. If it is not done, fruit spurs on the inside of the framework go barren from lack of sun. An alternate treatment sometimes used with these and other vertical-growing varieties is to tie vertical branches down toward the horizontal. This opens up the tree and also encourages fruiting on the tied branches. After being tied down for a season, a branch can be untied without much chance of its growing too nearly vertical again.

Fruit spurs of European and Damson plums are mainly on long, thin lateral branches. They are long-lived, like the Japanese spurs, but their first year is unfruitful. On that account, be careful not to prune away new lateral branches unless they are crowded, poorly placed, or so growthy that they unbalance the tree form. Prune some of the longer ones back halfway, a process that will also serve to keep down fruit set to a good level.

The annual pruning of European and Damsons is really a thinning-out process. Remove older fruiting wood, including older short spurs on framework branches, to make room for new. Keep the tree form open to let in sun. As much fruit thinning as most European plums need will be supplied by the annual pruning, and like Japanese plums, Europeans should have fruit 2 to 4 inches apart. Damsons are seldom thinned at all as thinning does not make the fruit any bigger and the trees have no trouble supporting their crops.

Since prunes are plums, they are handled the same as any European plum.

Harvesting

A plum is ready to pick when a little twist can separate it easily from the tree. At that time, the skin will have a bloom—the powdery coating that denotes ripeness—and the flesh will be elastic rather than hard. Very juicy varieties should be picked most promptly, but none except Japanese should be harvested until they are quite ripe unless you prefer the tang that slightly unripe plums have. Pick Japanese plums just as they start to feel soft, and ripen them in a cool room. For canning, plums need not be completely ripe—though this is also a question of preference.

Plums usually ripen in waves, so that you'll be picking them over several days. We harvested some of our Damsons by shaking the trees, and you can do so with any of the meaty plums and prunes, such as 'Bluefre'. Like cherries, as you pick, you can pile plums in a bucket without hurting them if they aren't over-ripe. They keep well in a cool room for at least a week, and longer, of course, in a refrigerator or cold storage. You'll start getting crops from your plum trees in three or four years. A healthy mature tree will give you a hundred pounds of fruit each season.

Leading Plum Varieties

SANTA ROSA. Ripening early in July, 'Santa Rosa' is a big handsome red fruit, changing to a purplish color a few days ahead of ripening. The clingstone flesh is yellow or reddish yellow. This is a good bearer and the plums keep well. It is an excellent dessert type.

'Santa Rosa' is a hybrid with predominantly Japanese-plum characteristics, but nobody knows all the crosses involved, since Burbank, the originator, never revealed them. However, 'Santa Rosa' is so good that it is widely grown not only in the United States (commercially in California where, as mentioned, it is the major shipping plum), but also in Europe, Africa, Australia, and New Zealand. Though commercial, 'Santa Rosa' is a good garden plum, too. Some nurseries supply it in dwarf size. Zones 5 to 9.

Pollinate with 'Redheart', 'Starking Delicious', 'Ozark Premier', 'Ace', 'MacVerna Delicious', or 'Elephant Heart'.

GIANT CHERRY.   Maturing the middle of July, this hybrid is the best cherry-plum that Stark's have tested, and is mainly for home gardens. It has a cherry flavor, is bright red, rather sweet and spicy, intended for both eating fresh and cooking. Zones 4 to 8.

Pollinate with 'Ember' or 'President'.

REDHEART.   Aside from its own merits, an important advantage of this plum, developed at the University of California, is that it is a companion tree for the luscious 'Elephant Heart', which it pollinates well—solving a problem that had plagued some growers of 'Elephant Heart' for a long time. Burgundy red in skin and flesh, 'Redheart' is a Japanese type, a hybrid of Burbank's 'Wickson' and 'Duarte', which means that 'Redheart' has some American plum blood in its makeup, too. The flesh is fine-textured and the fruit can be picked a little ahead of dead-ripe time if you wish. It ripens in early August. Zones 6 to 9.

Pollinate with 'Elephant Heart', 'Santa Rosa', 'Starking Delicious', 'Ozark Premier', 'Ace', or 'MacVerna Delicious'.

STARKING DELICIOUS.   This same name has been given to an apple, a pear, and a peach, an indication of Stark's regard. The 'Starking Delicious' plum is a Japanese type and the hardiest of the Japanese that Stark's have discovered. It is so persistent a bearer that trees in a test orchard have required fruit thinning after a winter when the temperature hit 17 degrees below zero. Trees also show resistance to disease and are long-lived. The large fruits are ruby red from skin to stone, well flavored, good both fresh and cooked. They ripen in early August. Zones 5 to 9.

Pollinate with 'Santa Rosa', 'Redheart', 'Ozark Premier', 'Ace', 'MacVerna Delicious', or 'Elephant Heart'.

OZARK PREMIER.   A new hybrid, Japanese type, 'Ozark Premier' is a yellow-fleshed plum almost twice as big as 'Santa Rosa', and is a mild, sweet fruit. It is semicling and the skin is scarlet vermillion. It ripens in mid-August. Zones 5 to 9.

Pollinate with 'Santa Rosa', 'Redheart', 'Starking Delicious', 'Ace', 'MacVerna Delicious', or 'Elephant Heart'.

EMBER. A Minnesota originated plum, 'Ember' is particularly hardy. It is red with yellow flesh, an American type, juicy and tender, ripening in mid-August. Zone 8 to as far north as Zone 4.

Pollination is sometimes a problem. Its best pollinators seem to be 'Giant Cherry' and a plum called 'Toka', large and sweet and carried by several nurseries.

RED ACE. This is a Burbank plum and the only non-standard-sized plum tree Stark's offer, 'Red Ace' being a natural semidwarf, growing 12 to 15 feet high. The variety was ready for introduction just as Burbank died. It is a medium-sized red plum with pale blue bloom, semi-freestone, rich and sweet. It is hardy and young-bearing, an all-purpose plum ripening in mid-August. Burbank did not specify its ancestry, but it is a Japanese type. Zones 5 to 9.

Pollinate with 'Santa Rosa', 'Redheart', 'Starking Delicious', 'Ozark Premier', 'MacVerna Delicious', or 'Elephant Heart'.

BURBANK GRAND PRIZE PRUNE. This is a European type that bears very large bluish purple fruits with yellow flesh, freestone but juicy. The quality is good, and the prunes ripen in mid-August. Zones 5 to 8.

Pollinate with 'Bluefre' prune. Next best: Green Gage plum, Damson plum, or 'Stanley' prune.

MACVERNA DELICIOUS. This new plum, developed in New Zealand, is becoming popular there, particularly with commercial orchardists because of exceptional keeping ability. The quality of the large fruit is good and it is attractive, both skin and flesh a wine-red. A Japanese type, MacVerna is a vigorous and young-bearing tree. It is supplied exclusively by Stark's. Zones 5 to 9.

Pollinate with 'Ozark Premier' or 'Redheart'. Next best: 'Santa Rosa', 'Starking Delicious', 'Ace', 'Elephant Heart'.

GREEN GAGE. A high favorite for centuries, this old European plum has been known by many other names, at least forty. Queen Claude, wife of Francis I, contemporary of Henry VIII of England, is supposed to have brought the Green Gage into France; there it is the 'Reine Claude'. Green Gage became known by that name after an English family named Gage had imported several varieties of plum trees from France and found no name tag on one—the 'Reine Claude'. Thereupon their head gardener, when the greenish yellow plum fruited, named it after the family, and the name stuck. Green Gage ripens about mid-August, and is a fine dessert plum, rich and juicy. It is a freestone, also a good cooking plum. It has several red sports; of them, 'Reine Red' is one of the best and most attractive, a Green Gage in all but color. Zones 5, 6, and 7.

Green Gage is a self-pollinator.

BLUEFRE PRUNE.   A yellow-fleshed freestone, this attractive blue prune is a hybrid of two European types, 'Stanley' prune and 'President' plum. The flesh is firm and sweet, well flavored and resembling, but better than, 'Stanley'. Hardy and young-bearing, 'Bluefre' is reported by Stark's as one of the most productive prune trees they have tested. The fruit is used fresh, cooked, and also dried, of course, being a prune. It ripens in early September. Zones 5, 6, and 7.

Pollinate with 'Burbank Grand Prize' prune, Green Gage plum, Damson plum, or 'Stanley' prune.

ELEPHANT HEART.   If you have the growing conditions this big red plum likes, it will be an ornament to your garden and a delight on the table. It is inclined to be a poor grower in the East and the Midwest, though not in every location; it likes rather arid and sandy sections. It also had been difficult to pollinate well until the plum 'Redheart' appeared. However, we grew it in Missouri years ago, before 'Redheart' arrived, and it flourished and fruited. Fruits are somewhat heart-shaped, and when thoroughly tree-ripened, the ruby flesh has a luscious flavor that suggests a sweet cherry. This is one of the Burbank plums and is undoubtedly the best of the red-fleshed Japanese types. Zones 5 to 9, especially the sandy sections of the Southeast and the semiarid sections of the West.

Pollinate with 'Redheart'.

PRESIDENT.   A European type, this is a large dark purple plum with sweet yellow flesh for eating fresh and for cooking. It is a good plum, though not superb. Fruit ripens in September. Zones 5, 6, and 7.

For best production, pollinate with 'Bluefre' prune or 'Stanley' prune.

DAMSONS. There are a number of varieties of Damsons though not every nursery offers even one of them. Those that do usually carry the 'Shropshire', and Stark's offer one they call 'Giant'. Damsons are quite productive. Some people like to eat a few fresh when they are fully tree-ripened, but the fruit is usually treasured for the distinctive jam it makes. Damsons have a habit of producing many suckers. These can be removed and planted to make new trees, as we did with the old Damsons on our farm. Such new trees take quite a few years before they bear, but then they go on bearing for about fifty years. The Damson is a fairly small tree, though some nurseries offer dwarfs as well. Fruit ripens in early September. Zones 5, 6, and 7.

Damsons are self-pollinating.

STANLEY PRUNE. Carried by more nurseries than any other variety of prune, this parent of 'Bluefre' prune is a New York State Experiment Station introduction that has proven popular both in home gardens and commercial orchards. 'Bluefre' is a little better fruit, but 'Stanley' is a heavier bearer. 'Stanley' ripens in early September, following 'Bluefre' by a week, and is an early bearer. The big fruits are deep bluish purple with firm greenish yellow flesh, freestone, of good quality for eating fresh and cooking, juicy, fine-grained, and tender. Don't pick them till they are soft-ripe. A reliable cropper, it is a European type, as are all prunes. Zones 5, 6, and 7.

'Stanley' is self-pollinating.

BURBANK PURPLE FLAME. We list this plum in spite of its being almost entirely an ornamental, because it does have crops of small red fruits that are of fair quality, and because the red leaves have made it a favorite accent tree for the home grounds. The tree is one acclaimed by Mrs. Lyndon B. Johnson, in the interest of a more beautiful America. 'Burbank Purple Flame' grows 15 to 20 feet and is a cloud of white blossoms in spring, the blooms having a pink blush and at the throat a rosy red coloring. Luther Burbank worked on several ornamental plums, most of them also bearing edible fruit. Zones 5 to 9.

It is self-pollinating.

Plum and Prune Troubles

Plums and prunes are not often victims of insects, though some can attack them. These are chiefly the plum curculio, peach borer, San José scale, and aphids.

If the plum gets a disease it will probably be brown rot, black knot, or yellow leaf. Brown rot acts the same as on the peach and is hardest on native and Japanese plums. Black knot is more apt to show up in a neglected orchard. It attacks the wood, and is most common on European plums, forming greenish knots that later turn black and hard. The remedy is simple: Cut the knots out as soon as you see them, preferably in the summer while they are green, and burn them. Yellow-leaf is caused by a fungus which discolors leaves, and the tree is weakened by losing them. Keep these fallen leaves cleaned up and burned, as the spores will live over on them and reinfect the tree the next spring.

Plum and prune schedule for combination spray

1. Spray as soon as petals have fallen.
2. Ten days after No. 1.
3. One week after No. 2.
4. Two weeks after No. 3.

Note: In wet seasons avoid brown rot by spraying with 1½ tablespoons of captan per gallon of water at weekly intervals, starting two to three weeks before harvest. Captan can safely be sprayed on fruit as late as a day before picking.

If borers are a problem, use a special spray for borers, cut them out, or spray tree trunk and limbs with DDT, malathion, or methoxychlor, 3 tablespoons per gallon of water. Apply twice at ten-day intervals in late spring or early summer—for instance, at the same time you apply sprays No. 1 and No. 2. Repeat borer spray a month later and ten days after that if needed. Delay this second spraying until after harvest for earlier varieties.

The Quince   15

Either you like quinces or you haven't the slightest desire for them. To some people, the best to be said for the quince, as a species, is that it makes it possible to dwarf pears. The 'French Provence' quince is now the rootstock on which most pears are grafted.

We'd like to put in a word for the quince as a lovely tree to have on the lawn or in the shrub border, no matter how you feel about quinces to eat. It is a gentlemanly tree, well behaved and with quiet dignity, and the bark is a pleasure to look at. The upper part is thickety, and there is an air about a quince tree that makes it look as if it intends to go quietly on living forever—a splendid specimen tree for the home grounds. We'd suggest a line of quinces along your front walk except that you wouldn't know what to do with all the fruit each fall.

Hardly anyone eats the quince raw but Luther Burbank bred one that can be eaten when dead ripe like an apple. It is called the 'Pineapple' quince, since it tastes a little like that fruit. However, it does not seem to be offered by any nursery outside California.

The quince listed today by most of the big mail-order nurseries is the 'Orange' variety, usually specified as of dwarf size, but all quinces are more or less dwarf. The 'Orange', popular in America since colonial days, is apple-shaped and yellow both in skin and flesh.

Apparently the quince originated in the Caucasus region of Europe. The ancient Greeks and Romans knew the fruit well and considered it healthy to eat as well as delicious. The name, *Cy-*

donia oblonga, comes from Cydon, a city in Crete, where the quince seems to have first attracted attention, at least the attention of someone able to publicize it.

Preserves and jelly are made from the quince, and it is sometimes added to cooked apples for more flavor. In England, it was used to make quince wine, and in earlier days the fruit was *the* fruit for marmalade. A famous English horticulturist, John Gerard, gave this recipe for marmalade in his *Herbal* of 1636.

> Take faire Quinces, paire them, cut them into pieces and caste away the core, then put unto every pound of Quinces, a pound of Sugar, and to every pound of Sugar a pinte of Water; these must be boiled together over a stil fire till they be very soft, then let it be strained or rubbed through a strainer or an hairy sieve, which is better, and then set it over the fire againe untill it be stiffe, and so box it up, and as it cooleth put thereto a little Rose water, and a few graines of Muske mingled together, which will give a goodly taste to the Cotiniat. This is the way to make Marmalad.

A popular columnist in our local newspaper asked if anyone had a recipe for quince preserves and got so many answers that for three days the column was monopolized by quinces—how to cook them, where to get fruit, where to get trees, and so forth. He finally had to say: "Please—no more quinces!" But the response proved that even if you seldom hear much about the quince, it has supporters.

A light fuzz on the skin is characteristic, though it was barely noticeable on a variety growing on a place we owned in the South. We didn't have much use for the fruits as food but they were so handsome in an offhand way and smelled so good that we used to bring them into the house just to have them around. Incidentally, this aroma makes it advisable not to store them with other fruits, which will get to tasting like quinces.

Culture

Ideally, soil for the quince should be well drained and warm. In practice, the quince gets along on various soils, including heavy clay. We grew ours in sandy soil. Give shallow cultivation, if any, and mulching is preferable.

In dry periods quinces can use some watering, though they'll get along on a minimum. Fertilizer is seldom needed.

Pollination
The quince is self-fruitful, so that one tree standing alone will set fruit quite well.

Pruning
Prune the quince as if it were an apple tree, but prune it lightly, for fruit is borne on wood grown the same year. Keep an eye on possible fire blight, promptly breaking off any blackened branches and burning them. Don't confuse these with blackish knots on the trunks and branches of old trees, which are normal characteristics of age and should not be cut off.

Harvesting
Not much, if any, thinning is needed for the quince to produce good fruit. The quinces ripen late in the year and are ready for picking when they turn yellow. Handle them carefully—they look tough, but the skin is easily bruised.

Leading Quince Varieties

ORANGE. The fruits look like yellow apples and are of good quality. They ripen early—in the first part of September. Zones 6, 7, and 8, and the West Coast.

VAN DEMAN. This is a hybrid with 'Orange' one of its parents. When exhibited in 1891 at a meeting of the American Pomological Society, it won the coveted Wilder Medal, and was sold by its originator, Luther Burbank, to Stark's. It ripens in the first half of October in northern Missouri and grows well on the West Coast except in low desert regions. Zones 5 to 8.

BURBANK JUMBO. This follows 'Van Deman' in ripening, coming in the last half of October. 'Burbank Jumbo' is an attractive little tree and like 'Van Deman' bears fruit young. It is also a Burbank development. Zones 5 to 8.

Quince Troubles

Aside from risk of fire blight, the quince is little troubled with pests and disease. If it gets anything, it will be an apple pest, and a combination spray or dust will take care of it. In case of persistent troubles, follow the spraying program for apples.

'DOUBLE DELIGHT' PEACH TREE. Exquisite in flower, this also bears superb fruit and thrives over a wide area. A fine ornamental, this has many possibilities for the home landscape. (ARMSTRONG PHOTO)

GENETIC DWARF PEACHES. Excellent for growing in planters are these new little peach trees, such as 'Stark Starlet' or 'Bonanza,' developed by Armstrong Nurseries of Ontario, California. These tiny trees carry a load of fruit and the luxuriant foliage gives a graceful effect.

(ARMSTRONG PHOTO)

APRICOTS AND NECTARINES. *Above:* The 'Wilson Delicious' apricots, large, yellow-fleshed, and freestone, grow on a beautiful tree for your yard. *Below:* 'Stark Delicious' nectarines are quick to come into bearing, produce handsome fruits that can weigh a pound each. (STARK PHOTOS)

CHERRIES, SOUR AND SWEET, RED AND YELLOW. *Left:* Montmorency types, the most popular sour cherries, young-bearing and hardy, are good fresh or cooked. *Above right:* The Canadian sweet cherry 'Van' becomes deep red, tastes like the very good 'Bing'. *Below right:* 'Stark Gold', spicy flavored and almost translucent, bears heavily even after winters of 30 below. (STARK PHOTOS)

Berry Fruits *16*

You can harvest an astonishing lot of superb fruit—and in a great hurry—from a little space by planting berries. The smallest garden can grow berries, and they are interesting little fruits, easy to raise. Even the best nursery stock is cheap—and will continuously provide you with new plants every year from the first planting, as well as with heaps and heaps of beautiful, epicurean fruit.

Strawberries

In the sixteenth century a physician named William Butler ate a dish of the little wild strawberry *Fragaria vesca* and uttered a remark that made him famous. Said Dr. Butler, "Doubtless God could have made a better berry, but doubtless God never did." It is one of those benevolent coincidences that the delectable strawberry will grow practically anywhere, in the smallest space, even in a flowerpot, and give fruit the same season it is planted—as fast as a vegetable garden.

Furthermore, the strawberry is an easy little plant to grow, and even the best nursery stock is not expensive, costing from five to twenty cents a plant in home-garden quantities. Each plant will give you about a quart of berries plus a little family of new plants to bear next year's crop. These new plants spring up from joints on stems (runners) that grow out from the mother plant along the ground. Simply dig up the new plants or let them grow where they root. A few varieties produce new plants in a cluster close around the mother plant; with these, dig up the whole group and pull the young plants free.

The best place to plant strawberries is on a gentle slope and in any good garden soil, preferably a little acid. Soggy soil discourages strawberries and so does lime. If you plant them as a border for decorative effect, don't put them with plants that require lime.

Strawberries are low growing, forming mounds a foot or so across and 6 to 8 inches high. The modest white flowers with golden centers are succeeded by berries that increase in size as they change from green to straw-yellow to flashing cardinal-red. The generic name of *Fragaria*, is Latin for fragrant; it refers to the fruit, which is a delight to smell.

When you order plants, you'll find that nurseries usually sell them in lots that are multiples of twenty-five, and that twenty-five plants are the fewest you can buy. This may seem a good many if you have little space. However, you can plant fairly close or even in a strawberry jar. This is an urn with a number of side openings where plants can grow; you can put it on a porch or patio.

Some gardeners grow strawberries on a pile of earth 2 to 3 feet high, covering the small hillsides with plants. A commercial variation of this is a triple stack of disks of soil, each 5 inches deep, each inside an aluminum band, the three stacks forming a kind of pyramid. The lowest disk is 6 feet across, the center one is 4 feet, and the top one about 2 feet. With a little crowding, fifty plants will fit on the shelves of soil and be watered by a sprinkler on a pipe that runs under the stack and comes out at the top. Along with a birdproof net covering, the outfit costs between fifteen and twenty dollars.

You could build something that would do the same job, using corrugated metal edging strips or whatever comes to hand. Everbearing strawberries take well to the pyramid arrangement, as they are compact-growing. Runners must be kept cut off, of course, in such close quarters, but many varieties of everbearers don't form runners. Also, everbearers ripen berries over a long period instead of all at once, and this makes them more attractive for such a planter.

Planting systems

The time to plant a strawberry bed is as early in the year as your soil can be handled. When beds are laid out in rows, the usual way of planting, you have the choice of three systems. We give them in the order of our own preference.

HILL SYSTEM. The simplest version of this is to set plants 18 inches apart in rows 2 feet apart, and to cut off all runners. This will result in large strong plants and will produce the best and biggest berries. Keeping runners cut off takes time but weeding is easier with the hill system. "Hill" here doesn't mean a mound, but refers to the spacing. Calling it the single-plant system would be clearer. (The pyramid planting just described is the Hill System on three levels.)

HEDGEROW SYSTEM. This is simply the Hill System somewhat crowded. Set plants 24 inches apart, in rows 3 to 4 feet apart. Cut off all but two runners per plant; let these two form new plants in the same line as the mother plants and about 8 inches away on each side. Thus you'll end up with one strawberry plant every 8 inches, forming a row that looks like a miniature hedge as plants grow up and touch each other.

MATTED-ROW SYSTEM. Set plants 18 inches apart in rows 4 feet apart. Allow runners to make new plants in all directions as long as plants are at least 6 inches apart. When the rows become 18 to 24 inches wide, chop off any additional runners that form.

Culture

The best place for strawberries is in garden soil that has been growing flowers or vegetables, except tomatoes or potatoes. Don't plant in ground that has been in grass until after it has been dug and cultivated for two years to kill white grubs, or has been treated with dieldrin, chlordane, or aldrin—chemicals that kill grubs at once.

Prepare soil as for a seed bed, and work in 1 bushel of rotted manure for each 20 feet of row, if you can get it, which you probably can't. Alternates are a bushel of compost, or a bushel of moist peatmoss, or 4 pounds of cottonseed meal. With the peatmoss, which will do a good job, add a handful of a balanced fertilizer— a 5-10-5 formula or something of the kind.

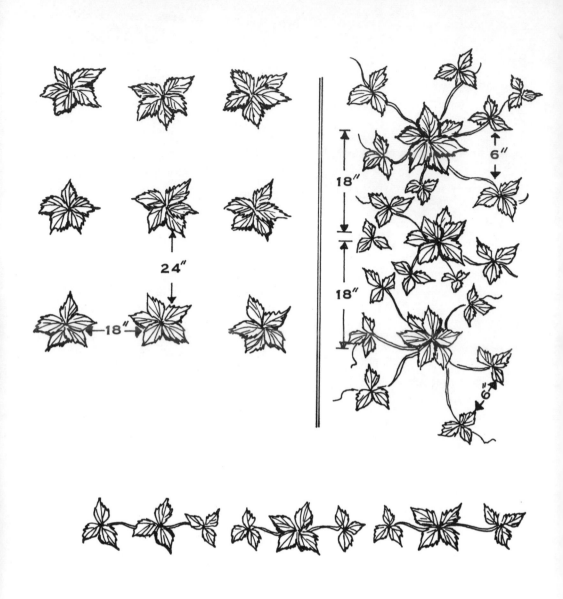

When plants arrive, if you cannot set them out soon, a simple way to keep them happy for as long as a week or two is to put them in the refrigerator, in the package they arrived in if it is a plastic wrapping. If not, put them in a plastic bag to store them in the refrigerator; this will keep them moist.

When you plant, dip roots in water first; carry plants in a box with a damp cloth over it to keep sun and wind from drying them. Once planted, strawberries are hardy and even late frosts or snow won't harm them.

Dig holes 8 inches deep and plant with the base of the crowns just at soil level. The crown is the solid part between roots and top. Press soil down well with your feet after planting. Then snip off all but two or three new leaves of each plant, all old leaves, and any blossom buds. Give each plant a pint of water with soluble fertilizer in it.

Cultivate around plants for the next day or so, to keep soil from crusting. Keep weeds down for two weeks; then spread a mulch all around the plants and between rows. Make the mulch 4 inches deep unless you use sawdust, which should be only an inch or two. To be on the safe side, sprinkle a handful of chemical fertilizer

STRAWBERRY SPACING. Above left: Hill System with no runners, for the best berries. Above right: Matted-Row System, with new plants in all directions. Below: Hedgerow System with two runners and two new plants each.

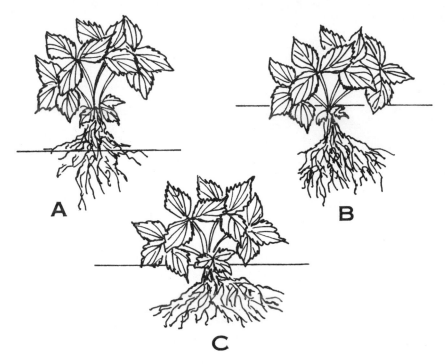

PLANTING DEPTH FOR STRAWBERRIES. A. *Too shallow, crown high, roots showing.* B. *Too deep, crown buried.* C. *Proper depth, crown at ground level.*

per yard of row to hold the nitrogen balance in the soil as the mulch disintegrates. Do this for any organic mulch. We have used red-cedar twigs, cut from growing trees, for mulching, also pine needles, sawdust, redwood chips, grass clippings, leaves, and straw. We use whatever we have; if it is something that tends to mash down into an airtight layer, we add some twigs. There are sheet plastics on the market for mulching, too, and other synthetics are being developed.

Now that the bed is planted and mulched, how soon can you start picking berries? If you have planted a June-bearing (non-everbearing) variety and want to rush things, you can have strawberries in two months. The usual procedure is to grow strong plants this year and gather the crop next, but if you want a fast crop, do this:

Before mulching plants, rake into the soil around them about a teaspoonful of a balanced chemical fertilizer per plant. Make sure they get the equivalent of a two-inch rain each week—a good soaking. If you are using the Matted-Row System, let each plant form no more than six new plants from runners. Finally, *don't remove blossoms.* They will start forming a month or so after planting and will give you fruit a month after that. In August, fertilize for the next year's crop. Apply to each 20 feet of row one-third pound of chemical fertilizer or a generous 5 pounds of cottonseed meal.

The slower, orthodox method gives plants a year to develop for a bigger and better crop. With this, keep down weeds, and water as for a fast crop during the first year. However, you can let plants make as many new plants from runners as a matted row will accommodate, if you are using that system. Most important of all, *pinch off all flower buds as soon as they form during this first year.* Fertilize in August for the next year's crop. Apply to each 20 feet of row one-quarter pound of a balanced chemical fertilizer or 4 pounds of cottonseed meal.

When winter comes, cover plants with a strawy mulch 4 inches deep in areas where temperatures go below zero and snow will not be sufficient to form a natural mulch all winter. Apply the mulch after the ground is frozen; leave it on until you can look under it in spring and see new leaves starting.

Then rake most of it into the space between rows, leaving a little to sift down among plants and help keep berries clean. No fertilizer is needed now or wanted. Fruit will start ripening in June or a little later, depending on variety. Flowers will still be opening when you start to pick the first ripe fruit.

Here's a tip that will give you strawberries more delicious than any you've ever tasted: After picking them fully ripe (all-over red, and slightly soft to the touch), rinse them quickly in cold running water; drain them *stem-side down* on crumpled paper towels. When they are dry, and not until then, hull them (remove stem and cap). Most people hull strawberries first and then wash them, which loses a great deal of flavorful juice to the sink.

Everbearers

An everbearing strawberry is a type that ripens a crop in fall after spring planting, ripens another crop the next spring before the standard (June-bearing) varieties do, and then ripens another fall crop. After that, plants are usually chopped out and discarded, for they become diseased and unproductive if left much longer. Some everbearers go along through the season ripening a few berries continuously, so that from twenty-five plants you may get a little bowlful every day from spring till late fall of the first full season. For most families a combination of everbearers and June-bearers is ideal.

Another feature of everbearers is that most produce few or no runners, so that they are excellent to grow in the Hill System or in the stack type of bed. The year you plant them, culture is the same as for June-bearers except that you give half again as much fertilizer, and remove flower buds only until about the middle of July. You'll then get a crop of berries in fall, and two more the next year.

How long do strawberry plants last?

If you want to take a chance on diseased plants and are willing to get fewer and smaller berries, you can let your strawberry bed go on growing for a second, third, and fourth fruiting year. In general, we advise you not to. However, the 'Ozark Beauty' strawberry will give you three or four years of *good* crops. For other varieties you are better off planting a new bed in a different spot each spring and spading up the old one.

You can dig up rooted runner plants for the new bed. Even better, you can root them in 4-inch flower pots sunk in the soil next to the mother plants. Just lay a runner's rosette of leaves on top of the soil in the pot, and soon the soil will be full of roots. Cut the runner loose then, and you have a new plant ready to grow quickly wherever you plant it. Or you can buy fresh plants from a nursery —a very good idea if your own plants have been troubled with disease.

But if you still want the old bed to stay where it is for another year or so, and the plants are healthy, do this: Remove all mulch and burn or compost it. Narrow the rows by chopping out the poorest plants. As soon as you've gathered the crop, cut down the remaining plants with a lawn mower set high, but don't cut off the crowns. Spread a half-inch of good garden soil over the mowed plants. Then cultivate between rows and fertilize as if you were planting a new bed. From there on, manage the planting the same as when you originally put it in.

Pollination

Although some varieties of strawberries need other varieties nearby to pollinate them, this is not the problem it used to be for the home gardener. Nearly all the newer varieties will set fruit alone.

Leading Strawberry Varieties

There are dozens of good varieties offered by the big nurseries, plus many more popular in certain sections. Stark's carry three June-bearing and one everbearing strawberry. We list these below, plus two other varieties that deserve mention. You will find new strawberries appearing on the market every year.

STARK RED GIANT. This is a variety introduced in 1967; the Nursery considers it the best strawberry they have ever handled. It is big, firm, and juicy, with burgundy-red flesh, well flavored. It originated in Minnesota and the large-leaved plants are sturdy and healthy. Crops are plentiful, good for eating fresh, for preserving, canning, and freezing. Zones 4 to 8.

SURECROP. A high-yielding and vigorous strawberry, this is as adaptable to various climates as is 'Red Giant'. 'Surecrop' is a United States Department of Agriculture development, and produced well over a quart per plant in tests by the University of West Virginia Agriculture Extension Service. The glossy red, firm fruit is widely sold commercially, but when ripened on the plant, it is a very good home-garden strawberry, too. It does well on land too dry or poor for some other strawberries, and is, in fact, such a vigorous grower that you must keep a sharp eye on any over-production of runners. The variety is particularly well flavored, rich and sweet, and excellent for freezing as well as all other uses. Zones 4 to 8.

DUNLAP. Properly called 'Senator Dunlap', this is quite an old variety for strawberries, originating in Illinois before 1890. It is sometimes called a domestic strawberry with wild-strawberry flavor.

It has been popular with commercial growers for years, being a dependable cropper and quite winter-hardy. Berries must be handled gently to avoid bruising, and are well worth such care. 'Dunlap' is good fresh and for preserves. Zones 4 to 8.

OZARK BEAUTY. Probably the best and heaviest cropping everbearer, this yields up to two quarts per plant under good care. The large berries are well flavored, and there is a minimum of undersized fruit produced over the long season. Stark's found plants still loaded with fruit late in October in Missouri when a first frost was overdue. Plants are quite winter-hardy. Though an everbearer, 'Ozark Beauty' produces runners, is easy to grow, and all-purpose as to fruit. Zones 4 to 8.

GENEVA. Another good everbearer, this was introduced by the New York State Experiment Station in 1962 after eight years of testing, the first everbearing strawberry the Station has put on the market. It is considered an excellent home-garden berry for taste and looks. The principal drawback of the large, soft, and highly flavored berries is a susceptibility to fruit-rot in poor weather. Plants are large, vigorous, and productive. Berries begin ripening in June and continue until frost. Zones 4 to 8.

FLORIDA 90. This is one of the very few strawberries Florida gardeners can grow for it needs little cold weather to break its dormancy. The variety bears large red berries of good flavor, which are a commercial crop in Florida. Zones 9 and warmer parts of Zone 8.

Strawberry Troubles

If you treat strawberries as a one-season crop (two seasons in the case of everbearers, counting their fall crop the year you set them out), and do not plant in the same spot twice in succession, or crowd them, they will probably have no insect or disease problems worth bothering about. For cutworms, spread poison bait; hand-pick caterpillars. Use a combination spray or dust if leaves are badly chewed or discolored, but stop when berries start ripening. Weed out and burn any seriously diseased plants. Today's newer varieties of strawberries are healthier than most old ones, and resist a good many diseases that once made strawberry growing difficult or even impossible.

Raspberries

At the supermarket, we saw some red raspberries, locally grown, that had arrived in fair condition for so delicate a fruit. The price for a skimpy cupful was fifty-nine cents. We thought of the 'Indian Summer' red rasperberries grown on our farm that lavished us with such heaps of fruit we couldn't keep up with them fresh, even with giving basketfuls away, and we froze the surplus. We aren't blaming the supermarket, but if you want prime red raspberries, you have to pick them off the bushes. Black raspberries and purple ones are not so fragile, but there too you can raise better ones than you can buy, even if you can find them on the market at all.

A few raspberry bushes planted in a corner of your garden in spring will begin giving you fruit the very next year, or that same year in the case of everbearers. And you can count on getting heavier crops each year after that for five to ten years. Raspberry bushes make attractive summer hedges, too, and the thorns serve to keep out of your yard or garden some of the four-footed visitors you'll be glad to do without. Bushes will supply you with their own replacements so that you can have new plantings coming along as you remove old ones—which you do to keep up the quality of the fruit. Old plantings give smaller berries.

Culture

Any garden soil will suit raspberries so long as it isn't soggy, but avoid ground that has just grown tomatoes, potatoes, peppers, or eggplant to keep from giving the raspberries verticillium wilt. Turn the soil beforehand, digging at least a foot deep and working in some humus, such as compost or peatmoss. Ideally, plant red raspberries in sandy loam, blacks and purples in heavier soil, but we have grown both reds and purples in heavy clay soil and they got along fine.

Commercial fertilizer isn't essential, but a sprinkle of it is called for if you use peatmoss to lighten the soil, and plants respond to a mulch of strawy manure a few inches thick. We had plenty of this on the farm but we don't have it now. We recommend compost as a good substitute, plus a straw mulch, which you can pile 6 inches deep. Peatmoss or grass clippings also make good mulches. Add a handful or two of a balanced chemical fertilizer for each bushel of these, and for each three or four bushels of straw. In the South, the secret of growing red raspberries is to mulch them well. Mulch keeps soil cool.

As to site, raspberries will get along in partial shade. Though they prefer protection from strong winds, they didn't get it on our farm but they prospered just the same. You can grow raspberries in rows like hedges or as separate plants in the so-called Hill System. For rows, plant the reds 2 feet apart and space rows 6 feet apart. Plant blacks and purples 3 feet apart and space rows 7 to 8 feet. For hill planting, space individual plantings of reds 5 feet apart each way, blacks and purples 6 feet.

Spring is the best time to plant. Set red raspberries deep enough to cover all roots, and firm the soil around them with your feet. Since new shoots will come from the roots, prune severely at planting time—leaving just 2 inches of *red* raspberry stem sticking out of the ground.

Plant *black* and *purple* raspberries a bit shallower, with the crown (the place where stem and roots join) just at the ground surface. Then make a little mound of soil to cover the crown and the lower 2 inches of stem. Cut off the rest of the stem. As the season goes along, this mound will level off with the help of a little cultivating from you.

If you mulch, you won't need to cultivate much, but do keep weeds down. When you cultivate, don't go deep. Raspberry roots are near the surface. When they are bruised or cut, they make so many suckers, you'll be kept busy chopping them out.

To make new red raspberry plants, you need only dig up some of those suckers and plant them. They will come right through that 6-inch straw mulch we recommended, even though most weeds won't. You can also get new plants by planting pieces of root as long as your finger.

To make new *black* or *purple* raspberry plants, toward the end of summer, throw a spadeful of soil on the tips of any canes that

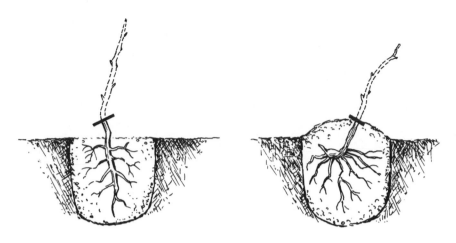

PLANTING DEPTH FOR RASPBERRIES. *Left: When planting red raspberries, prune back stems to 2 inches. Right: When planting black and purple raspberries, prune back stems to 2 inches; then cover with a soil mound. Level mound later in season.*

are arching down and touching the ground. By the next spring, they will all have rooted, and you can simply cut them free from the mother plants, dig them up, and plant them where you wish.

One caution: If you are having a disease problem with raspberries, you'll be wise to start fresh with new plants from a nursery rather than to grow your own. This is also a good chance to try another variety. You may find one better adapted to your place or one that has more resistance to disease.

Pollination
Raspberries need no cross-pollination in order to set fruit.

Pruning
Pruning raspberries is simple (except for the thorns, though an exception is the variety 'Canby'). Canes grow for one year, bear fruit the next, and then they're through, so after a cane has fruited, cut it off at the base. The only other pruning needed is to encourage good growth. Do it this way:

REDS. In spring, cut back canes to 4 to 5 feet. Remove weak ones entirely, leaving three or four canes per foot of row, or about eight per hill for the Hill System.

BLACKS AND PURPLES.   In spring, while plants are still dormant, cut back *lateral branches* of last year's canes to about 10 inches. Fruit will be borne on these branches this year. Then, in early summer, pinch off tip buds of new shoots coming up from the ground when the shoots are 3 to 4 feet high. This is to make them grow strong lateral branches that will bear fruit next year. As with the reds, remove weak canes, leaving about the same number of strong ones.

EVERBEARERS.   Everbearing varieties are available in reds, blacks, and purples. "Everbearing" in raspberries means that, instead of ripening their entire crop during a few weeks in midsummer, they bear a small crop then and a bigger one in late summer or fall. You have a choice in pruning these. You can prune them exactly as you prune other reds, blacks, or purples. But, if you want a bigger fall crop and are willing to sacrifice the earlier one, cut off *all*

PRUNING BRAMBLES. *Above: Typical bush of black or purple raspberries before and after pruning. Center: Red raspberry planting before and after pruning. Below: Blackberry planting before and after pruning.*

canes to 2 to 3 inches from the ground when plants go dormant late in fall. This second method is gratifyingly simple, and it has another advantage—it cleans out fungi that could make trouble next season.

Supports

You don't have to use supports for raspberries but supports make a neater planting and one easier to harvest. The simplest support is one stake to which each clump is tied. A better way is to stretch two parallel wires between posts, at heights of 3 feet and 5 feet, and tie canes to the wires.

Another method is to string two wires at the same level, from crossarms on top of posts. Make the crossarms 3 or 4 feet from ground-level, and space the wires about 30 inches apart. Let the canes grow up between. You needn't tie the canes; they'll lean on the wires. We used this method and liked it.

THREE TYPES OF SUPPORT FOR RASPBERRY PLANTS. *Left: Two wires, at 3 and 5 feet above ground level. Center: Single post support. Right: Two wires, both 3 or 4 feet above ground level and 30 inches apart.*

Harvesting

Be gentle with raspberries when you harvest them. Hold your hand palm-up and cupped, and pick berries with thumb and forefinger, letting them drop into your palm until you have four or five. Then let them roll off into a shallow bowl or basket—and don't heap it or you'll get bruised berries. For best quality, shade the berries in your basket from the sun.

Needless to say, raspberries are not for keeping, no more than is uncorked champagne. We pick them early in the morning before the sun is on them, then wash them gently under cold water, and spread them on crumpled paper towels to dry. We sprinkle a little sugar over those we freeze. Raspberry preserves are absolutely wonderful, and our purple raspberries bore so prodigiously we even made purple raspberry jelly. Years ago homemade raspberry wine was popular and was considered the most delicious and fragrant of any home wine. As a rule, you can expect about a pint of raspberries for each foot of row, but we've gathered two and three times this much in good seasons.

Leading Raspberry Varieties

New varieties appear a little faster than those in tree fruits because breeders don't have to wait so long for results. For the home gardener, this is fine. Berry plants cost much less than trees, they start bearing in a hurry, and you can sample a lot of varieties during just a few seasons. The ones we list here have been on the market for enough years to have proved themselves first rate. We omit everbearers in blacks and purples because we think none has yet been as thoroughly tested as the red everbearers.

NEWBURGH. This good red raspberry, introduced in 1929, makes a more compact plant than most others, and should be supported to keep canes from bending to the ground when weighted with fruit. Early spring pruning is especially important to keep this from bearing so many berries that they won't ripen properly. Well grown, the fruit is quite large, firm, and good. 'Newburgh' is outstanding in its resistance to mosaic, a virus disease. An origination of the New York State Experiment Station, 'Newburgh' ripens in early summer. Zones 4 to 8 and cool-summer areas of the West Coast.

CANBY.   Originated by the United States Department of Agriculture, this red raspberry came from Corvallis, Oregon, a few years ago. The extra-large, conic berries are very good and are easily picked when ripe. This is hardy, vigorous, and highly productive, with good disease resistance. It also has another very big plus—it is practically *thornless*, especially in the upper part, where you pick the berries. The strong, tall canes should be given some support. 'Canby' is an early midseason variety, following 'Newburgh' in ripening. Zones 5 to 8.

LATHAM.   This is a late red raspberry, following 'Canby', with a good name for producing heavy crops and doing well in only fair soil. We raised it and liked it, though it did not bear as heavily for us as it does in some locations. 'Latham' also has a reputation for good health and for berries free of seediness—large, bright red, and delicious. Hardy in cold climates and dependable in warm ones. Zones 4 to 8.

SEPTEMBER.   Developed by the New York State Experiment Station, this is now offered by most nurseries and is considered generally the best of the red everbearers. It also does better in the South than other everbearers. Plants are vigorous, productive, and hardy. Berries are of medium size, unusually firm, and the quality is good. 'September' ripens a first crop early, in June. The fall crop, borne on tips of the current season's canes, starts ripening in August. Fall berries are better flavored than early ones. Zones 4 to 7.

BLACK HAWK.   If dry, hot weather is your problem, consider this for a black raspberry. In addition to vigor under such conditions, it is also a heavy producer of big glossy berries full of juice and sweetness. 'Black Hawk' was produced at Iowa State University. Zones 5 to 8.

STARKING BLACK GIANT.   This patented variety is owned by Stark's, who consider it the most productive black raspberry the Nursery has ever tested. The uniformly large berries have a purplish tint and are juicy and good. Like 'Black Hawk', 'Starking Black Giant' can live and bear through drouth. Zones 5 to 8.

SODUS.   This husky purple raspberry from the New York Experiment Station was introduced in 1935 and continues to be very popular. Like all purple raspberries, it is a hybrid offspring of a black and a red—'Newburgh' and 'Dundee'. 'Sodus' berries are big and firm, with a sprightly taste, and the bush is an amazingly generous bearer. Plants are healthy and resistant to drouth. Zones 5 to 7.

In 1961, the New York station released another purple raspberry for testing, 'Clyde', which it considers most promising. It is both a market and a home-garden berry.

Raspberry Troubles

A dormant spraying or dusting in early spring with a combination product will help prevent some raspberry diseases, but in home gardens the best course is to remove promptly and burn any cane showing signs of trouble, or remove the whole plant. Always cut diseased canes low, leaving no stumps. The long-term remedy is sanitation. Keep down weeds, don't crowd plants, and know your fruit garden so well that you notice signs of trouble before it gets bad. In spraying or dusting, be careful not to get chemicals on berries that are so nearly ripe they show color.

Blackberries

Blackberries grew wild in most places where we've lived, as do their creeping cousins, the dewberries. Blackberries are delicious, wild or cultivated, when allowed to ripen to perfection on the plant—and if rains come at the right times. A Missouri neighbor who was deathly afraid of snakes braved them every summer just to pick wild blackberries. Her berry outfit included her husband's gum boots, and her son's baseball bat to brain the snakes with.

Blackberries respond to the same conditions as black raspberries, and take almost identical care. Space and plant blackberries the same way. Prune them the same, removing canes that have fruited, pinching back new shoots in June—at 3 feet for blackberries—to encourage growth of laterals. Prune back these laterals early the next spring to 15 inches. Wild blackberries need no support, and neither do garden-grown ones. New plants can be had by digging suckers. If they occur where you want new plants, let them go on growing there.

Blackberries are such tremendous bearers that the fruit gets dumped into buckets when picked, and so loses quality from bruising. Handle berries gently and they will repay the favor. Pick only the berries that are full black and that part easily from the canes. When picking for jelly, include a few half-ripe berries to get a shimmery mold when you turn it out of the glass. A foot of row gives about a quart of berries.

Leading Blackberry Varieties

Only a few varieties are offered by nurseries. 'El Dorado' is an old one that is still popular; 'Darrow' and 'Bailey' are fairly recent introductions by the New York Experiment Station. Stark's handle two other new ones, 'Midnite' and 'Raven'.

MIDNITE. This is favored for dependable fruiting, unusually healthy growth, and small-cored berries of large size and high quality. It is for Zones 5 to 8, but there are varieties of blackberries for every zone in the country.

RAVEN. Here is a new variety from the Maryland Agricultural Experiment Station. Also tested at the Arkansas Station, it is considered an excellent variety, vigorous and winter-hardy, healthy, and an upright grower. It is a heavy yielder of attractive fruits that are free of any astringent after-taste. Berries are ripe three or four days after turning black. 'Raven' freezes and cans well, and is of dessert quality when fresh. Zones 5 to 8.

Blackberry Troubles

Blackberries are usually healthy, with few troubles if you don't
crowd the planting and if you run a clean garden. As with raspberries, it is important to remove and burn promptly any affected
canes. A combination spray or dust will take care of most leaf troubles and will get rid of mites that occasionally prevent ripening.
Don't spray or dust after berries start to ripen.

Both wild and domestic blackberries occasionally suffer from a
sterility problem that results in small, poor fruits, and from a rust
that appears as orange spots on leaves and canes. In both cases,
get rid of the plants. Dig them up and burn them as soon as you
notice the trouble.

Blueberries

Blueberries require two things: an acid soil and a bird-fooler.
Both are easy, and the reward is luscious dining and a plant of four-
season beauty—for a blueberry bush is one of the most attractive
shrubs you can put in your yard. It is a shimmer of little white
bells of blossoms in spring, the prettiest glossy green in summer,
presently a picture of plump blueberries, and in autumn foliage
in sunset shades of red. Finally as leaves flutter to the earth, the bare
graceful lines of olive, rich green, or reddish branches are revealed
on this lovely plant.

The best guide to culture is the method worked out by Research
Professor of Horticulture, Stanley Johnston, at Michigan State
University in South Haven. Here we follow the University's Cir-
cular Bulletin 188.

Culture

If your garden soil is acid, you can grow blueberries without doc-
toring it. An acidity of pH 4.4 is ideal. The acceptable range is
pH 4.0 to 5.1.

But in non-acid soils you can still raise good blueberries by
planting in halves of fifty-gallon metal drums sunk in the ground

and filled with a mixture of two parts acid peat and one part garden soil. A metal shop can cut the drums in half. Also have four two-inch holes drilled in the bottom of each half for drainage. Burn out any residue of what the drum held.

Choose a sunny open site, well drained, and plant the bushes an inch or two deeper than they grew in the nursery. Two weeks later give each plant two tablespoons of a balanced acid fertilizer. You can repeat this in early summer. Each year thereafter follow this feeding schedule, gradually increasing the amount to a quarter pound of fertilizer per plant per season. Water enough to keep soil moist. Keep plants mulched with straw, old sawdust, old oak leaves, or peatmoss. Blueberry plants in drums grow 4 to 5 feet high and fruit freely. As harvest time approaches, throw a net over them to keep off the birds.

You can get new plants by rooting cuttings of shoots grown the previous season. Cut them in early spring, choosing shoots bearing leaf buds, which·are smaller than fruit buds. Make cuttings about 4 inches long, slant each end with your knife, plant at an angle in moist peatmoss, leaving only the top third of the cutting above ground. Keep the peatmoss moist enough so that you can squeeze water from it in your hand. If cuttings root, they will do so in about three months.

Pollination
Cultivated blueberries should be planted in groups of at least two varieties for a good crop. Almost any combination of varieties works out well.

Pruning
At planting time, cut off about half the length of the upper branches. Like the peach, the blueberry bears fruit on wood made the previous season. No further pruning is needed until after the third growing season. From then on, at each dormant pruning (which can be as soon as leaves fall, or any time during winter and spring), thin out top growth by removing slender twigs entirely, also low branches, and weak and dead wood. Most important, remove branches when they become grayish black with age and produce few fruit buds. Cut them off at the base.

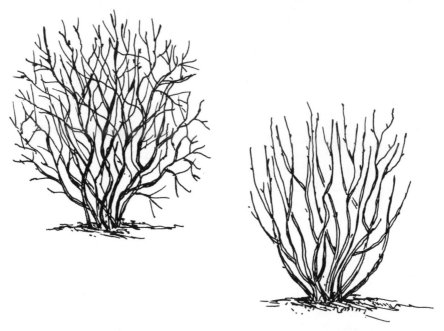

PRUNING BLUEBERRIES. Bush, before and after pruning.

Heavy pruning will give you larger berries but a smaller crop and an earlier maturing one. A full-grown blueberry bush in open ground can grow to 6 feet or more and about as wide.

Harvesting

You can spread the harvest by a wise choice of varieties. We list four that extend the season for about a month. In the East the first blueberries ripen early in June; in the Midwest, from two weeks to a month later.

Blueberries ripen on a single bush over a period of a few weeks. They need about half a dozen pickings, and they cling to the bush well. You can expect to gather eight to ten quarts per plant after bushes are eight years old. They live on for many years after.

Leading Blueberry Varieties

EARLIBLUE.   One of the first to ripen, this United States Department of Agriculture introduction bears large berries resistant to cracking—firm, mild, and sweet. They are borne in tight clusters.

The vigorous and hardy plants have fine upright growth. Zones 4 to 8 in the East and Midwest, and in blueberry areas along the West Coast.

BERKELEY. This bears large berries in big loose clusters, flavoring up nearly as quickly as they turn blue. Plants are vigorous, spreading, and productive. 'Berkeley' is a good home-garden blueberry, ripening in midseason, about two weeks after 'Earliblue'. It is for the same areas, with the exception of the coldest parts.

RUBEL. A selection from a wild blueberry, this retains the esteemed wild flavor and is liked for home plantings. The season is late, following 'Berkeley'. Medium-sized berries are borne on vigorous winter-hardy plants. For the same areas as 'Earliblue'.

COVILLE. This very late variety ripens a full month after 'Earliblue'. The sturdy bushes produce big crops of large berries. For best flavor, pick them about a week after they turn blue. For the same areas as 'Earliblue'.

Blueberry Troubles

Aside from birds, blueberries in the home garden have few troubles. If plants become diseased, they should be dug up and burned. The schedule for cherries can be followed if spraying or dusting is needed, but the most likely trouble is yellowing of leaves. Fertilizing with ammonium sulphate will cure it; allow a quarter pound per bush. Iron chelate is also good, dissolved at the rate of one tablespoonful per gallon of water; apply to leaves and soil.

Grapes 17

Like Professor Henry Higgins of *My Fair Lady*, the grape is a most forgiving thing. Sometimes it seems almost to thrive on neglect. If you find an ancient vine growing in blowsy abandon all over a broken-down arbor of the old house you buy, as we have more than once, it will welcome you and treat you as an equal and, unless violently overpruned, will load you with deliciousness in due season. The date, the fig, and the grape—this triumvirate are the ancient fruits, the friends of man when man was learning to grow his own food. Of them, the grape is the hardy one, living willingly through winter's cold. The grape recommends itself to you even in limited space, for it will cling to a fence, taking no room to speak of, a healthful, luscious, cheerful companion in the garden.

Culture

Grapes grow just about anywhere and on almost any soil. If given a choice, they like a slope of well-drained loam that isn't very rich. In fact, in soil as rich as bottom land, what you'd get would be rank growth of vine but not well-flavored grapes. You'd be better off even planting on a steep and rocky hillside, a place most other fruits would spurn. Also, the slope is apt to give better drainage, and this is important.

Grapes in a home planting will do a little better if you can cultivate them. If grown on the lawn, mulch your vines and feed them with a fertilizer high in nitrogen, such as ammonium nitrate, especially while they are young. Feed them in the spring. A vine you planted last spring could use three or four ounces of nitrogen this spring—call it a good half-pound of ammonium nitrate, which is 33 percent nitrogen by weight. Next spring give a pound of ammonium nitrate; after that, change to a balanced fertilizer each spring at the rate of about two pounds for each vine.

A very dry spell can hurt the crop since grape roots are not so extensive as tree roots. Water vines if leaves droop. Keep a mulch extending two to three feet all round the trunk.

Pollination

Most grapes are self-fruitful and so need no cross-pollination. Three that are not are 'Brighton', 'Lindley', and 'Herbert'—varieties you aren't likely to be dealing with.

Pruning American grape vines

When one of the writers was young, the family had a grape vine— a 'Concord', naturally—on an arbor alongside the garage, and early each spring a cousin who had a farm would come by to prune it. None of the family would have dreamed of tackling this riddle, and nobody knew exactly what the cousin had done after he'd done it. He never said, either, and this air of mystery about grape pruning is pretty common, now as then.

It needn't be. What grape pruning amounts to is this: You save some of last year's wood to grow this year's grapes.

There are elaborations and refinements of this basic rule, and some people will say we're over-simplifying. Just the same, if you don't ever learn anything more about grape pruning than this, you can now prune a vine better than ninety-nine out of one hundred persons can. To identify the last year's wood that you save, look for clean, trim canes about the size of a pencil, with buds spaced a few inches apart. The buds rise from nodes—the places that look like joints.

You'll need four of these canes if you are growing grapes on two parallel wires stretched between posts, which is the best way. (The southern grapes or muscadines require a little different handling; we'll take them up separately.) This two-wire, or four-arm Kniffin System, as it's called, gives you a vine which, when pruned, looks like two letter T's, one standing on top of the other.

The top wire should be about five feet above the ground, and of substantial No. 9 hard-galvanized stuff. Stretch it tight between two posts set ten feet apart. Stretch another wire halfway between the first one and the ground. Use a turnbuckle on each one to take up slack in summer and to ease the wire when it contracts in cold weather.

If you'd rather grow your grapes on a trellis, a fence, an arbor, or whatever, it will work. Almost anything will work. But the four-arm Kniffin System is the easiest to manage and you'll get more grapes. If you are growing several vines, *use the same ten-foot spacing between posts for each one.*

Now, here is how you prune a grape vine. You prune it once a year, early in spring, say the first week of February in Missouri, which is more like late winter but we'll call it spring for convenience. Do your pruning in these three easy steps, for American grapes, *Vitis labrusca*. (We'll take up the pruning of the other two species, European and muscadine, later.)

1. First decide which of the new canes that grew last season you want to keep as fruiting canes for this year. You'll need four, you remember, pencil-sized and spaced along the trunk so that they can be trained out easily along the wires to form the four arms, two on each side. Now tie strips of old nylon stockings to these four canes as reminders, for the moment, not to cut them.

2. Near the base of each of the four canes you are saving, select two or three other strong canes; cut them back to stubs bearing a couple of buds each. *These are your renewal spurs.* They will grow new canes this year, to give you a good selection of fruit-bearing canes for next year.

3. All you need to do now is to cut away, fairly close to the trunk, all the other canes except the four to which you tied the nylon stockings. Fasten the four saved canes to the wires with the stockings. As you do so, shorten each of these four canes to about a dozen buds, cutting each cane at a point about an inch beyond the last bud. The four buds nearest the trunk aren't apt to produce fruit, but the others will send out short shoots that will bear from one to three bunches of grapes each, plus leaves and tendrils.

Opposite. SEMI-ARBOR AGAINST A GARAGE WALL. Slanting side arms of 2 x 4's, with diagonal braces, support three strong wires. A vine is trained up each end with three fruiting canes led out to meet in the middle. Good hot-climate support since grapes are shaded by a canopy of leaves.

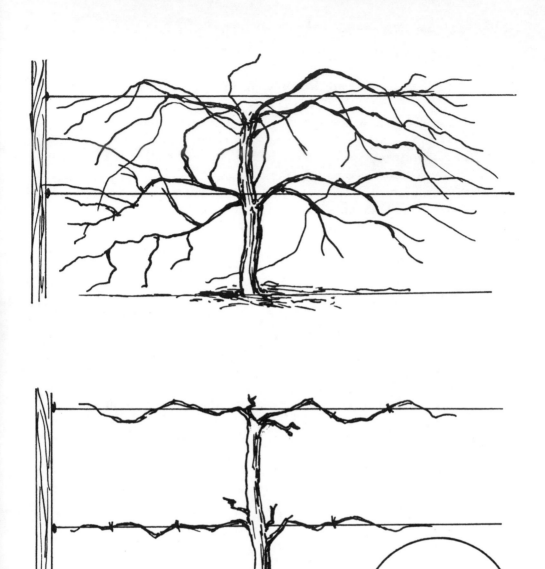

GRAPE PRUNING. A mature grape vine, before and after pruning, using the Four-Arm Kniffin System of training.

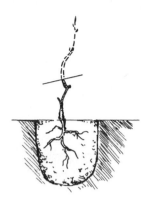

PLANTING A YOUNG GRAPE VINE. *Above: After covering the roots well, and firming the earth, cut the vine back to two buds.* TRAINING A YOUNG GRAPE VINE. *Below: Tie a string to the top supporting wire, to lead the strongest cane upward so that it becomes the trunk.*

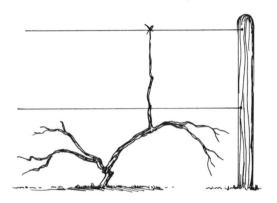

Each cane can use another tie or two at this time, and we suggested nylon stockings because they are usually available and they do a good job.

Don't be alarmed at the amount of wood you'll have pruned away, or at the skinny look your grape vine will now have. All that this severe pruning does is to make it, as the French say, furiously to grow.

Care of young grape vines

The grape vine you get from a nursery this spring will start giving you fruit next year if you want it to. Most home gardeners do want it to, though commercial growers prefer to let their vines put all strength into developing a strong trunk through both the first and second years. But here's how to get grapes fast.

FIRST SPRING: After planting the young vine deep enough to cover all the roots, firm the soil and pour a bucketful of water, with soluble fertilizer added, into the hole. Then finish filling it with earth. Prune the vine back to two buds. Set posts and wires. The vine should be planted halfway between the two posts. Spread a mulch four to six inches deep and extending two feet out from the vine.

When new canes have grown out from the buds and are about two feet long, choose the strongest one and fasten loosely to it a string, which you then tie to the top wire so as to lead the cane straight up. This cane is to be the trunk of your grape vine. The string will encourage it to grow vigorously upward; as it does so, it will sprout lateral canes to form the four arms.

SECOND SPRING: Tie the trunk to both wires. Tie two canes to the bottom wire, one on each side, and two more to the top wire, to form the arms. Prune back all four canes to five or six buds for this season. Prune back the top of the trunk to just above the level of the top wire.

Now form renewal spurs to grow next year's fruiting canes, near the base of each of the four arm canes, by cutting one or two other canes back to two buds, just as you do with a mature vine. Prune off any other canes.

When growth begins, fertilize with half a pound of ammonium nitrate. Add fresh mulch and extend it to cover an area three feet around the trunk.

Through the growing season, pinch off any new shoots on the lower trunk. This will send all the strength where you want growth and fruit.

Third spring: Prune as for a mature vine.

Pruning a neglected grape vine

A neglected grape vine, especially an old one, can look absolutely hopeless. The mind boggles, you might say, at what to do about it. If you want to be drastic, save a one-year-old cane growing from the ground level, or near it, and cut everything else away. Then proceed to train the cane into a new trunk. Let lateral canes grow out from it on each side. Tie these to parallel wires in the Kniffin System. (This is also a good way to put new life into a vine that has been giving less and less fruit each year.)

But if you don't feel this drastic, prune away everything except four to six one-year-old canes, plus some renewal spurs. Choose pencil-sized canes, as in other grape pruning for fruit, and shorten them to half a dozen buds each. Incidentally, never save thick new canes in *any* grape pruning you do. They are called bull vines, and they run to leaf, not fruit.

If your neglected old grape has a *sound* trellis, you may as well use it. Old grape vines usually grapple a trellis like an octopus anyway.

Pruning European grape vines

European grapes, *Vitis vinifera,* have generally a more compact growth habit than our American grapes. Most European varieties will produce fruit from buds near the base of canes, instead of only leaves, and their total crop is heavy. Outdoor culture of European grapes is confined to parts of California and Arizona, some protected valleys of New Mexico and west Texas, and some milder sections of Washington and Oregon. But there are hybrids of European and American grapes that can take rougher weather and that require the same sort of pruning.

Of the various types of pruning for European and for European-American hybrid grape vines, the one most likely to be useful to you is called cane-pruning. It is nothing more than the four-arm Kniffin System all over again but in a slightly more compact form to suit the less rampant growth of European grapes.

Follow the directions for American grape pruning, but set the bottom wire three feet from the ground, the top wire one foot higher.

Allow a healthy, mature vine to keep eight to twelve buds on each of the four arms you select as fruiting canes each year. Since European grapes are heavy producers, thinning is a good idea. Pinch out some flower clusters on varieties bearing non-compact bunches. On those with compact bunches, such as 'Thompson Seedless', pinch off some bunches while they are still quite small. Thin at least enough to make sure that no bunch of grapes will be touching another when the bunches are full grown.

Varieties that do well when cane-pruned include 'Himrod Seedless', 'Interlaken Seedless', 'Thompson Seedless', 'Steuben', 'Buffalo', and 'Golden Muscat'.

Pruning muscadine grape vines

These grapes, *Vitis rotundifolia,* are native to America. They are the grapes of the South, thriving through most of Zone 9 along the

South Atlantic and the Gulf states. The best-known varieties are the 'Scuppernong', which bears white-to-bronze fruits, and the 'James', bearing black grapes.

Though some varieties have fair-sized bunches of up to twenty-five grapes, most muscadines average only about five grapes to the bunch. However, the vines are so vigorous that old ones may produce dozens of bushels of high-quality fruit in a season.

Two types of training are usually recommended—a three-wire horizontal trellis and an overhead arbor. In both cases the grapes hang free of the vine. Since most varieties drop individual grapes as they ripen (berry grapes is another name for muscadines), this form of training is convenient for gathering the fallen fruit. We once owned a place on the Mississippi Gulf Coast that had an old muscadine planting. This had been allowed to grow into a bulky hedgerow fifty feet long and ten wide. It was so hopelessly snarled that we let the birds harvest the grapes, which usually fell into the tangle anyway. In this case, it was better to plant new vines and train them right than to battle the old planting.

FOR THE OVERHEAD ARBOR SYSTEM, set up a framework of posts that support a series of horizontal stringers. The posts should be 4 x 4's or thicker, and the stringers either 2 x 4's or 2 x 6's, set high enough for easy walking underneath. Plant the vine at the foot of a post and let the strongest cane that develops during the first season become the trunk. Lead it up the post; prune off other canes until the trunk reaches the top of the arbor. Then pinch off the growing tip to make it form shoots that can be trained to arms radiating across the arbor top.

These arms are a *permanent* part of the vine, just like the trunk. Muscadines are apt to bleed a good deal if you wait until spring to prune, so do it in November or December. Starting with November or December of the second season, prune back canes of that season's growth on the arms to six to eight inches, each bearing about two buds. These are the fruiting spurs. Space them about a foot apart on the arms. Prune away the other canes. Repeat this pruning each year.

IN HORIZONTAL TRELLIS TRAINING, select the strongest cane of the first season's growth to become the trunk. Train it up a six-foot

'BURBANK GRAND PRIZE' PRUNES. Fine freestone fruits for home gardens. A prune is a plum; when fresh, it looks and tastes like a plum; because prunes are very sweet, they can be dried well. (STARK PHOTO)

RASPBERRIES, BLUEBERRIES, AND STRAWBERRIES. *Above left*: 'Newburgh' raspberries are delicious fruits for the home garden, and you can harvest a quart or more from each bush every year. (MORSE PHOTO.) *Above right*: Beauty of bush and delights of fruit are yours when you grow blueberries like these. (GROFFMAN PHOTO.) *Below*: Each plant of 'Ozark Beauty' strawberries, possibly the best everbearer on the market, yields up to two quarts of berries from late spring until frost. (STARK PHOTO)

BOUNTY OF GRAPES. *Above:* 'Golden Muscat' sometimes bears five-pound bunches. *Below:* 'Buffalo' is an early bearer, exceptionally vigor-ous even in hot, dry weather. Clusters hang on the vine in good condition longer than most other grapes. (STARK PHOTOS)

PLUMS AND NUTS. *Above:* The old European 'Reine Claude' is the Green Gage, a freestone dessert plum as well as good for cooking. The neat trees suit the home landscape. (STARK PHOTO.) *Below:* A nut tree on your lawn will give shade in summer and in autumn a bountiful delicious harvest like this. (GROFFMAN PHOTO)

post, pinching it off at the tip when it reaches the top. Three wires are usually used for the trellis, spaced about two feet apart and fastened to posts about twelve feet apart. Train the best six canes to form arms five to six feet long on each side of the trunk along the wires. As with the arbor training of muscadines, these arms are *permanent* parts of the structure. They should be spur-pruned each November or December on the mature vine, in the same way as with the arms of the arbor-trained muscadine.

Southern gardeners may do well to try some of the muscadine hybrids, a new development in grapes. 'Lake Emerald' is a good one, highly resistant to disease, the emerald-green fruit borne in large bunches. Another, particularly adapted to Florida conditions, is 'Tamiami', which has yielded thirty or more pounds of grapes per vine in bunches that weigh half a pound or more. It is a dark purple grape.

Harvesting

The yield of a grape vine depends on the variety and on the growing conditions. For the bunch grapes, about fifty bunches a season is average for a healthy vine. For muscadines there is no average that we know of, since the older they are, the more the vines seem capable of producing, and a hundred-year-old muscadine may ripen several thousand pounds of grapes in a good season.

As grapes ripen they change color, the green ones becoming yellow or whitish and more translucent than opaque. Red and black grapes turn those colors, and the central stem of all grapes becomes dark and woody. The taste test is best of all—the ripe grape is sweet. Clip ripe bunches with hand-pruners and remove any poor berries. The ideal day for gathering is a dry one. Handle bunches gently, particularly if you are going to store them. Don't pile them high.

Red grapes are usually the best keepers, 'Delaware' having been held more than ten months, for instance, in cold storage (from 35 to 40 degrees above zero). Before refrigeration was possible, gardeners used to store their surplus grapes this way: They laid the bunches on shelves for two or three days, two bunches deep. The grapes were then taken out and aired for a few hours. Then each bunch was wrapped in soft paper, packed in a shallow box and stored in a cool, dry, room. In this way, late grapes were kept all winter long.

Leading Grape Varieties

BUFFALO.   This is a hybrid grape with three special merits—earliness, disease resistance, and ability of the fruit to hang on the vine for as long as you want it to, and stay good. 'Buffalo' is also a well-flavored grape, juicy, sweet, and tender, with attractive medium-large, blue-black berries in large and medium-loose clusters with light blue bloom. It was bred by the New York State Agricultural Experiment Station at Geneva, which has a seventy-five-year history of work with grapes. Vigorous and hardy, 'Buffalo' is a regular bearer and a heavy one as well. It ripens in mid-July. Vigor and earliness have also enabled 'Buffalo' to produce well in hot, dry weather. A good grape for home gardens, it is excellent for eating fresh and for juice, wine, and jelly. Give the European cane-pruning. Zones 5 to 8.

DELAWARE.   This is a very good red grape, rather small and round. The bunch is compact, the skin thin and translucent, the flavor sweet and sprightly. Delaware's origin is not known but it has been widely popular for perhaps a hundred and fifty years. It was discovered growing in a garden in New Jersey. The vine is hardy, vigorous, and very productive in rich, well-drained soil. It is tolerant of other soil types but grows less satisfactorily in thin ones. It is used fresh, for jelly, and as a wine grape. It ripens in early midseason—early or mid-August—and keeps well. It is one of the grapes that, like 'Concord', can take cold weather. Give the American pruning. Zones 5 to 8.

HIMROD SEEDLESS.   Related to 'Interlaken Seedless', 'Himrod' is another outstanding grape from the New York State Agricultural Experiment Station. It is a hybrid of the well-known 'Thompson Seedless' (thought to have originated in Persia) and the 'Ontario'. The 'Thompson' is a pale greenish yellow, the 'Ontario' a white grape. This offspring, 'Himrod', is a darker greenish yellow than 'Thompson' and better flavored, crisp and sweet. Though early, ripening soon after the very early 'Buffalo' in mid-July, 'Himrod' is an excellent keeper and can be held in storage until Christmas or close to it. It can be grown farther south than most grapes listed here, and is hardy in colder climates. It is a reliable annual producer of excellent eating and wine grapes and has a good record of vigor and freedom from disease. Give the European cane-pruning. Zones 5 to 9.

INTERLAKEN SEEDLESS.   This seedless grape, developed by the New York State Experiment Station in cooperation with the Boyce Thompson Institute, is the hybrid offspring of 'Thompson Seedless' and 'Ontario', like 'Himrod'. Ripening in mid-July with 'Himrod', it is of lighter color and suited for planting in the same zonal range though it may need winter protection in cold sections. It enjoys the good health of 'Himrod' and is a good producer of crisp, solid table grapes. Give European cane-pruning. Zones 5 to 9.

GOLDEN MUSCAT.   This is a hybrid and a very good one, again from the New York State Experiment Station. The color is golden yellow, sometimes with a greenish tint. The large grapes are oval and juicy, the bunches large, some weighing as much as five pounds. The flavor suggests the rich and distinctive one of the famous European muscat grape, from which muscatel wine is made. This is not surprising since 'Golden Muscat' was produced by crossing the 'Muscat Hamburg' grape with 'Moore Diamond', a good old golden yellow American grape. Their offspring is vigorous and hardy, doing well even on poor soil. It ripens the latter half of August and is used as a dessert grape and for juice, wine, and jelly. Give European cane-pruning. Though sometimes recommended for planting in warmer sites, 'Golden Muscat', according to Stark experience, is widely adapted through Zones 5 to 8.

NIAGARA.   A white, or more correctly light green grape, this is the 'Concord' of its class, probably the best-known and most popular white. In most areas it also ranks with 'Concord' in vigor, something you might expect on learning that it is a hybrid with 'Concord' one of its parents. 'Niagara' has been an important grape for some eighty-five years. It ripens at about the same time as 'Concord' or shortly before—during the second half of August. Noted for hardiness and resistance to cold, 'Niagara' produces well, bearing large grapes in medium-sized bunches. It adapts to a wide range of growing conditions and soils, and is a usually dependable bearer of good-quality grapes, sweet and delicately flavored, for dessert use, juice, and jelly. This is one of the few American bunch grapes that do well in such parts of Zone 9 as northern and central Florida. Some others are 'Fredonia', 'Carmen', and 'Florida Beacon'. These are black grapes, ripening in June and July in Florida. Give 'Niagara' the American pruning. Except as noted, it is for Zones 5 to 8.

VINERED.   Newly arrived from Ontario, this grape is deep red, has a mild and rich flavor, and is very sweet. The medium-sized grapes are borne in large and fairly loose clusters, ripening in late August. They are used fresh, for jelly, and for wine. 'Vinered' is thought to have a bright future, and it is well timed for bringing a red grape into succession ripening at this seasonal point. Give the American pruning. Zones 5 to 8.

STARK BLUE BOY.   Another brand-new grape, this one so important in Stark's eyes that they say flatly, "We consider this to be the best in dessert quality of all the American grapes." The bunches are large, and the attractive medium-sized grapes are blue-black, juicy, and slip-skin. Though quite sweet, they are spicy and vinous, with an agreeable tartness. They become well flavored long before the final harvesting date, which is the second half of August. The vigorous and hardy vines are highly productive and are recommended for home planting. Give the American pruning. Zones 5 to 8.

CONCORD.   This is the best-known American grape, though not the best in quality. It originated in Concord, Massachusetts, from a seed planted in 1843 by E. W. Bull. It was introduced commercially in 1854. Vigor, good bearing, and dependability have made it the commercial leader for about fifty years, as well as the most widely planted in home gardens. 'Concord' is the grape used commercially for jelly and grape juice. It will thrive in all types of soils. The grapes are large and blue-black, heavily overlaid with bloom; bunches are also large. The flesh is firm, sweet, and juicy. 'Concord' is used fresh as well as for juice and jelly; it will keep better if picked before it is dead ripe. It is an early-midseason variety, ripening the second half of August. Zones 5 to 8; Zone 4 if given winter protection.

A strain of Concord that Stark's consider a somewhat hardier and stronger bearer is called by them 'Stark Hicks'. It ripens with 'Concord'. Give both the American pruning.

STEUBEN. This is a fairly new and highly acclaimed dessert grape that has a flavor variously described as spicy, perfumelike, and exquisite. 'Steuben', also from the New York State Experiment Station, is a medium-sized, bluish lavender grape, borne in large, long, and tapering bunches. It is midseason, ripening in August after 'Concord', and is thought by many grape authorities to be even better than 'Concord' in adaptibility to growing conditions. It has produced a normal crop following a winter with a reading of 20 degrees below zero, and has shown excellent resistance to disease, especially mildew. A fine table grape, 'Steuben' is also good for jelly, and it yields a pale pink juice. The grapes store well. Give European cane-pruning. Zones 5 to 8.

STARK DELICIOUS. This good red grape originated in Illinois about sixty years ago, bred by viticulturist E. A. Riehl as a hybrid with 'Niagara' blood. Stark's bought it, named it, and have been pleased with its performance, considering it a fine late red grape for home gardens. The medium-sized grapes are borne in long clusters and ripen in early September, being of best quality when allowed to ripen completely on the vine until they are a deep crimson with a pink bloom. The vine is hardy and fairly productive. Give the American pruning. Zones 5 to 8.

CATAWBA. An excellent American grape, popular for more than a century, 'Catawba' was discovered about 1820 in Maryland by a Major John Adlum of the District of Columbia. Too late in ripening for some of the eastern and northern states, it matures in late September in the Midwest. It requires a favored location and a warm season. The color is red to copper, with a lilac bloom. The grapes are roundish, medium in size, and come in large loose clusters. They are juicy and sweet with a rich, musky flavor. Let the bunches hang till fully ripe. 'Catawba' is one of the best-keeping grapes. It is mainly used for jellies and juice, and is excellent for wine. Give the American pruning. Zones 5 to 8.

Grape Troubles

A lot of things can happen to grapes, but most of them won't, especially if your vines have plenty of sun and good air circulation. The insects that do most damage are: leafhoppers, which suck juice from leaves; phylloxera, sucking insects that won't be of concern unless you grow European varieties, on which they can cause galls on leaves and roots; the grape berry-moth, which causes wormy fruit; mites, flea beetles, root worms, and grape curculios.

Grape diseases are usually caused by fungi. Black rot is the worst, shriveling the half-grown fruit. Destroy affected grapes to break the cycle. Mildews may cause some trouble, and so may anthracnose. This attacks leaves and shoots, as well as fruits, appearing as sunken brown dots on the grapes, which harden and split.

But an open site, sanitation, and this simple spraying program will keep your grapes clean.

Grape schedule with combination spray

1. Spray when shoots are 6 to 10 inches long.
2. Two weeks after No. 1—just before vines bloom.
3. Two weeks after No. 2, if blooming is over; if not, wait for it to finish.
4. Two weeks after No. 3.

Nut Trees   *18*

You can grow a nut tree right on your lawn as if it were just a shade tree—it gives a filtered shade, superior to the hard maple—and be rewarded each fall by some of the world's best food. Some trees bear so prodigiously that their owners give, barter, or sell a yearly surplus of a thousand pounds of nuts. Also, nut trees are famous for taking care of themselves. They may get no more attention than a fence post from their owners, but go right on showering down a rich and comforting harvest each summer's end. Nuts are energy foods, whereas fruit is low in energy but high in protective value. Together they provide excellent nourishment.

Most of the nuts covered in this chapter we have grown. Others we have known as native to the place where we were living. In the past twenty-five years, horticultural science has greatly increased the northward range of some important nut species. If you've always thought you couldn't grow certain nuts, take a new look. You may be surprised.

Culture

Many nut trees have a long tap root, so it is especially important when you plant to dig the hole deep enough to accommodate this root without bending it. As you fill the hole, tramp the earth firmly and prod it with a hoe handle. Pour in a bucketful of water, with soluble fertilizer added, when the hole is partly filled. After the solution has soaked in and you have filled the hole with earth to the ground level, prune off the top third of the tree which will be a whip (unbranched). Finally protect the trunk with a cylinder of hardware cloth reaching from a few inches underground to within four inches of the top of the tree.

Nut trees are not choosy about where they grow and as we have said, they get along with minimum care. They will respond to some feeding, though they don't demand it. If you fertilize, do so in spring, at the rate of a pound or less of ammonium nitrate for a young tree, and up to ten pounds for a full-grown one. Hazelnuts are small, more like shrubs, and mature ones need no more than half a pound of ammonium nitrate. The best way to apply fertilizer to a nut tree is to put it in holes in the earth. Punch them with a crowbar, about two feet apart, in rings, with the tree in the center. Space the rings two to three feet apart, the outer one being a little farther from the trunk than the spread of the branches.

Pollination

Except where noted, pollination is not usually a problem with nut trees. Even where cross-pollination is an advantage, it is not essential to getting a crop.

Pruning

Hazelnuts are often grown in vase shape or almost bush form and need little shaping except the removal of persistent suckers. Other nut trees are grown in pyramid form. Here are the points to watch:

When the tree is mature, the lowest limb should be about six feet from the ground, which means you'll eventually need to cut off any limbs below this height. But let these lower-growing limbs remain until the tree grows tall enough to give you a choice of limbs to keep and to cut. Then select framework branches that are a good eighteen inches apart, up and down the trunk. This spacing allows for the growth a nut tree makes.

Species of Nuts

BUTTERNUT, *Juglans cinerea*. The name of this hardy and productive native North American nut suggests that it should be high in oil content, and it is. Closely related to the walnut, the butternut is often called the white walnut. The rich and spicy kernel is enclosed in a thick, rough shell. The nuts are for eating fresh and for cooking.

The butternut is a useful—and tall—shade tree, reaching up to fifty feet, sometimes quite a bit more. It is also spreading, so don't plant it where its shade will become a nuisance. Considered a good timber tree, it grows over a wide area and starts bearing two to three years after planting, and it is long-lived. Zones 5 to 9.

Before using the nuts, cure them for two to three weeks by spreading them out in an airy place. Leave the husks on while they are curing. Later, when the nuts have been husked and are ready to eat, crack them by standing them on end and tapping with a hammer (we use a light maul). This way, you can expect a good many unbroken halves.

HAZELNUT, *Corylus.* If you don't have much room for a nut tree, the American hazelnut is the most obliging little thing you'll find. It is more shrub than tree, taking up about the same space as a lilac bush. There are also European hazelnuts, most of which form small trees. Both European and American species are of the same genus, and the nuts of both are also called filberts.

The best nuts come from some of the European species, such as the 'Barcelona', but the hazelnut most apt to succeed in your garden is the American hazelnut, *C. americana.* It can grow six to eight feet tall, though the ones that grew wild in Missouri near our farm averaged nearer five feet. The nuts are small but good, ripening in late summer and having the characteristic aromatic flavor of the hazelnut kernel. We've liked them in cookies, but they're good to eat fresh, too. Plant trees on a north slope to protect the flowers (catkins) from late frosts, and plant two bushes, any two, for better pollination. The American species will grow from Zones 4 to 8.

Space hazelnuts 8 to 10 feet apart and prune them back to about 2 feet when you set them out. Mature bushes are pruned later in the season than most other plants—after blossoming. Cut out suckers and old wood that has borne nuts, and head back strong shoots to encourage spur growth.

To tell when nuts are ready to harvest, watch for them to start turning brown. They fall quite soon after that. Spread them out to dry thoroughly in an airy place for a week or so. Then husk and store them where it is cool and dry. Some people say hazelnuts keep better if you sprinkle them with salt.

HICKORY, *Carya*. Few big nurseries bother to carry hickory nut trees, an indication that the demand is small. Also, they are troublesome to propagate. Those nurseries that do carry them usually offer grafted improved strains of the shagbark hickory, *C. ovata*. We had both shagbark and shellbark hickories growing in the woods of our farm; we found that the shagbark nuts were a little bigger and easier to crack. Hickory nut meats are decidedly good, and we preferred them to black walnuts for many things because they are less assertive in flavor and have a good character of their own. Let them cure in an airy place for a week or two after harvesting.

When you plant a hickory tree, tie it to a stake to keep wind from loosening it while it establishes roots. Also, keep young hickories watered the first season or two, and mulch them well. They can get to be quite large and noble looking trees, over a hundred feet tall and of moderately spreading shape. The shagbark is particularly tall growing. Zones 5 to 8.

PECAN, *Carya pecan*. Paper-shell pecans used to be strictly for southern gardeners. We had never grown them in Missouri. When we moved south to the Mississippi Gulf Coast in Zone 9, we were entranced with the crops of big thin-shelled pecans from the huge trees growing on the lawn of the house we bought. Today we could grow a quite similar pecan in Missouri, or farther north where the growing season lasts five months. The distinctive feature of these new pecans is that they don't need so long a growing season as the southern paper-shells.

There are a number of new varieties of such pecans, trees that have in most cases appeared as seedlings in the Midwest. Several nurseries carry one or more, such as the 'Colby' or 'Major' varieties. Stark's have one called 'Starking Hardy Giant' that will take a little more sub-zero cold than most other hardy paper-shells.

The nuts of these hardy types are smaller than some southern pecans, though good-sized—about an inch and a half long and nearly an inch in diameter. They ripen in the latter half of September. The Hardy Giant nuts average four to the ounce. Flavor is comparable to that of the better southern pecans. The hardy paper-shells are for Zones 5, 6, and 7.

Stark's are the only big mail-order nursery, so far as we know, to carry, in addition to a hardy paper-shell pecan, both southern paper-shells and native pecans. 'Stuart' and 'Schley' are their southern varieties. We raised Stuarts, probably the most popular with both commercial and home-growers. 'Schley' is much the same. We would plant trees of either, or top-work them on healthy seedlings grown from any pecan nut if we found ourselves again in the Gulf Coast area. Zones 7, 8, and 9.

The native pecan carried by Stark's is a seedling that grows wild in some Missouri woods. The nuts are a third the size of paper-shells, and the only reason for planting seedlings, now that paper-shells are available, would be if you prefer the taste. Good seedlings are usually oilier and richer than paper-shells, but we don't think they're worth the extra work of shelling out. Furthermore, the *new* hardy paper-shells have high oil content.

You can eat pecans as soon as they fall, but the flavor improves if you give them a week or two in storage. Burlap sacks are convenient to keep them in. A mature paper-shell tree will give you upward of fifty pounds of nuts. Some have yielded three to four hundred pounds, but one hundred is what most home-growers count on in a good year.

Pecan trees are huge, growing more than a hundred feet high. Squirrels can get to be a real pest, picking off green nuts and never seeming to get it through their heads that the crop won't be ripe until fall.

One pecan planted alone can produce nuts, though larger crops are usually obtained when others are near. Space the trees about seventy-five feet apart. Don't plant them near the house for you will have a temporary staining on walls and walks from fallen leaves.

The pecan likes good garden soil, deep, well drained and fertile, though it will get along with less. A spring feeding of ammonium nitrate is appreciated, from half a pound for a young tree to ten to fifteen pounds for a big one.

The tree searches for water with a powerful tap root, and develops a mattress of feeder roots. Many of these will be only six inches underground, so don't cultivate deep or you'll cut them. In fact, you can grow pecans on the lawn and omit cultivation. Like fruit trees, the pecan and other nut trees do better when mulched.

BLACK WALNUT, *Juglans nigra*. We had an experience with black walnuts in California that almost made us forget how much we d liked these fine emphatic-flavored nutmeats in taffy and cookies when we were children. We were in Santa Rosa, and we'd leased a house with great old tall black walnuts growing all around it. We were delighted with the prospect of a good harvest, not with taffy in view but for cookies and because we had a chicken recipe that called for black walnuts. Then one day in October the autumn rains began and the autumn winds blew, and the black walnuts in their thick green husks began dropping like soggy bombs on the roof, on walks and terrace, on outdoor furniture, and now and then on us. It went on for days, and by the time we had finished cleaning up, we didn't care if we never saw another black walnut the rest of our lives. The moral of this is: Don't plant black walnut trees closer than fifty feet from your house.

The black walnut grows wild as a forest tree, but the tree you buy from a nursery will be one of the new grafted varieties that has bigger nuts, easier to crack. At least that's what you should buy if you want nuts worth your time. Most nurseries carry the 'Thomas', a good variety of the native black walnut. According to an experienced breeder and grower of nut trees, Bill Erickson of Louisiana, Missouri, 'Victoria' is a variety known for healthy foliage and for doing well in valley locations. 'Sparrow' is another good one; though the nuts are somewhat small, they fill well. Most black walnuts will start bearing four to five years after you plant them, and a mature tree can produce thirty to forty *bushels* of nuts, or enough to feed an army.

Stark's carry a hybrid of the native black walnut called 'Kwik-Krop' because trees may start bearing when only two years old. The nursery has found that trees still in field rows usually have a few nuts their second year. 'Kwik-Krop' nuts are of good quality. They drop during the first half of September, and have shells that are thin for black walnuts, though a long way from those of paper-shell pecans. The tree gets to be about sixty-five feet tall; native black walnuts can reach a hundred and fifty feet. Plant both in Zones 5 to 9.

Some vegetables and fruits—tomatoes, plums, and sweet cherries especially—don't grow well near black walnut trees. The roots seem to be toxic to them.

After the nuts drop, cure them by spreading them to dry in an airy place for three weeks. You can leave the husks on during the drying, but if you take them off, it will hurry matters. Crush the husks a little, and you can remove them with your fingers. But wear heavy rubber gloves or the husks will color you walnut.

ENGLISH WALNUT, *Juglans regia.* A missionary's discovery a few years ago has put a type of English walnut trees in cold-winter home gardens that can no more raise the usual English walnuts than they can grow oranges. The missionary was the Rev. Mr. Paul Crath, and the walnut trees he discovered were growing in cold country—the Carpathian Mountains of Poland, where it goes to 30 degrees below zero. To him they looked exactly like the English walnuts he knew. Selecting nuts from about fifty trees, Mr. Crath planted them when he returned to his home in Ontario, Canada. When the new walnut was introduced into the United States by the University of Wisconsin, it was a sensation. There are now quite a few different varieties of Carpathians on the market. (They are basically similar, but being grown from seed, differ enough to be distinct varieties.)

The Carpathian is a variety of the English walnut. The smaller Carpathian trees, such as the Lake strain, grow forty to fifty feet, about half as high as the usual English walnut, and come into bearing three to five years after you plant nursery trees. They are deep rooted and strong limbed, less particular about soil and site than the other English walnuts, and they make good shade trees on the lawn.

When the crop ripens, the Carpathian husks open and the nuts drop to the ground. Shells are thin and kernels crack out easily. Breeder Bill Erickson mentions, as another good productive Carpathian, the variety 'Colby'. For best pollination, plant two trees. They are quite hardy, though sometimes nipped in bud by late frosts because they start growing early in the season. Zones 5 to 9.

No one is sure yet as to the maximum crop you can get from a mature Carpathian tree, but the guesses are that it should run up to three hundred pounds. Cure the nuts for two to three weeks before use, spreading them out in an airy place. If they seem soiled when you first gather them, wash them in plain water before curing, especially if you want to pack some for gifts.

Nut-Tree Troubles

For the home gardener, spraying nut trees is not practical. They are much too large. It is fortunate therefore that a dormant spray is all they usually need, and this can be applied by a commercial tree-man. On the whole, nut trees are little bothered with either insects or disease. Aside from burning out nests of web caterpillars with a torch on a pole, the home gardener's best weapon against nut tree troubles is to keep the trees growing well. Feed and water as needed, prune away any blackened wood (caused by bacteria and fungi), and any limbs showing open wounds (caused by cankers), and practice garden sanitation. Coat pruning cuts three inches or more across with a protective tree paint. If leaves that fall are diseased, burn them.

The hazelnut is small enough to spray but has so few pests that you can forget about spraying unless aphids become outrageous. Then a little malathion or a combination spray or dust will handle them.

Black walnut trees may develop crown rot in damp locations. Remove a few inches of soil from around the trunk and replace with gravel.

Experimenter
in the Garden   *19*

We were talking to a bright high school boy who had become interested in grafting, and we asked what plants he was thinking of working with. He said he was going to graft a rose bush onto an apple tree. We agreed the effect could be pretty. We told him that the graft wouldn't take but that he might as well try it and find out for himself. We admired his curiosity. He was going to have fun in the garden, and he was going to learn things he could use all his life.

In this chapter we're going to touch on grafting and suggest some other experiments you can do in your own fruit garden—to create new fruits, to change the form of a tree, to grow different fruits on the same tree, and more.

Grafting

All the high school boy's rose and apple had in common was membership in the family *Rosaceae* and that's a fairly distant relationship in plants. Too distant for them to be grafted, which is a sort of marriage-of-convenience between two plants.

You can usually graft one *variety* of the same fruit onto another variety—an apple on an apple, a pear on a pear, and so on. What the varieties have in common is that they belong to the same species. (Species is spelled the same, singular and plural.)

Also, you can graft some *species* onto other species. They must almost always belong to the same genus and even then the graft doesn't always take. Peaches and plums both belong to the *Prunus* genus, for instance, and you can usually graft a plum to a peach but seldom a peach to a plum. Cherries and apricots are also members of the *Prunus* genus, but they will not graft successfully to each other.

But grafting a plant of one *genus* onto a plant of a different genus is almost always wasted effort. The two are too different. One of the rare exceptions is the graft of the pear to the quince. The pear is of the *Pyrus* genus and the quince is *Cydonia*. The quince becomes the root of the new plant, the pear the top, and the effect on the pear is to dwarf the tree.

Botanical classifications

To indicate some of the chances of grafting success between the plants covered in this book, here are their botanical classifications.

FRUITS	FAMILY	GENUS	SPECIES
Apple	Rosaceae	Malus	domestica
Apricot	"	Prunus	armeniaca
Cherry	Rosaceae	Prunus	avium (sweet cherry)
Cherry	"	"	cerasus (sour cherry)
Grape	Vitaceae	Vitis	labrusca (American)
Grape	"	"	rotundifolia (Muscadine)
Grape	"	"	vinifera (European)
Nectarine	Rosaceae	Prunus	persica
Peach	"	"	persica
Pear	"	Pyrus	communis
Plum	"	Prunus	various (American)
Plum	"	"	domestica (European)
Plum	"	"	insititia (Damson)
Plum	"	"	salicina (Japanese)
Quince	"	Cydonia	oblonga

BERRIES	FAMILY	GENUS	SPECIES
Blueberry	Ericaceae	Vaccinium	various
Blackberry	Rosaceae	Rubus	various
Raspberry	"	"	various
Strawberry	"	Fragaria	various

NUTS	FAMILY	GENUS	SPECIES
Butternut	Juglandaceae	Juglans	cinerea
Hazelnut	Betulaceae	Corylus	americana (hazelnut)
Hazelnut	"	"	maxima (filbert)
Hickory	Juglandaceae	Carya	ovata
Pecan	"	"	pecan
Black Walnut	"	Juglans	nigra
English Wal- nut	"	"	regia

Don't let the Latin discourage you or convince you that grafting is mysterious. Most home gardeners do think this, but it isn't so. Listen, grafting is nothing more than transplanting. Instead of transplanting in soil, you're transplanting to wood. You take a piece of one tree and transplant it to the trunk or branch of another tree.

Here are the main reasons for grafting: It is a fast way of multiplying trees. It keeps varieties true to type. It brings trees into bearing quickly. It controls the size and form of a tree. It can renew an old tree. It builds hardiness or health or adaptability into varieties that lack these qualities. *It can give a choice of flavors and ripening times of fruit on a single tree.* It can provide cross-pollination if the branch of a good pollinator is grafted onto a self-sterile variety.

Terms defined

To make matters clearer, let's define some of the terms used in grafting and propagation.

BUDS.   The places on a stem from which leaves, wood, or flowers grow.

BUDDING.   Growing one plant on another by attaching a bud of the first plant to it.

BUD STICK.   New wood at the end of a branch, cut off to provide buds for grafting onto another tree.

CAMBIUM.   The thin, moist layer of living tissue just under the bark, which produces both bark and wood.

CUTTING.   A piece of a plant, usually stem or root, that will grow into a complete plant if rooted.

DOUBLE-WORKING.   Grafting that builds a new tree with three or more units—usually the root of one tree, a bud or scion from another (which will become the top), and in between them a stem piece from still a third tree to form part of the trunk. The three are intended to grow into a better tree than any one of them could be. One of the main objects of double-working is to build a hardy framework, adapted to cold areas.

FORCING.   Making a bud grow by cutting off the part of the limb that extends beyond the bud.

GRAFTING.   Growing one plant onto another plant by attaching twigs, called scions, of the first plant to it.

GRAFTING WAX.   A protective covering for cut surfaces after a graft is made.

LAYERING.   Producing rooted sprouts by burying a branch that is still attached to a plant, or by bending down the whole plant and covering it with earth.

POLLINATOR.   A plant that produces pollen that can pollinate the flowers of another to enable it to set fruit. The one so pollinated is usually of a different variety that is not able to pollinate itself.

SCION.   A shoot of a plant that is bearing buds and is cut off in order to graft it onto another plant.

SEEDLING.   A plant grown from a seed.

STOCK.   The plant onto which a bud or scion is grafted.

SUCKER.   A shoot growing up from an underground root or stem of a plant.

TOP-WORKING.   Grafting or budding onto the branches of an established tree, usually done to change the variety bearing the fruit, or to add other varieties to the same tree.

WATER SPROUTS. Upward-growing suckers arising from branches. Unless well placed, they are usually removed.

WHEN THE BARK SLIPS WELL. When it peels easily from the wood.

A distinction is usually made between grafting and budding, but this is only for horticultural convenience. Both methods are really grafting, but since most stone fruits are easier to bud, and since budding is faster and cheaper and more convenient than grafting, by using the term "budding," a nurseryman saves a lot of needless conversation.

Grafting comes first in the season's work, so let's consider it first.

Techniques of grafting

To get the scions you need for grafting, you can save wood you trim off trees at pruning time in winter or early spring, or you can get scions from other gardeners, or buy them from a nursery. A scion should be healthy young wood of last year's growth, a little bigger around than a pencil and with several buds along its length. It is usually best to cut off the last bud or two on the tip, as the middle ones grow more strongly.

You can keep scions in the refrigerator until you are ready to graft them. Wrap the bases of a bundle of scions in slightly damp paper towels and fasten a plastic sandwich bag around this wrapping. If kept moist, the scions will live for several weeks.

The time to do the grafting is in spring during the six weeks before full bloom. Unwrap your bundle of scions, and with a sharp knife, cut the bases at a slant. The shape of the cuts will depend on your method of grafting. Cleft grafting, bark grafting, and whip grafting are three good methods.

CLEFT GRAFTING. This is often employed for top-working trees. Select a limb that is one to four inches in diameter; saw it off six inches or so from the place where it joins trunk or framework limb. If the tree is small, you can graft onto the trunk itself, cutting it off at a convenient height from the ground. (For a slender trunk, use a whip graft instead.)

Cut the scions as shown in A, to form a wedge on one end that will fit snugly into the stock.

Split the cut end of branch or trunk with a blade, as at B; a grafting iron is shown but a chisel will do. Also use it to hold the split open while you insert the scions. Two scions are usual, though only the better one is kept after they have grown for a season or two; the other is then stubbed back and is removed a year later.

In placing scions in position, as shown in C, it is important to have the cambium layers—the part immediately under the bark—of scion and stock touching each other. Slant the scions slightly outward to help ensure this. No tying is necessary with a cleft graft, as the pressure of the stock D will hold the scions tight. But the cut end of the stock should be covered with grafting wax on top and as far down the sides as the split reaches.

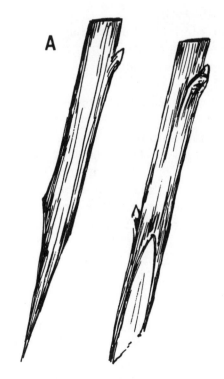

CLEFT GRAFTING. *Often used for top-working a fruit tree of one variety to one or more other varieties, as three different apples or peaches or pears on one tree.*

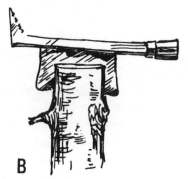

B

C

D

BARK GRAFTING.   Like cleft grafting, this is a method of top-working a tree. It is simple and satisfactory, and one of its merits is
minimal damage to the stock. It must be done in early spring when
bark begins to slip. Gather scion wood beforehand and store it so
that it will still be dormant when grafted.

As the illustrations show, the scion is cut to a wedge on each
side at the bottom A, so that the long cut rests against the wood
of the stock when the scion is pushed down into a kind of pocket.
This is made by slitting the bark of the stock as shown at B. Two
slits are made, as far apart as the scion is wide. These slits are just
long enough to accommodate the scion without splitting the bark
on the stock below it.

When the scion is in place, a little of the inside cut should show
above the top of the stock. Cut off about half the strip of bark
between the two slits. Hold the scion in place with two nails, one
driven through it into the stock, just above the bark flap, and another through it and the flap, as shown. Use No. 20 flat-headed
wire nails three-quarter-inch long. Make sure the lowest bud on
the scion is on the *outside*, slightly above the top of the stock.
Cover all cut surfaces with grafting wax.

*Opposite: BARK GRAFTING. Another good way to top-work a tree to a
different variety.*

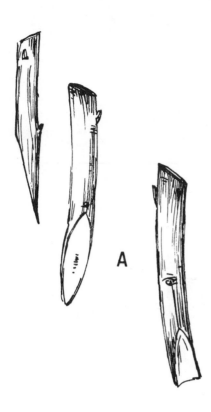

A

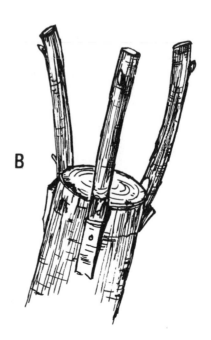

B

A

B

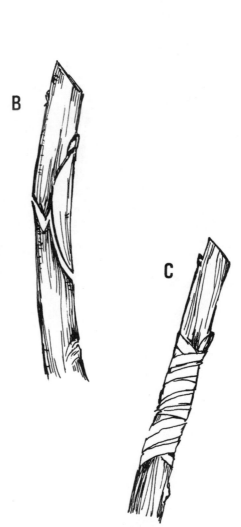

C

WHIP GRAFTING. Here is a convenient way to top-work a small tree, or to graft together two branches of about the same diameter, providing they are not big branches. A branch the size of a broomstick would be too big.

Cut both stock and scion in wedge shape, as shown at A, the cut being a long one with about an inch and a half of cut surface showing.

Then make a slit in each, about halfway between the pointed end of the wedge and the center core of the branch. When you slide the scion firmly onto the stock, these slits open up and scion and stock make a kind of tongue-and-groove joint as at B.

If the scion is a little smaller than the stock, be sure the cambium layers touch by making the bark of the scion come flush with that of the stock on one side. All you need is *one* such point of contact for the two to grow snugly together.

Wrap the graft well and seal it, as at C.

When you make a graft, be sure to leave some branches on the stock. They will nourish the plant while the graft is growing. Leave them even though you are changing over the tree entirely to a new variety. These branches on the stock are called nurse branches. The time to remove them is at the next dormant pruning.

Opposite: WHIP GRAFTING. *To graft two branches of about the same thickness to each other, or to top-work a young tree, use this whip graft.*

A word about grafting wax: You can buy it at garden-and-farm stores. Traditionally it is an equal combination of tallow, beeswax, and resin; it is applied while warm. A more convenient and safer product for a home gardener is an *asphalt water emulsion,* such as Tre-Kote. You paint it on cold and it stays flexible. This product is also approved by professional fruit growers, and it is used to protect pruning wounds, too. In a pinch you can use Vaseline to protect a small graft or bud graft, though hot sun may melt it. Whatever you use, the idea is to keep out air. Check the graft several times, and renew the seal if you see any cracking.

To tie grafts that need it, and buds, use string, cloth strips, raffia, plastic tape, friction tape, masking tape, adhesive tape, or rubber bands. Rubber bands are the most efficient and they won't girdle the tree if you forget to remove them. Select wide ones, about quarter-inch, and cut them into strips. Then wrap them like a legging around the graft (in the examples here, only the whip graft needs wrapping). Tuck the end of the rubber strip under the last lap to hold it in place.

Budding

You can graft onto wood of any age, but budding is only for young wood because bark must be thin and flexible. Budding is the usual form of grafting on young trees, especially in nurseries.

Though a bud may seem small and inconsequential, it is, in A. J. Downing's phrase, ". . . a distinct individual, capable of becoming a tree under favorable circumstances." To bud, simply cut a bud off one tree and fasten it onto another. There it will proceed to grow as if it had never left home.

You can make another variety become the fruit-bearing part of a young tree by planting a bud of it on the trunk of another. Or you can put the bud on only one branch of a tree and grow the new variety there. This is a way of producing several kinds of peaches, say, on the same tree, by budding several varieties on different branches. With older trees this same thing is usually accomplished by grafting, though not always.

Techniques of shield budding

Budding has timing advantages over grafting. You do it after the spring rush is over and also during a longer period. This gives you a chance to repeat if the first effort or two isn't successful.

Budding is done in summer and early fall. The time for it is while the bark of the stock can be easily separated from the wood —"when the bark slips well," the phrase is. You can find this out by making a T-cut in the stock at the point where you want to insert a bud. Then see if the bark lifts up easily, so that you can slide a bud into place as shown in the illustration on the next page.

To get the bud, cut a vigorous shoot of current-season growth several inches long (a bud-stick, as in Figure A), and select one of the buds in the middle. You want a bud that grows wood; these are always narrower than flower buds. Buds that grow wood are located in the axils of leaves, where leaf stems join a branch. Cut off all the leaf except a quarter-inch piece of its stem. Leave this for a handle. Then cut the bud off the bud-stick along with a piece of wood and bark, B. Do so by making a shallow cut with a sharp knife, starting about half an inch below the bud and cutting upward to half an inch above it. This will give you a shield-shaped sliver of bark and wood with the bud in front at top center. It should be just big enough to fit easily into the T-cut on the stock, C. You may have to trim a little off the top of the shield.

To insert it, hold the bud upright, using the leaf stem for a handle. Then ease the bud gently down into the T-cut as you hold the cut open at the top. The cambium of bud and stock should touch—and they will if your timing is reasonably good, D.

Now wrap the stock with rubber-band strips or tape to hold the bud tight to it, but don't cover the bud itself, E. You don't have to seal it. However, sealing will keep out curious insects.

If the bud takes, it will unite with the stock in two to three weeks. The leaf stem will drop off, which is a way to tell. At the next dormant pruning, cut off the stock just above the bud. This will make the bud grow when spring comes. Rub off all other growth on the stock.

An older tree is ordinarily top-worked by grafting instead of by budding, but sometimes a graft fails to grow. In that case, shoots

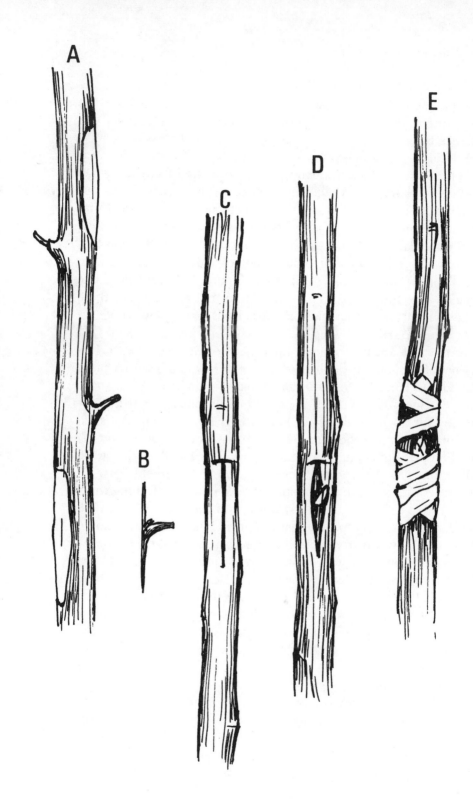

that spring up from the stump of the stock can be budded the next summer or fall.

Budding a peach tree

Here is the way to grow a peach tree by budding:

1. Plant a peach seed this fall.

2. Next spring it will sprout and by summer it will be about three feet tall. This is the time to bud it. Place the bud in the trunk a few inches from ground level.

3. Early the second spring, if the bud looks healthy and strong, cut the stock, as described. From now on, rub off any other growth on the stock.

4. The third spring, prune the young tree as described in Chapter three. You may get your first peaches the fourth summer.

Stock for budding

Planting a seed is only one way to get a young tree on which to bud a different variety. Another way is to root a twig. Cut a six-

Opposite: SHIELD BUDDING. Most stone fruits and most nursery trees are grafted by using buds rather than twigs for scions. (See page 252.)

inch shoot of the current season's growth from a tree in late summer. Dip the cut end in a rooting hormone such as Rootone and plant it in the garden. Put a handful of sharp sand into the hole. Insert about two-thirds of the shoot in the soil, and keep the soil moist. If the cutting takes root, it will put out leaves in spring. It will be big enough to bud by summer of the next year.

However, apples, peaches, apricots, most plums, pears, and sweet cherries grow poorly, if at all, from stem cuttings, so use a piece of root instead. Take a three- to four-inch length of young root about as thick as a pencil and cut the lower end on a slant. Plant the root barely under the soil surface, lower end down. The upper end will produce a shoot that will grow into a small tree by the end of summer. Since this will be the same kind of tree as for the root of the tree you took it from, it will be a good one to bud to. You can bud the second summer.

Some cherries and plums sucker freely from the roots. These suckers, which come up near the trunk, can be pulled loose and planted, to grow into trees you can then bud. Like root cuttings, they make good stocks.

Hybridizing

Having learned how to graft one tree onto another and how to grow a tree that you can graft onto, you'll want to find out how to get new material to work with. You can get buds and scions from established varieties of fruit trees, of course, but if you want to try something much more risky but also more adventurous, create a brand-new variety of your own. Impossible? Not at all. With Nature's help you can do it easily—and of all garden pastimes, there is none more exhilarating.

Grafting is a vegetative process, not a sexual one; you don't create new plants by grafting—you remodel existing ones. To create a new fruit, you must work with a seed. One way to manage this is to deliberately mate a blossom of one plant with another of a different variety. This will give you a fruit whose seed will grow into a hybrid plant with characteristics from both parents.

Another and simpler way to bring a new fruit into being is to plant any fruit seed. Almost every one from a domesticated fruit will grow a new variety. This is due to old genetic variations in its makeup, and possible natural hybridizing when the blossom that grew it was pollinated.

We'll call the deliberate handmade matings *hybrids;* the other ones, *seedlings,* even though each is both hybrid and seedling.

Techniques of hybridizing

Manmade hybrids in plants are a fairly new development in civilization. This is because it was only about two hundred years ago that we discovered plants had sex. And it was an enormous discovery.

If a plant could make a new plant by itself, as yeasts do, you could not get useful combinations of characters in the new generations by mating two distantly related plants. Instead, you would get exactly the same old plant over and over, a rubber-stamp reproduction. Since plants have sex, however, you get in their progeny a combining of two individuals. This opens the way to a vast number of changes that multiply as generations go on.

This combining is a complicated process that geneticists only partially understand. It is sometimes further complicated by polyploidy, an increase in chromosomes, the carriers of the units of inheritance, the genes, in the new individual. Through polyploidy the Duke cherries and the loganberry arose.

In spite of all this, the techniques of hybridizing are surprisingly simple. Let's say you want to cross a 'Van' cherry with a 'Napoleon' cherry. First decide which one is to be the female parent, the bearer of the fruit from which you'll get the seeds you are going to plant. Let's say it is the 'Van'. When the tree begins to bloom in spring, make sure the male parent, the 'Napoleon', is also blooming or about to bloom.

Next, choose a 'Van' blossom that is not yet open, and with a pair of cuticle scissors or a very sharp knife cut off the petals and all the stamens. As the illustration shows, the stamens are a group of little stalks surrounding the pistil. Stamens are the male organs. You are cutting them off so they cannot pollinate the pistil. Instead, you want to use pollen from the 'Napoleon'.

To prevent mishaps, tie a small paper bag around what is left of the 'Van' blossom. Come back to it a day later with a fully opened 'Napoleon' blossom. Hold the 'Napoleon' blossom upside

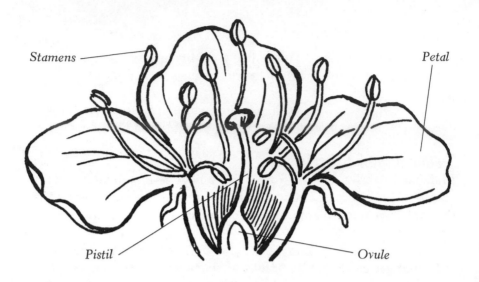

CROSS-SECTION OF A FLOWER. *This cherry blossom is cut away to show the organs of reproduction. The stamens, carrying pollen, surround the central pistil. The stamens form the male element; the ovule or rudimentary seed, is located at the base of the pistil, the female element.*

down, touch the stamens to the pistil tube of the 'Van'. Tubes get slightly sticky on the ends when ready for pollen. The pollen itself looks like yellow dust.

If you are successful, this procedure will pollinate the 'Van' blossom. Presently the ovule will prove it by swelling at the base of the blossom. After this, you need not keep it covered with the bag, though this is a convenient way to keep track of the blossom that you have hybridized. Make several such crosses so that you'll be sure to get enough seeds to give you a good selection of trees.

Taking petals off blossoms you are going to hybridize has no effect on pollination. It is done for working convenience. Petals are purely decorative.

In making crosses, try to combine two or more good characteristics in the hybrid. Say you've got a beautiful peach but it is small. Try crossing it with a peach that is big, and perhaps unattractive. Or cross a very early fruit with a choice late one. If they don't bloom at the same time so you can cross them, store the pollen for a while. From several opened blossoms, tap pollen into an envelop. Dry it by placing the envelop in a warm place for a few hours, as beside a table lamp. Then put the envelop in a plastic bag and store it in a food freezer. It will keep for several months. This is a way to get a hybrid that could never occur naturally because of difference in blooming times.

Improving the peach

Here are a few practical suggestions for possible improvements in a peach for home gardens. They are offered by plant breeder Grant Merrill of Exeter, California, a professional with the enthusiasm of an amateur.

1. A fruit-set moderate enough so that no pruning or thinning would be needed.
2. Resistance to peach-leaf curl (which would reduce the need for a dormant spray).
3. Less need for winter chilling, so a variety could be grown in climates too mild for most peaches.
4. High flavor, of dessert quality.
5. Adaptability to freezing, to keep the surplus.
6. Double blooms, if possible, to increase ornamental value.

This is an ambitious program for a home gardener to tackle. A professional breeder would also have his eye on getting variations of this ideal peach to spread the ripening season, to get both white- and yellow-fleshed peaches, to get an appealing color, to get a minimum of fuzz, etc.

When the fruits from your crosses mature, save the seeds, plant them, and label the spots.

Though professional breeders go to some pains to prepare their seeds for planting, the simple way for most of us at home is to follow nature's example—just plant the seeds when you have them. This is when the fruit they are in is ripe. A seed planted this summer or fall will sprout next spring.

Give each sprout a card in your file. Show the male parent, female parent, date pollinated, date picked, date planted, date sprouted. Later, record any grafts you make, the date that any resulting fruit is picked, and a description of it (color, size, taste). The first fruit borne by a seedling tree is not always final indication of quality. This was discovered years ago in England by a famous experimenter, Thomas Knight, who raised a seedling cherry that seemed worthless at first and that later became a success.

Since trees grown from seed often take years and years to come into bearing, you can shortcut this by grafting the twig of a seedling onto a mature tree of the same species, especially a dwarf. The whip graft is a good one for this. Graft to an outer part of a branch and you may get fruit the next season from the scion. This is the way Luther Burbank tested his new fruits to save time. In a biography of the plant wizard, we said: "He used this grafting system all the rest of his life and got still another advantage from it—an immense number of grafts per tree. Burbank actually had something like five hundred varieties of fruit growing on a single tree at times, making each such tree a testing station in the field."

New Varieties from Seedlings

Seedlings are the oldest source of new varieties. They are still one of the professional fruit breeder's best friends. These natural hybrids (usually) are also called chance seedlings and open-pollinated seedlings.

One value of natural seedlings is that when they are of self-pollinating fruits—as most peaches—the seeds they produce will grow an inbred generation of plants. Such plants show all sorts of interesting variations. This is the F_2 generation, famous for bringing out recessive characters, some of which may be very good. (The F stands for "filial," and the subscript 2 here means the second generation of offspring.)

To show you how this works in practice, we'll quote Mr. Merrill on some recent projects of his. One involved fifty peach seeds he was preparing to plant. They came from a natural seedling tree growing in a friend's yard. The parents of the tree were believed to be 'Early Sungrand' nectarine and 'Merrill Gem' peach. Thus the tree was a hybrid, and its seeds were expected to grow an F_2 generation that might include some good performers.

Another project dealt with two plums: " 'Champion , a very large but poorly flavored plum, interplanted with 'Santa Rosa' plum. Hope to retain size and add 'Santa Rosa' flavor." The interplanting insured cross-pollination between these two Japanese-type

plums. Mr. Merrill was planting about eight hundred seeds of this
cross with the hope of getting perhaps fifty plants, as only 10 percent of seeds from the same cross the previous year had germinated.
This is one of the hazards in plant breeding—after the work is all
done, you are at the mercy of the seed.

A third project dealt with a try at extending the season for a
certain type of peach: " 'Carnival', open-pollinated. This is the
highest-colored September peach I have bred, and I hope in the
F_2 generation (this is F_1) to get August and October peaches with
as good color and flavor. Will plant about two hundred seeds."

As you look over the varieties described at the end of each of
the fruit chapters, notice how many good fruits originated as seedlings. Both of the original 'Delicious' apples were seedlings, and
today they are the world's most important apples. One of the very
newest good apples is also a seedling—'Stark Splendor', which
sprouted from a seed of 'Golden Delicious' in New Zealand.

One of the famous names in fruit breeding, that of a Belgian
chemist, Dr. Jean Baptiste van Mons, is associated entirely with
improvement through seedlings. Although he had to raise eighty
thousand pear trees to do it, van Mons created some splendid
varieties, the 'Beurre Bosc' being one. His method was to crowd
and hard-prune his trees to reduce vigor, as odd-sounding as that
is for a program that required early bearing trees. The moment a
tree bore fruit he gathered it green, let it rot, then planted the
seeds immediately. By the time he had the fifth generation up
and bearing, Dr. van Mons said, he could confidently expect to
find some good new varieties among it. His method was based on
inbreeding, and he termed it "regenerating in a direct line of de-
scent." The procedure was controversial and time-taking and never
gained wide acceptance, but it did show some good results during
the fifty years Van Mons followed it.

Whether you find a new fruit by growing a seedling or in any
other way, the one element you cannot do without is observation.
"Selection" is the word for it in plant breeding, and it means an
awareness of fruits and fruit trees, so that when something different shows up, you notice it. This is the very oldest tool of all in
the plant breeder's kit, and it continues to be the most important
one even today when many new ways to change plants are being
used and others are being invented. Because . . . unless you know

a good thing when you see it, nothing will happen. Make it a habit to notice fruits on a tree, and to notice particularly any that are different from their fellows. Many a new wonder has been found by a gardener strolling through his home garden.

Mutations

A mutation is a change in the genes of a plant. Genes determine the qualities it inherits. The change that a mutation causes makes the plant different in an obvious and important way from the variety it came from. This difference may be an earlier- or later-bearing habit, an altered color or taste, a different tree form, or any of many other characteristics or combinations of them. Most mutations are useless to us, but when a good one does show up, it has the merit of being a permanent change.

Scientists are learning more about how to bring about mutations. In nature they occur because of such factors as severe heat or cold, physical damage, and the reaction of plants to other plants and plant products. Perhaps you can detect a mutation if one comes to your attention and you are alert to such possibilities. This may lead to your finding a new variety, and some of the best fruits we have were discovered in this way.

Sometimes one limb of a tree will grow fruit different from that on the other limbs. This is called a bud sport, "sport" being another word for mutation. Though bud sports have been prominent only since the 1920s as sources of new fruit varieties, they are not new. Nature, quite plainly, was making bud sports all along, but nobody was paying attention to the propagation possibilities. In 1845, Andrew Jackson Downing mentioned what appears to have been a bud sport on a 'Mayduke' cherry tree of his, but the reason for his mentioning it was not its possibilities for producing a new variety by grafting. He wrote: "In the gardens here, we have noticed a peculiar habit of this tree of producing very frequently some branches which ripen much later than the others, thus protracting for a long time the period in which the fruit is in use."

Severe pruning will sometimes cause mutations in a fruit tree, particularly the pruning back of large framework limbs. This is called bench cutting or dehorning. The effect on the tree is to produce rank sucker growth from adventitious buds. Keep a close eye on any trees so pruned, especially pears and apples. In the past fifteen years several good new apples have so arisen in fruit-growing sections in the Northwest.

Some seedling trees are mutants, and it sometimes happens in these cases that still other mutations show up in the second generation. The characteristics thus exhibited are recessive and so were not seen in the first generation. For more information on mutations and what you can do about them for your enjoyment and possible profit, see Chapter 23, in which pomologist Paul Stark, Jr. discusses how new fruits come about or are brought about.

Suburbia...
The Young Family
Plants a
Fruit Garden   20

Several times in our lives we've had to take a piece of reluctant earth and make a garden out of it. In the East, we gardened in a spot that seemed to be a pudding of boulders under a thin crust of loam, and in the South we raised pears and pecans in soil so sandy we could walk dry-shod across it five minutes after a drenching downpour.

But raw clay is as stubborn as anything so far as gardening is concerned, and there is more of it—especially in new housing developments in the suburbs. We've dealt with midwestern clay that we had to dig with a pick because it bent our spade. The reason for this chapter is to let a man who recently moved into a new suburban home tell what he is doing about planting a fruit garden in such clay, and about some of the other typical problems of his time and place.

He is Jim Law, a fruit-tree specialist in charge of production at Stark's, where he is a vice president. So he knows fruit gardening. He and his wife Norma were college sweethearts, and now are parents of a small blonde beauty and of a boy who looks startlingly like his father.

This is what he's doing to change bare earth into an inviting and fruitful bower, and here it is in his own words.

Jim Law's Fruit Planting

When Norma and I went house-hunting we were looking for space (reasons: an eleven-year-old son and an eight-year-old daughter), a view of the sheltering hills half-ringing this old river-bluff town on the broad Mississippi, and ground enough for a fruit garden. We found it all, with a little compromising. The house is roomy, the view spacious. And the lot is big enough though roughly trapezium-shaped, 200 feet wide in back, 90 in front, with one side on a long slant. We're on a slope, which is good—fruit trees need air drainage. But the soil! A tight clay, and the contractor dumped more on top—free. You can live with subdivision clay, though; buy topsoil and fill planting holes with it, use fertilizer with a free hand, and plenty of mulch.

Now about fruit trees; we thought of apples first because all four of us like them fresh and cooked. We're planting five double-dwarf trees just inside the rear lot line and opposite a patio, onto which the family room opens. And we're making these double-dwarfs do triple duty. We're espaliering them so they form a screen six feet high. We'll get privacy and apples, too. And each spring a garden wall of blossoms. Here's what we're planting for successive ripening:

'Starkspur Lodi' is a really good dessert apple, ready the middle of July. We eat it fresh and love it baked, with a dollop of whipped cream when it's served. About a month later, 'Starkspur Earliblaze' will be ready to take along on late summer hikes into the hills— and it's another mighty good baker. 'Starkrimson Delicious' comes in about a week after the children start back to school in September, a big sweet red apple for their lunch boxes. Nearly a month later, 'Starkspur Golden Delicious' is ripening, and this beautiful apple is probably our family favorite, delicious fresh, superb cooked. Finally, I'm top-working a dwarf tree to a new apple, 'Stark Blushing Golden'. This follows 'Golden Delicious' by ten days or so and has its merits plus a little more tartness, along with a very big plus—exceptional keeping quality. We can store apples in a cool corner of the basement, and we've also held onto our twelve-year-old refrigerator to use for other fruit storage.

Dwarf peaches and cherries are going into one corner at the

back, the peaches being a mother-daughter twosome. Burbank July Elberta' is a wonderful garden peach that ripens here in early August (just in time to make peach ice cream in our old-fashioned crank-up freezer). It is the mother of 'Starking Delicious' peach, a fine freestone that comes along in mid-July. Our cherries are both sweets—'Van', a Bing type, and 'Stark Gold', which follows it by a few days. If we had room, we'd add a 'Montmorency' for pies and freezing and to remind us of happy years among the tart-cherry orchards of northwestern Wisconsin's Door Peninsula. But we need space for pears—two good dwarfs. They're 'Seckel' and 'Moonglow', both resistant to blight, which is a problem here in the Midwest. If there's anything better than a bowl of apples and a hearth fire on a frosty fall night, it's a bowl of spicy pears and a hearth fire.

One of the agreeable things about grapes is the small space the vines take. We're growing ours on a miniature arbor fastened to the back of the garage. It is merely two braced struts with three wires between as illustrated in Chapter seventeen. A vine is planted at each end, and fruiting canes are led out along the wires. We're planting 'Buffalo' and 'Himrod', delicious new table grapes. The bunches will hang down, shaded by the leaves on top from hot summer sun. This arrangement is also good outside a south window, giving shade in summer and dropping the leaves to let sunshine in through winter.

We also wanted an apricot tree, and its beauty of bloom and structure made it a natural choice for the front yard. We selected 'Wilson Delicious' for hardiness and rich tender fruit.

One more point; since we can get our trees free you may be thinking: Yes, but what would such an order cost *me?* Well, I bought a big balled-and-burlapped shade tree last spring and I've just compared that bill with the catalogue price of this total fruit order. The shade tree was $70.00, the fruit planting comes to $72.25. We'll get a lot more value from the fruit trees, and we think the example of producing some of our own food with our own work is a good thing for the children to see and share. If they were younger, we might be saying what one of the nursery customers said of a young cherry tree in her yard. It had exactly two cherries its very first year, and both her children were entranced with this miracle. "The tree was a perfect baby-sitter," she told us. "And thank goodness it had enough cherries to go around!"

(*Authors' note:* Jim Law has overlooked one item. We visited the new home and heard Norma and him planning this fruit garden. We remember very well that strawberries were mentioned. They were mentioned by Norma, and she was looking hard at Jim who was looking hard at the ceiling. Add $5.00 to the order, Jim. Norma and the children will love twenty-five 'Ozark Beauty' plants.)

Sharing the Bounty—
Beautifully

21

(*Authors' note:* This chapter was not co-authored, but was written by Pat Kraft because she takes responsibility for the arrangement of our home-garden fruit when it is presented as a gift.)

We know a rancher who has a small fruit garden and who grows the most luscious peaches I've ever seen. He is very generous and often arrives at our door with a large brown paper bag filled with them—just a plain paper bag, exactly as if he had suddenly thought of bringing us some and had picked them up at the supermarket. It always reminds me of a time when we were living on our Missouri farm and were invited to a friend's housewarming. As any new farm-owner will tell you, the farm demands all your spare money . . . so, what was I to take to the festive occasion?

One of our old peach trees was just ripening its crop. I decided our gift would be peaches. I found a graceful basket that curled slightly to the sides and with a curved handle, the kind advertisements show lady gardeners using for their cut flowers. Then I bought a few yards of peach-colored, narrow velvet ribbon. On the day of the party, we carefully picked each choice peach with a short piece of stem and a few leaves attached. I dusted the peaches with a tissue, and wiped the leaves with a damp cloth (never wash the lovely bloom from a peach). I placed the fruit in the basket with a branch to follow the line of the handle, and one peach anchored at the base of the curve, tied with the velvet ribbon.

We covered the basket with shining plastic and went off to the party. The present was almost *too* successful. Host and hostess insisted on posing for pictures while holding the basket, and the flower arrangement on the dining table was whisked off to make room for our peaches. But they deserved it for they were tree-ripened delicious, as well as beautiful.

Later one of my farm neighbors was wishing she could think of something for a great occasion. Their son's grandparents-in-law were about to celebrate a fiftieth wedding anniversary—and as my neighbor pointed out, that meant *gold*. We thought this over together, and came up with a gleaming idea.

In their garden grew that king of fruit trees, a 'Golden Delicious' apple. What better gift for a golden anniversary? My neighbor covered a bushel basket with two coats of gilt paint. Then she bought a few sheets of pliable gold-colored florist paper, the kind that is wrapped around gift flowerpots. She hoarded the ripening apples, and on the great day she had fifty ready to wrap in the gold paper and arrange in the golden basket. She tied a wide gold-colored ribbon from handle to handle, with a flowing bow. Fifty golden apples for fifty golden years—symbolic and beautiful. And the grandparents loved apples.

One spring we wanted to cheer up a bachelor friend in the hospital. Our Montmorency cherries were at their best. I had stashed away a tiny creel, a fisherman's basket, just like the big ones but about pint size. I put crumpled tissue paper in the bottom and carefully filled the basket with the shiny tart cherries, each one (or two, as they're usually in pairs) with its stem. I piled them up and let them spill over the rim a little—a creel bursting with ripe red cherries—and tied onto it a spring-green bow. The bachelor swore that the cherries accounted for his rapid recovery and were far and away the best things he had to eat while incarcerated.

Tree-ripened, beautiful fruit is too elegant not to have a proper setting. And the setting can so easily suit the fruit. It need not be expensive; the fruit is the present. Nor need it be a new container, for nothing is lovelier than an old bowl or platter picked up perhaps secondhand or at an auction. I once had a fruit bowl I intended some day to have replated. Then I came across it as I was about to visit a friend on her birthday. The garden had just bits and pieces of things to offer—some at the end of their season, others just starting—so I arranged a fruit salad bowl in the old silver dish. I considered some beautiful marzipan apples, peaches, and bananas to decorate the handle, but after I'd filled the bowl with the real fruit from our trees, it blended so beautifully with the sheen of the silver, it needed nothing more than plastic covering and a multicolored ribbon bow.

We knew a man on the Mississippi Gulf Coast who had inherited a pecan grove. He had trouble finding help when harvest time came, so we'd occasionally volunteer to pick the nuts—a touchy job because he had hundreds of hybrid azaleas planted under his trees.

One day I noticed several attractive little nut bowls on a shelf in his kitchen, and some rather impractical looking nutcrackers. When I mentioned them, he looked somewhat abashed and said a little defiantly, "Well, they make my pecans appreciated."

He told me that for years he'd been taking bags of nuts to friends: "I'd arrive at a dinner with my gunny sack of big beautiful Stuarts or Mahans, and the hostess would say how nice and would I please just set them on the porch? And some woman with a few flowers in a coffee can she'd pasted some pretty paper on would get the rave notices."

So one day shortly before Thanksgiving he noticed these little nut bowls in a hardware store. On impulse he bought a bowl and a nutcracker. He filled the bowl with huge paper-shell Mahan pecans he'd polished, tucked the nutcracker in on top, and covered the whole thing with sheet plastic to keep the nuts in place. This was the gift he took his Thanksgiving hostess instead of the usual gunny sack of nuts—and it was an enlightening experience. No dumping on the porch for these nuts. No indeed. The hostess bore them proudly to the holiday table, and everybody there knew who had brought them.

The next day he told his friend at the hardware store about it. The man's wife was a famous cook. She was always baking her nut bread and nut cookies for bazaars and fairs, so our friend proposed to her husband that they barter nut bowls and crackers for pecans, and so they did.

"I'm getting better at it all the time," the pecan-grower told us. "I keep my eye out for a few nicely colored leaves in the fall to tuck under the nuts. Of course, people don't get a tenth the pecans they used to—but I take them refills, a plastic bag of Stuarts to load up the bowl again, and after dinner everybody cracks a few nuts, and those ladies with their coffee cans of flowers hardly get a look-in any more."

When we were ready to go, he had a gunny sack of pecans ready for us. "When anybody works as hard as you," he said, grinning, "they don't need nut bowls to appreciate pecans."

We knew a woman doctor in Virginia who was planning to retire to a little place in the country. When she took us to see it, I started talking about the flowers she could raise—roses, lilacs, iris, lilies. She stopped me short. "Not I. I just don't have any luck with flowers. Can't even arrange them, and if I plant a seed it dies. I guess I see too many flowers in my rounds at the hospital; I don't like them much and the flowers know it."

There were several old but healthy fruit trees on the place, and before the first year of her retirement was up, she had found her true talent. She was a born artist with fruit—the growing, the harvesting, the arranging. She had her first success when a luncheon coincided with her first harvest, 'Montmorency' cherries. She cut twigs with bunches of cherries and leaves, and piled them in a milk-glass epergne. She also had a pair of old milk-glass hens. She filled them with cherries, the hens tilted up to show what they were "setting" on. Her guests were delighted, but they refused to touch the cherries for fear of spoiling the effect and she had to pick more from the trees.

And so it went through the season: peaches, velvety and fragrant in a green Mexican pottery platter; grapes with bloom still on piled high and dripping over the rim of a champagne basket. When the bounty of fall arrived, her table was dazzling with polished apples, pears, late grapes, and nuts.

She told us, "It works so beautifully for me. I love to cook but I'm a meat-and-potato cook and I never was good at desserts—and you remember that I couldn't even fix flowers for the table. Now my beautiful fruit does everything. There *was* a problem for a while—nobody wanted to spoil the centerpiece by eating it. But I solved that by bringing in an eating-bowl of the same fruit with fruit plates and knives."

Then with the enthusiasm of the true gardener, she remarked: "I used to wonder if I'd miss my practice and be bored when I retired. But I've found that in an orchard there's *always* something that needs doing, and I won't get everything just the way I want it if I live to a hundred. I'm telling all my old patients to get busy with a fruit orchard. Keeps you too busy to bother with worries; it's healthy exercise, and the harvest is good for what ails you. You know what? Fruit trees are a way of life—the good life."

Fruit
And
Your Health   22

An Eldon Dedini cartoon in *The New Yorker* shows an elderly patient roaring at his doctor: "An apple a day! *This* is Medicare?" But the happy fact is, fruit really *is* good for you—and even for what's wrong with you at times. Apples especially are thought of as the fruit of health, and they have excellent rating for minerals and vitamins. But apples also cherish the human constitution in ways not fully understood, although they are recognized. They help the nervous system, they promote intestinal health and improve digestion; they strengthen capillaries, the tiny blood vessels that cause bruises when they are ruptured. Apples also carry substances that encourage the health of skin and eyes, and they are an aid to the general growth of the body, including the building of good teeth and sturdy gums.

In emphasizing the need for fruit of all kinds in the diet, a noted contemporary Swiss physician and psychiatrist, Dr. Paul Tournier, in *The Healing of Persons*, cited the case of a young woman suffering from asthma that was complicated by an intolerance for sugar and consequently for fruit. At the time treatment began, the patient required two adrenaline injections daily, and actually had not eaten a single piece of fruit for twenty years. "I explained to Marcelle," Dr. Tournier recorded, "that fruit was man's basic food." He then prescribed "a tiny portion of grated apple daily," and gradually increased the amount. In a month the patient was eating half an apple a day, receiving only one adrenaline injection, and was well along to the complete recovery that followed.

An interesting corollary here is that scraped raw apple is a medically approved remedy for diarrhea. In *Our Most Interesting Diseases*, Dr. Harold Burn cites the use of apples by those on holidays abroad to arrest acute attacks. He writes: "The most probable explanation of this action is that apples diminish the entry of bacteria through the wall of the intestine into the blood stream, and that this is of importance in the large intestine." He says it is also surmised by medical investigators that eating apples lowers the risk of appendicitis and of serious infection of the urinary tract by a colon bacillus.

One of the most revealing investigations of how apples affect health was made at Michigan State University and published in the bulletin of its agricultural experiment station in 1961. This study was made over a three-year period. Each year five hundred volunteers were selected at random among men and women students and regardless of their medical history or general health, in order to have a true sample of the student group. Each ate from one to three ripe apples a day for twenty weeks each school year. Their health records were compared at intervals with those of all the other students.

The results were amazing. Nobody was trying to prove anything, but all were leaning over backward to let whatever they found speak for itself. After three years, here are the results:

The apple-eating students had one-third fewer colds, sore throats, sinus attacks, and other upper respiratory infections as the other students.

For every apple-eating student who had a tension-pressure problem (nerves, headaches, trouble concentrating, etc.), *six* of the other students suffered.

So not only were apples found to be healthy but they were also natural tranquilizers. Furthermore, the apple-eaters had fewer skin troubles, less indigestion, fewer eye and ear disorders, allergies, mouth infections, and less hay fever and asthma.

(Although we know of no slightest difference between varieties of apples in their effect on health, you may be interested to learn that the apples used in this study, which was outlined and directed by Dr. E. H. Lucas, were: 'Cortland', 'Delicious', 'McIntosh', and 'Golden Delicious'.)

Everybody understands that eating an apple helps clean the teeth; more important, it gives the gums a healthy workout, massaging them and stimulating the mucous membranes. As your dentist will tell you, if your gums aren't healthy, you're in trouble, no matter how good your teeth are. Eating *any* kind of fruit does something more for teeth and gums. Scientific investigators don't know exactly how it comes about, but what is called a "bacteriostatic condition" is set up in the mouth when you eat fruit, particularly raw fruit. This condition halts the development of bacteria, and it may be due to a stimulation of certain cells by the appealing taste of the fruit. Some researchers have concluded that eating a piece of fruit for dessert or at bedtime seems to be particularly helpful. (They don't say you shouldn't brush your teeth just the same.)

As for digestion, fruit has two values. It contains cellulose, and because we cannot digest cellulose, this adds bulk needed in normal diets. The other value, particularly with the more acid fruits, is to contribute to the body's non-acid, or alkaline, reserve—contrary as that may sound. The object of this reserve is to neutralize acid substances from such other foods as eggs, cheese, cereals, and meats.

Minerals and vitamins are concentrated in fruits—particularly in the fruits you pick from your own trees and bushes. The former medical director of the Metropolitan Life Insurance Company, Dr. William P. Shepard, in his *Executives' Health Secrets*, made this point: "Fortunately, considering the increasing distance between food producer and urban markets, refrigeration, canning and quick freezing preserve most, though not all, the vitamin content of food. But the family who can eat vegetables and fruits the same day they're picked is still most fortunate."

Yellow fruits, such as apricots and peaches, will give you Vitamin A, the vitamin that helps you see better, especially in poor light. Vitamin A is also an infection-fighter, and is good for the skin.

Almost all fruits are fair providers of the B-complex vitamins. These help steady nerves, improve your morale, sharpen your appetite, and confer other blessings.

Vitamin C, which aids in healing wounds, is plentiful in fruit. This vitamin also gives good muscle tone and assists you in throwing off infections.

Among the minerals, iron is one you'll find in fruits, mostly in apricots, peaches, plums, and blackberries. Iron is essential for the manufacture of blood.

In summary here, the Swiss Dr. Tournier put the value of fruit in the diet this way: "A simple reform, and one which would have a considerable bearing on health, would be to eat some fruit at each meal, including breakfast, and particularly at the beginning of the meal. A fruit is a germ which contains in essence the life-force of a whole plant."

Then there's the reducing diet, that specter of the cupboard for so many of us. Here, fruit is an all-things-to-all-men, good for over-weights as well as underweights. Serious reducers who know their calories realize that even a large apple logs in at only one hundred calories. (That's a raw apple, you understand; baked with sugar and butter and drenched with cream, it is something else again.)

Fruits are protective foods, so light on fat that in spite of their natural sugar, you can eat them without a qualm about what the bathroom scale is going to say about it later. In fact, and on the authority of experts in nutrition, you can even add fruits to your present diet without running the calorie count up more than a few units. This table will give you a working idea of how unfatten-ing fresh fruit is. For a comparison, keep in mind that a slice of bread has about 100 calories, and a glass of whole milk nearly 200.

1 small apple	60 calories
5 apricots	100 calories
1 cup of blackberries	80 calories
1 cup of table grapes	150 calories
1 large peach	75 calories
1 large pear	60 calories
3 medium-sized plums	50 calories
1 cup of strawberries	60 calories

Notice that we didn't include any nuts in the list. They are loaded with calories, about 30 or 40 in a single paper-shell pecan, for instance.

In conclusion, may we give fruit some credit for bringing health to those who raise it? Gardening is far and away one of the health-iest pastimes and pleasures you can choose. The Florida Department of Agriculture, recommending home gardening as the oldest and most wholesome occupation, states: "Today, physicians and psychiatrists alike often recommend gardening as a therapeutic measure. Gardeners find that their work has a relaxing and restful effect on them mentally, even though they may become tired physically." Incidentally, gardening is also reducing. If you are about average size, an hour of weeding will melt off 300 calories. Forty minutes of spading will do the same thing.

Almost five hundred years ago a soldier and scholar named Bartholomaeus de Platina wrote a cookbook. It was the first cookbook that was ever printed—since movable type had been invented just a few years before. In his book, Platina gave his readers the benefit of his thinking "concerning the exercise of the body." What he had to say may be of interest to today's fruit gardeners, as it must have been to those of the year 1475.

Walking and shopping exercise a man well, as do walking up and down hills, the carrying of a thing not too heavy from place to place when we are at home, hoeing, harrowing, planting and pruning while we are cultivating gardens and orchards for the sake of our souls.

Fruits Today—
and Tomorrow   *23*

Paul Stark, Jr. is an internationally known pomologist, graduate of Cornell University and one of the few world authorities on deciduous fruit varieties. A fifth-generation Stark, his work for the nursery, of which he is a vice president, is currently in research and fruit improvement. He is exceptionally qualified to write on the subject of new fruits and how they are found—and in some cases brought about. He has been active in this work in Europe, Australia, and New Zealand, as well as the Americas, for more than twenty-five years. His father is one of the notable pomologists who pioneered in recognizing the immense value of mutations in producing new fruit varieties. Here, now, is Paul Stark, Jr. on the subject of new trends in fruit and the fascinating new techniques being used to change old varieties and bring new ones into being, and to simplify and improve fruit gardening:

Paul Stark, Jr. Reports

Variety improvement in fruits during the past two decades has been nothing short of sensational. In earlier days, perfection in fruit quality came only at the peak of the season, as in 'Early Elberta' and Hale peaches, 'Golden Delicious' apples, and 'Comice' pears. Now we have high-quality fruits throughout the season, also better-keeping and preserving fruits to give abundance all winter long.

Probably the biggest and most important step forward for home fruit gardening has been the selection of dwarfing stocks and methods to give smaller, more easily managed, attractive, and productive trees. With them we can grow many varieties of fruits in very limited space. Size control has come about through research, first at the East Malling research station in England, where A. T. Preston and Robert John Garner and their predecessors and associates worked with apples and pears. In France the Angers experiment station pioneered in better quince stocks for dwarfing pears. The late Tom Maney of Iowa State University, and Stark's own research director, H. W. Guengerich, made contributions in control of apple-tree size with dwarfing stem-pieces. Karl Brase of the New York State Experiment Station pioneered in reducing the size of peach and cherry trees, while Karl Sax at the Arnold Arboretum was perfecting dwarf peaches, plums, and apricots. Tasmanian tree-trainers and the French Louis Lorette led the way in mold-and-hold pruning. Orchardist Grady Auvil of the State of Washington adapted this pruning to American commercial plantings.

Then there has been the discovery of genetic dwarf and semi-dwarf varieties with much more fruiting wood throughout the trees. By means of these dwarfed types, and other tree-size controls, we can produce a bearing unit to order, as to shape, size, and space required. Patio and penthouse gardening with fruits thus become realities. Espalier training, once a nightmare for an untrained amateur, is easy with these new tree combinations.

Now let's take a look at some of the tools we have at hand today to tailor trees to our needs, and at some of the results.

Tools and techniques

Research into virus diseases is giving us more productive trees, free of harmful virus problems and more reliably hardy and uniform in growth. More surprising, we have isolated what we might call "good" viruses. These have given us dwarf cherries on spur-type trees, producing more and larger fruits. Other "good" viruses are being used to fight the "bad" viruses that threaten the life of trees.

Progress has been made in breeding hardier fruits such as the 'Reliance' peach from the work of E. M. Meader of New Hampshire. This gives us reliable production in areas with long cold winters. In Virginia, George Oberle has built frost resistance into his new peaches, 'Madison', 'Washington', and 'Jefferson'. The new Alar sprays, which modify plants for favorable fruiting and compact growth, also when properly timed, help to improve hardiness. This is accomplished by stopping growth of terminal buds and too-vigorous shoots, and by building stouter limbs that store more food reserves.

Disease-resistant varieties of pears, apples, and plums are now a reality, and reduce the need for spraying and for removal of diseased wood. Ralph Shay, while stationed at Purdue University and in co-operation with Fred Hough of Rutgers University, bred scab immunity into apples. Fred, along with Catherine H. Bailey, is giving us brown-rot resistance in nectarines and peaches. John Magness, recently retired from the United States Department of Agriculture, and the alert selections of Marvin Cook of Tipp City, Ohio, gave us blight-resistant and high-quality pears.

Atomic radiation is producing spectacular results. It causes mutations, and through these, we are getting genetic dwarf and semi-dwarf trees—some mutations also carrying immunity to mildew and other diseases. Self-fertility in Lambert-type cherries has been achieved by crossing irradiated seedlings from the John Innes Horticultural Institute of England with American and Canadian types at the Summerland Research Station in British Columbia. There, Charles Lapins and Don Fisher have already introduced a truly compact 'Lambert' from their irradiated selections. Other fruits are in process of being selected, including the great Canadian apple, 'Spartan', that I feel should replace 'McIntosh' in North American orchards.

Control of insects by predators is well on the way to practical application. I see in the future the happy disappearance of chemicals for pest control in home fruit gardening. What a day that will be! Already, new and better weed-killers and weed-depressers are here.

Hormones play a part in fruit life, as in human life. New hormones, well along in development, will help control tree size and will increase fruit production. Others, for commercial planters, will help in thinning fruit more efficiently, regulate fruit set, and bring about heavier and more regular crops.

Seedlings and mutations
One of the ways that varieties have been improved and new ones

found is not at all new—but is still one of the best. It is, in fact, nature's own method—the production of *chance seedlings* and of *bud mutations* (bud sports), and the discovery of these by alert people. Some such discoveries have enriched those who found them for the Plant Patent Act gives both professionals and amateurs the protection that inventors have long enjoyed. The discovery of the highly productive, semidwarf 'Starkspur Golden Delicious' apple, for an outstanding example, paid the owner $51,000.

What, now, is a chance seedling? It is a tree from an accidentally planted fruit seed. It might spring up in a back yard, or in a fence row on a farm. Hunters find many in the woods, growing from seeds of fruit that other hunters ate. Seedlings bear fruit a little different from others of their species because fruit trees almost never come true from seed. The fact is that practically all of our important apple and pear varieties, as well as many other fruits, have come from chance seedlings.

As to bud mutations—or bud sports as we usually say—they come about when the genetic makeup of a single bud changes. The fruit on the branch that grows from this bud may mature earlier or later than that on the rest of the tree, or it may be a better color or a poorer one, or be more heavily equipped with fruit spurs, and so on. What causes a bud to mutate? Most mutations seem to occur following winter injury, or after a severe pruning (dehorning) that forces a deep-down adventitious bud into growth—a bud that ordinarily would remain dormant all its life.

Obviously, bud sports are not new. What was new was our recognition of their importance, and this was brought about by the discovery of the 'Starking Delicious' apple. That was in 1923. The original 'Starking Delicious' apples grew on one limb of a Delicious tree in New Jersey. On this limb the apples colored a deep, rich red weeks before other apples on the tree were colored. The owner of the tree, Lewis Mood, wrote my father about it, and he inspected the tree and immediately arranged for propagation testing. It proved the mutation true, and Mr. Mood received $6000 for exclusive propagation rights, a tremendous sum then for a single limb of one tree.

At the time, some in professional horticulture were skeptical of the worth of such a mutation, so they were invited to come and see for themselves the original limb and the young grafted trees in fruit. Seeing was believing—and the era of bud-sport variety improvement was under way. No variety of modern times has been more talked about, more widely planted, or more generally appreciated by growers and consumers both than this 'Starking Delicious' apple. It rapidly replaced its parent as the leading apple, and soon Starking trees spread their branches over the deciduous orchard areas of the world.

We now have earlier-ripening and later-ripening selections of our best varieties to extend the season. Giant pears and apples have resulted from a doubling of chromosomes, the inheritance controllers, in the tetraploid mutations. Golden russet mutations in 'Gorham' and 'Bartlett' pears have given us delicious and longer-keeping fruit. All the important apple varieties have better color through mutations. Probably the most important improvements are the limb mutations that bear up to twice the amount of fruit as the parent varieties—the spur-type apples, cherries, and others already on the way, the semidwarfs that greatly increase the efficiency of plants.

One big vacuum still to be filled, and one that will certainly reward the discoverer of the variety to fill it, is a true, early-ripening 'Delicious' apple to advance the harvest. So . . . keep an eye on your trees, 'Delicious' and others. If you see one limb behaving differently from the rest—ripening its fruit far earlier, say—you may have discovered a gold mine in your garden. And a fruit nursery such as Stark's might make it pay you handsomely, not to speak of your doing the world at large a big favor.

Index

6-8 feet   8-10 feet